Trusting Records in the Cloud

Trusting Records in the Cloud

Edited by

Luciana Duranti and Corinne Rogers

facet
publishing

Published by Facet Publishing,
7 Ridgmount Street, London WC1E 7AE
www.facetpublishing.co.uk

Facet Publishing is wholly owned by CILIP: the Library and Information
Association.
The editor and authors of the individual chapters assert their moral right to be
identified as such in accordance with the terms of the Copyright, Designs and
Patents Act 1988.

British Library Cataloguing in Publication Data
A catalogue record for this book is available from the British Library.

ISBN 978-1-78330-402-8 (paperback)
ISBN 978-1-78330-403-5 (hardback)
ISBN 978-1-78330-404-2 (e-book)

First published 2019

Text printed on FSC accredited material.

Typeset from editors' files by Flagholme Publishing Services in 10/13pt Palatino
and OpenSans
Printed and made in Great Britain by CPI Group (UK) Ltd, Croydon, CR0 4YY.

Contents

List of figures and tables

Figures

Tables

Contributors

Gabriela Andaur Gómez is a Lecturer and Researcher in the Information, Library and Archives Management Program at Alberto Hurtado University, Chile, and Archivist in the Modernization Project of the National Archives of Chile. She holds a Master's degree in Archival Science from the University of British Columbia School of Library, Archival and Information Studies. She is interested in archival theory, description and access to public information, with a focus on the preservation of digital records.

Karen Anderson, Professor Emerita, was appointed Foundation Professor in Archives and Information Science at Mid Sweden University in 2008. She was Director of the InterPARES Trust European Team 2013–2016. She is an Editor-in-Chief for Archival Science, a member of the editorial board of the International Journal of Public Information Systems and a member of the Swedish Standards Institute's Committee for Records Management.

Richard Arias-Hernandez is an Instructor at the University of British Columbia School of Library, Archival and Information Studies. He teaches and researches on socially just design of information technologies in the Master's degree in Library and Information Science and in the Bachelor of Media Studies. His current research is on Library and Information Science and Media Studies program evaluation, evaluation of community-based experiential learning, postcolonial/decolonial perspectives for digital libraries and archives, and linked data for digital libraries and archives.

Alicia Barnard is a researcher and consultant for developing digital records policies. She is a trainer in digital preservation and records management and has published and presented papers in Mexico and abroad. She was head of the Documentation Centre of the Ministry of Health for 20 years and has twice received the Award for Archival Merit from the National Archives of Mexico, as well as funds from UNESCO for training on digital records preservation from the InterPARES project.

Eduardo Bonilla has a Master's degree in Records and Archives Management from the Universidad La Salle, Bogotá, Colombia. He has focused on information governance in his roles as General Management and Quality Director of the Mexico President's Office, Director of Information and Management Studies of the Federal Institute of Transparency, Access of Information and Personal Data Protection, and, currently, Director of said office at the National Institute of Transparency, Access of Information and Personal Data Protection.

Jenny Bunn is a Lecturer and Programme Director for the MA in Archives and Records Management at University College London. She has previously worked for institutions including the V&A Museum, The Royal Bank of Scotland and The National Archives in the UK and is actively involved with the work of the Archives and Records Association as a part of the editorial team for *Archives and Records* and as a member of the Committee of the Section for Archives and Technology.

Yingfang Cai is the Director of the Business Section, Economic Science and Technological Business Guidance Division of The State Archives Administration of China, and an Executive Member of the Section on Business Archives, International Council on Archives. Cai has a PhD in Management Science and Engineering, has held a Post-doctoral Researcher in Project Management, and is a Professor. He has long been engaged in business archival work and has taken part in the formulation of different rules and guidelines regarding Enterprise Records Management and archiving, accounting archives and specifications on archives outsourcing services.

Mark Crookston is Associate Chief Librarian of the Alexander Turnbull Library in the National Library of New Zealand. He has worked in a range of archive and library roles across New Zealand, the UK and the Pacific. He has previously been Secretary General for the Pacific Branch of the International Council on Archives and is a member of the International Council on Archives' Expert Group on Appraisal. Mark has a Master's in Library and Information Studies from Victoria University of Wellington, New Zealand, and has presented and published many papers on the collection, preservation and use of digital archives.

Adrian Cunningham works as an independent archival consultant. Previously, he spent 36 years working with documentary heritage collections in national and state governments in Australia in positions including Director of the Digital Archives Program at Queensland State Archives (2011–2017) and Director, Strategic Relations and Personal Records at the National Archives of Australia. Currently, he serves as the Liaison for the International Council on Archives to the International Standards Organization's Committee on Records Management and Archives, TC46/SC11.

Ineke Deserno was appointed the NATO Archivist in 2010. She is responsible for preserving and providing access to the institutional memory of the Organization. Ineke arrived at NATO having accumulated 15 years of professional experience managing the records of the United High Commissioner for Refugees, the International Olympic Committee and the World Health Organization. She holds a Master of History and Archival Studies from the Netherlands, a postgraduate degree in archives and records management from Canada and a PhD from Australia.

Carlos Augusto Silva Ditadi is an archivist at the National Archives of Brazil and a member of UNESCO's Memory of the World Committee for Brazil. Carlos has been involved with several phases of InterPARES.

Luciana Duranti is Professor of archival theory, diplomatics and the management of digital records in the master and doctoral archival programs of the School of Library, Archival and Information Studies of the University of British Columbia, Canada. She is the Director of the Centre for the International Study of Contemporary Records and Archives (www.ciscra.org) and InterPARES, the Digital Records Forensics and the Records in the Clouds Projects.

Laura Dymock began working in digital asset management after completing the Master of Information program at the University of Toronto, Canada. She worked at a rights management company before moving to the Canadian Red Cross where she implemented a DAM system and migrated key audio-visual assets. Maintaining her interest in music, she has also spearheaded digital archives and digitisation projects in Toronto's non-profit arts community.

Tove Engvall has been a Graduate Research Assistant in the InterPARES Trust project. She has a Master's degree in Archives and Information Science at Mid-Sweden University, where she is currently an Adjunct Lecturer. She previously worked as a municipal archivist and on national e-archive projects in Sweden. Her research interests focus on trust, accountability and power in relation to records and an open global environment.

Lois Evans is a PhD Candidate at the University of British Columbia, Canada, where she is studying the automation of retention and disposition in the digital environment. She was a records manager in local government for over 12 years and is the working group chair for the Canadian General Standards Board's Electronic Records as Documentary Evidence. Lois has participated in InterPARES since 2008, contributing the Shared Drive Migration Toolkit (IP3) and participating in the Social Media and Trust in Government study (IPT).

Andrew Flinn is a Reader in Archival Studies and Oral History in the Department of Information Studies, University College London. He is also vice-chair of the UK Community Archives and Heritage Group and a steering committee member of the ICA's Section on Archival Education. His research interests include community-based archives, archives and social justice, and the significance of records and rights of access to information in people's lives.

Fiorella Foscarini is Associate Professor in the Faculty of Information at the University of Toronto, Canada. In her teaching and research, she uses diplomatics, rhetorical genre studies and information culture concepts to explore issues related to the creation, management and use of records in organizational contexts. She is co-editor-in-chief of the *Records Management Journal* and senior associate editor of *Archivaria*.

Patricia C. Franks is co-editor of the *International Directory of National Archives* (with Dr Anthony Bernier) and the *Encyclopedia of Archival Science* (with Professor Luciana Duranti). She is author of *Records and Information Management*. She led two InterPARES Trust research projects: *Retention and Disposition in a Cloud Environment* and *Social Media and Trust in Government*.

Georg Gänser studied Archival Science and obtained a doctoral degree in Contemporary History in Austria. He has worked in several archives in Germany and Austria, and as archivist at the International Atomic Energy Agency and at UNICEF. He is currently a MAS candidate at the University of British Columbia School of Library, Archival and Information Studies and a graduate research assistant in the InterPARES project.

Arina Grazhenskaya, Master of Information Sciences, is a graduate of Geneva School of Business Administration and Moscow Institute of History and Archives (Russian State University for Humanities). Her Master's thesis was focused on the information governance nature and implementation from the European public administrations' perspectives.

Maria Guercio was State Archivist at the National Archives in Italy (1979–1998), full professor of archival science and electronic records management at the University of Urbino (1998-2011) and at the University of Rome La Sapienza, where she has contributed to many national and international initiatives for electronic recordkeeping and digital preservation (such as InterPARES and Moreq) and EU-funded collaborative projects (such as ERPANET, CASPAR and APARSEN). She is co-director of the journal *IJLIS* and the author of many articles and manuals on archival science, electronic records management and digital preservation.

Pekka Henttonen is an Associate Professor at the Faculty of Communication Sciences, the University of Tempere, Finland and has a PhD in information studies. His special field is electronic records management. He has published research about requirements for electronic records management systems, metadata, knowledge organization and Finnish archival history. Besides scientific publications, he regularly writes for professional journals. Before his university career, Pekka worked in the National Archives and Military Archives of Finland.

Darra Hofman received her MSLS from the University of Kentucky and her JD from Arizona State University in the US. She is currently a PhD candidate at the University of British Columbia School of Library, Archival and Information Studies. Her research focuses on the intersection between records, technology and human rights, with a special focus on blockchain technology and privacy.

Paige Hohmann is Archivist, Records Manager and Special Collections Librarian at the University of British Columbia – Okanagan Campus in Kelowna, British Columbia, Canada. Her work is focused on digital readiness, from shared drive management to policy development. Paige holds Master's degrees in Archival Studies and Library and Information studies from the University of British Columbia.

Grant Hurley is the Digital Preservation Librarian at Scholars Portal, the information technology service provider for the Ontario Council of University

Libraries (OCUL) in Canada. He oversees the maintenance of the Scholars Portal Trustworthy Digital Repository and the development of digital preservation services, infrastructure and learning opportunities for OCUL members. He holds a Dual Master of Archival Studies and Master of Library and Information Studies from the University of British Columbia, Canada.

Shadrack Katuu completed his undergraduate degree in Kenya, Master's studies in Canada and his Doctoral studies in South Africa. He has worked in Austria, Botswana, Canada, Kenya, South Africa and the US. He is currently an information management officer at the United Nations Mission in South Sudan. He has authored more than two dozen publications.

Sevgi Koyuncu Tunç is a Computer Engineer and a PhD candidate. She has worked as a Microsoft Software Consultant and has been involved in many large-scale e-government projects. She saw the need for improvement in the human-computer interaction concept in Turkey because of usability problems in e-governments products. She is studying 'Usability Evaluation of Electronic Document Management Systems' at Hacettepe University, Department of Information Management, in Turkey.

Özgür Külcü is a Professor at Hacettepe University, Department of Information Management, in Turkey. He has an MS and PhD degree in Records Management from Hacettepe University, Department of Information Management. He completed three post doctoral programs at University of British Columbia School of Library, Archival and Information Studies Canada, University of North Carolina SILS and University of California Berkeley iSchools. His research interests are organizational information management, electronic archiving and records management, managing cultural heritage and metadata mapping.

Victoria Lemieux is an Associate Professor of archival science at the University of British Columbia School of Library, Archival and Information Studies in Canada. Her current research focuses on risk to the availability of trustworthy records, in particular in blockchain record-keeping systems, and how these risks impact transparency, financial stability, public accountability and human rights. She holds a doctorate from University College London (Archival Studies, 2002), and since 2005 has been a Certified Information Systems Security Professional (CISSP). She has received many awards for her professional work and research, including the 2015 Emmett Leahy Award for outstanding contributions to the field of records management, a 2015 World Bank Big Data

Innovation Award, and a 2016 Emerald Literati Award for her research on blockchain technology.

Elizabeth Lomas is a Senior Lecturer in Information Governance at University College London. She is a member of the UK Government's Advisory Council on National Records and Archives and Forum on Historical Manuscripts and Research. Her research focuses on the nature of information governance including digital evidence, information management, information security and information rights law.

James Lowry is a Lecturer at the Liverpool University Centre for Archive Studies in the UK. His recent publications include *Displaced Archives*, an edited collection published by Routledge in 2017, and *Integrity in Government through Records Management*, which he edited with Justus Wamukoya, published by Ashgate in 2014. James is Chair of the Association of Commonwealth Archivists and Records Managers, Secretary to the International Council on Archives (ICA) Africa Programme, an ex-officio member of the ICA's Programme Commission and a trustee of the International Records Management Trust.

Basma Makhlouf Shabou completed her PhD at the University of Montreal (EBSI). Since 2010, she has been a Professor at the University of Applied Sciences and Arts Western Switzerland, Information Science Department of Geneva School of Business Administration. Her recent research, publications, lectures and conferences focus on archival appraisal, information governance, information quality metrics and measurements, and research data management.

Julie McLeod is Professor in Records Management in the iSchool, Department of Computer & Information Sciences, Northumbria University in the UK. She has led research in digital records management (e.g. *Accelerating positive change in electronic records management (AC+erm)* www.northumbria.ac.uk/acerm and research data management *DATUM* www.northumbria.ac.uk/datum) and teaches information governance and records management. She is consulting editor of the *Records Management Journal* and received the Emmett Leahy Award for outstanding contribution to the field of information and records management in 2014.

Aída Luz Mendoza Navarro holds a Master's degree in Public Policy Management and a PhD in Law. She worked for 24 years at the General National Archives of Peru and directed it from 1992 to 2001. She is currently the Co-ordinator of the Archives and Records Management Program and the Research Department of the Faculty of Humanities and Education Sciences at the Catholic University Sedes Sapientiae in Peru.

Giovanni Michetti is an Assistant Professor at Sapienza University of Rome, Italy. He has been involved in national and international initiatives on records management, description models and digital preservation. He is heavily involved in standardisation as the Chair of the Committee on Archives and Records Management in the Italian Standards Organization and as the Italian representative in a number of ISO Working Groups on records management.

Umi Asma' Mokhtar is a Senior Lecturer in information science at the Faculty of Information Science and Technology, Universiti Kebangsaan, Malaysia. She was the recipient of the Oliver Wendell Holmes Travel Award from the Society of American Archivists in 2012. Her research interests are electronic records management, function-based classification and information policy. Her papers have been published in international and national journals including the *International Journal of Information Management* and the *Records Management Journal*. Currently, she is the co-researcher for the InterPARES Trust project for the Malaysian Team.

Jonathan Mukwevho holds a Master's degree in archival science from the University of South Africa. He works for the Auditor-General of South Africa as the archival consultant.

Lisa P. Nathan is Associate Professor at the University of British Columbia (UBC), Canada. She investigates the entanglement of ethics and information through her research and teaching at the UBC School of Library, Archival and Information Studies. She lives and works on the traditional territory of the xAməθkᘱyᗷm (Musqueam), currently occupied by UBC. Lisa collaborates with inspiring people to (re)design information practices – the ways we manage information – to acknowledge and address ethical quandaries (e.g. colonisation, social disparities and ecological degradation).

Mpho Ngoepe is a Professor in the Department of Information Science at the University of South Africa. Prior to his current position, Professor Ngoepe worked for the United Nations Children's Fund, Auditor-General South Africa and the National Archives of South Africa.

Gillian Oliver is Associate Professor of Information Management at Monash University in Australia. Previously, she led teaching and research into archives and records at Victoria University of Wellington and the Open Polytechnic of New Zealand. Her research interests reflect these experiences, focusing on the information cultures of organizations. She is currently leading research funded by the International Council on Archives (ICA) to develop an information culture toolkit.

Richard Pearce-Moses holds degrees in American Studies from the University of Texas and Library Science from the University of Illinois in the US. He is a past President and Fellow of the Society of American Archivists and a Certified Archivist. He has worked with a variety of records, including photography, regional history, Native American culture, state and local government, and electronic records. He is the author of *A Glossary of Archival and Records Terminology* (Society of American Archivists, 2005).

Christopher J. Prom holds a PhD in History from the University of Illinois at Urbana-Champaign in the US, where he is Assistant University Archivist and Andrew S. G. Turyn Professor. He is also Publications Editor for the Society of American Archivists and a Fellow of the Society. His work on the Archival Connections Project informs his contributions to Chapter 5 of this book.

Claudia Lacombe Rocha has been an archivist at the National Archives in Brazil since 1989. For the last 15 years, she has managed the Electronic Records Management and Preservation initiatives. She is President of the Electronic Records Committee at the National Council on Archives of Brazil, Director of TEAM Brazil for InterPARES 3 and a researcher on InterPARES Trust.

Corinne Rogers, Project Coordinator for InterPARES Trust (2013–2019), is an adjunct professor in the School of Library, Archival and Information Studies at the University of British Columbia, Canada, and a Systems Archivist with Artefactual Systems. From 2006–2012, Corinne participated in the InterPARES research and Digital Records Forensics project (2009–2011) and she is co-author of *Digital Records Pathways: Topics in Digital Preservation* – a suite of online educational resources produced by InterPARES for the International Council on Archives.

Eng Sengsavang holds Master's degrees in Archival Studies and Library Science from the University of British Columbia School of Library, Archival and Information Studies, Canada. She currently works as a Reference Archivist at the United Nations Educational, Scientific and Cultural Organization.

Anna Sexton is an archivist at The National Archives of the UK (TNA) and her interests include research use of government administrative data, participatory archive practice, community-based research, record access and rights issues, archival ethics and new thinking around digital records and computational methods. Prior to joining TNA, Anna was a Research Associate and Sessional Lecturer in the Department of Information Studies at University College London (UCL). She holds a PhD and MA in Archives and Records Management from UCL and has 20 years of experience working across the archive sector and academia.

Elizabeth Shaffer is Associate Director at the Indian Residential School History and Dialogue Centre at the University of British Columbia, Canada, located on the traditional territory of the xʷməθkʷəy̓əm (Musqueam). She is also a doctoral candidate at the UBC School of Library, Archival and Information Studies. Her current work and research include critical enquiry into how information policy, practices and systems emerge and evolve in contemporary digital spaces, with particular attention to social justice issues, impacts of colonialism and collections that document traumatic human events.

Silvia Schenkolewski-Kroll has published articles about archival science and archival education in *Archival Science* and other publications. She was a member of the International Council on Archives (ICA) steering committees of ICA/SAE and ICA/SBL. She has taught courses in the Escuela de Archivologia (Universidad Nacional de Córdoba, Argentina), delivered lectures in the VII, IX and XII CAM, University of British Columbia, Vancouver, and the Universidad Nacional de Chile. She is a member of the European Team of InterPARES Trust.

Elizabeth Shepherd's research interests include the relationships between records management and information policy compliance and rights in records (@MIRRAproject) and the development of the modern archive profession in England (*Archives and Archivists in 20th Century England*, 2009). A Professor at University College London, she teaches in the Master's programme in Archives and Records Management. Her service to the profession includes UK Research Excellence Framework REF2014 and REF2021.

Hrvoje Stančić teaches at the Department of Information and Communication Sciences, University of Zagreb, Croatia. He is a member of the board of the Croatian Archival Society (vice-president 2016/17), a member of the Croatian Information Documentation Society and a member of the Centre for

International Study of Contemporary Records and Archives (CISCRA, Canada). He is President of the Croatian mirror technical committee for the development of 'ISO/TC 307 Blockchain and Distributed Ledger Technologies' standard. He is the Director of the European research team at the InterPARES Trust research project.

Jim Suderman is the Director of Information Access at the City of Toronto, Canada, where he has been working for over ten years. In this role, he oversees the implementation of records and information management policy across the city through the delivery of access to information, records management and archival services. Prior to working at the city, Jim worked for 16 years at the Archives of Ontario, first as a senior archivist and then as the co-ordinator of the Archives' Electronic Records Program.

Joseph T. Tennis is an Associate Professor and Associate Dean of Faculty Affairs at the University of Washington Information School and Adjunct Associate Professor in Linguistics at the University of Washington in the US. He served as President of the International Society for Knowledge Organization from 2014–2018. He is on the *Library Quarterly* and *Knowledge Organization* editorial boards.

Kenneth Thibodeau, Director, Center for Advanced Systems and Technology (former) at the US's National Archives and Records Administration (retired), is an internationally recognised expert on electronic records and digital preservation. Among other accomplishments, he directed development of the Electronic Records Archives system at the National Archives of the US and led the development of the world's first standard for records management software, DoD 5015.2-STD.

Katherine (Kat) Timms holds Master's degrees in Library and Information Studies and in History (Archival Studies). She is currently a Senior Project Officer at Library and Archives Canada, supporting recordkeeping initiatives within the government records program. Her work in national and international standards development helped inform her contributions to Chapter 5.

Assaf Tractinsky works as a Knowledge Manager at the Israel State Archives. He has a PhD from the Department of Information Science of Bar-Ilan University and for the last five years has been a member of the European Team of InterPARES Trust on electronic records.

1

Introduction

Luciana Duranti and Corinne Rogers

This book presents the main findings of InterPARES Trust, the fourth phase of the InterPARES project, continuously funded by the Social Sciences and Humanities Research Council of Canada (SSHRC) since its inception in 1998. The InterPARES project is a collaboration among academics and professionals concerned about the continuing authenticity of electronic records over the long term. Hence the name Inter (among) PARES (peers), which is also an acronym for International Research on Permanent Authentic Records in Electronic Systems (InterPARES). The project name was carried on through its four phases to provide a continuing identity for the research – an overarching ongoing idea conveying its spirit and ultimate goal: the preservation of the evidentiary nature of records in different technological environments.

The overall challenges that InterPARES has addressed over 20 years were clearly identified at the outset of the project and have never substantially changed as new technologies renewed them over and over again. Gradually, the terminology changed as the adjective *electronic* came to be substituted by the more focused and precise *digital*, *authentic* by the more comprehensive *trustworthy*, and *record* began to be more and more frequently accompanied by *data*. The issues, however, stayed the same: digital records are vulnerable because they are easy to destroy, lose, corrupt and tamper with; they become inaccessible if not protected and persistent if their copies are not purposefully destroyed. Furthermore, digital records are not clearly and uniquely placed into a documentary context; their content, structure and form are not inextricably linked; and as stored entities they are distinct from any of their manifestations on a screen. When we save a digital record, we take it apart in its digital components, and when we retrieve it, we reproduce it from those components, thus creating a copy. Hence, it is not possible to preserve a digital record but only the ability to reproduce or recreate it (Duranti & Thibodeau, 2006).

Additional challenges presented by the digital environment relate to establishing digital records' accuracy, reliability and authenticity (i.e. trust-worthiness) and maintaining them over time so that the records' trustworthiness will be verifiable and provable:

- Developing an infrastructure that ensures a seamless controlled flow of trustworthy data/documents/records from the creator to the preserver and the user irrespective of changes in technology
- Providing transparency while protecting secrecy where warranted
- Guaranteeing that the conflicting rights of users, clients, employees and future generations are protected
- Ensuring a sustainable long-term preservation of the cultural heritage in digital form, regardless of where it is generated or stored.

The InterPARES name has also provided a continuing identity to the people involved in the project, conveying their own research and professional goals. Such identity has extended to all students involved through the years as research assistants: they helped develop, communicate and apply the research outcomes. Most of them became managers within potential partner organiz-ations or scholars in the general research area and eventually they turned into co-investigators in subsequent phases of InterPARES. For this reason, individuals who contributed initially as research assistants appear in this book either as co-authors or as contributors to findings.

Before presenting the content of this book, it is important to offer a brief overview of the phases of InterPARES that led to this point. Each phase of research has built upon the findings, recommendations and products of the previous one, culminating in a body of knowledge about digital records and data that applies regardless of the technological environment.

The goal of the first two phases of InterPARES was to develop the body of theory and methods necessary to ensure that digital records produced in databases and office systems, as well as in dynamic, experiential and interactive systems, in the course of artistic, scientific and e-government activities can be created in accurate and reliable form and maintained and preserved in authentic form, both in the long and the short term, for the use of those who created them and of society at large, regardless of technology obsolescence and media fragility. The key products were a framework of principles guiding the development of policies for records creating and preserving organizations (Policy Framework); recommendations for making and maintaining digital materials for individuals and small communities of practice (Creator

Guidelines); recommendations for digital preservation for archival institutions (Preserver Guidelines); authenticity requirements for assessing and maintaining the authenticity of digital records (Benchmark and Baseline Requirements); principles and criteria for adoption of file formats, wrappers and encoding schemes (File Formats Selection Guidelines); a glossary, a dictionary and an ontology (Terminology Database); two records preservation models, the Chain of Preservation (COP) Model (a lifecycle model), and the Business-driven Recordkeeping (BDR) Model (a continuum model); and two books presenting and discussing all the above (Duranti & Preston, 2005, 2008).

The third phase of InterPARES focused on the practical application of these products. Its goal was to enable public and private archival organizations and programs with limited resources to preserve over the long term authentic records that satisfy the requirements of their stakeholders and society's needs for an adequate record of its past. Different from the previous two phases, where the researchers were organized in teams according to their specific competence on the topics or research question addressed (e.g. the appraisal team or the policy team), in this third phase researchers were organized in teams according to country, so that all contextual perspectives could be taken into account. Among the most important reports of this phase were: Public Sector Audits for Digital Recordkeeping Analysis, Cost-benefit Models, Ethical Models, Open Source Records Management Software Analysis, Metadata Application Profile for Authenticity, Organizational Culture & Risk Assessment, E-mail Preservation, Preservation of Registries, Education Modules for Digital Preservation and a Multilingual Archival Terminology Database (MAT) (InterPARES 2012, International Council on Archives & InterPARES Trust, 2016).

The fourth phase of InterPARES (InterPARES Trust, hereinafter ITrust) resulted from the need to address issues of trust raised by the increasing creation, storage and/or preservation of data/records in online environments. Its goal was to produce frameworks that would support the development of integrated and consistent local, national and international networks of policies, procedures, regulations, standards and legislation concerning digital records entrusted to the internet. This was to ensure public trust grounded on evidence of good governance and a persistent digital memory. Its specific objectives were:

- To build the foundations for establishing a relationship of trust between the people and those organizations that hold the records and data related to and/or belonging to them on the internet
- To ensure the trustworthiness of data and records created in the course of interaction between people and organizations

- To develop a supra-national framework that embraces both developed and developing countries and all sectors and is capable of guiding the development of domestic legislation and regulatory instruments which are consistent across cultures and societies.

As the intent of this phase of InterPARES was to ground trust in the way organizations interact with a variety of client-groups in a digital networked environment and to preserve the by-product of such interactions, the partnership's activities required expertise in digital records and archives, diplomatics (i.e. records structure, form, function, and trustworthiness), information policy, information technology, communication and media, several types of law, internet security, cybercrime and digital forensics. This called for a team led by scholars grounded in theoretical and methodological research and professionals, bringing practical experience and opportunities for testing hypotheses and findings and for disseminating results among those who will use them in their own environment.

The goal of developing a framework and a policy network that are valid across cultures and can be easily contextualised required an international approach, involving as many countries as manageable in one research project. At the same time, because the issues to be examined presumed the existence of an advanced technological infrastructure, a widespread use of complex technology embedded in their daily routines by people and organizations, and the consequent surfacing of problems linked to it, the selection of both partners and researchers had to focus on those countries, organizations and individuals with the most experience in the use of network technologies and under the most pressure for addressing related existing or potential issues. In building the International Alliance, the management team aimed at parallelism in structure, composition and governance among regional Teams, ensuring some variation in knowledge and expertise, so that each Team could give a unique contribution to the Alliance. The large majority of the participants had worked in the previous phases of InterPARES, either as co-investigators or as graduate research assistants. Many new partners had worked collaboratively with members of previous InterPARES research teams, while others joined the partnership in this phase because of the reputation of the research network. This made for a harmonious, strong and effective collaboration.

The International Alliance, directed by Luciana Duranti and co-ordinated by Corinne Rogers, comprised seven regional teams: a North America Team, jointly led by the University of British Columbia (UBC) and the University of Washington (UW); a Latin America Team, led by the National Autonomous University of Mexico; a Europe Team, led by Mid-Sweden University; an Asia Team, led by Remnin University; an Australasia Team, led by the Victoria

University of Wellington; an Africa Team, led by the University of South Africa; and a Transnational Institutions Team, led by UNESCO. The Alliance also included Supporting Partners, who provided dissemination opportunities and ongoing feedback, and individual experts, who were consultants in specialised knowledge areas and contributed to the research *pro bono*. Neither group's members are described here for lack of space, but they are listed, together with all participants in the research, among the Partners and Contributors on the InterPARES Trust website (www.interparestrust.org). Each regional Team included both universities and organizations acting as test-beds, while the Transnational Institutions Team only included organizations/test-beds. The academics supervised the student assistants and the professionals guided data collection and testing in their respective organizations. All participants analysed the data and collaboratively found, tested and disseminated solutions and products.

ITrust used a theoretical framework strongly rooted in archival science and diplomatics, but the variety of issues and expertise required to address them called for a multidisciplinary approach. The methodologies used were provided by the knowledge areas most relevant to the research: resource-based theory, because it studies the technologic, managerial and relational means of maximising competitive advantage; risk management, because it studies vulnerabilities and ways to mitigate them; design theory, because it studies policy in situations with unknown variables; digital forensics, because it studies the authenticity of digital materials that do not reside in the systems in which they were produced and kept; human–computer interaction; aero-spatial, cybercrime and telecommunication law; and organizational theory. However, it is critical to emphasise here that the InterPARES Trust Team integrated the knowledge derived from the use of methodology from other disciplines into archival science, ensuring that the archival system of knowledge maintained its consistency and cohesion.

The research was organized into five domains and five cross-domains. The domains were Infrastructure, Security, Control, Access and Legal:

- The **Infrastructure** domain considered issues relating to system architecture and related infrastructure as they affect records held in online environments. Examples of studies: Contract Terms for Cloud Services, Economics Models for Cloud Storage Decisions, Dark Repositories as a Service, and Trusted Infrastructure as a Service.
- The **Security** domain considered records issues relating to online data security. Examples of studies: Standards of Practice for Archives, Use of Cloud in International Organizations, Security Classification, and Privacy and Security Techniques.

- The **Control** domain focused on the management of digital material in online environments, addressing authenticity, reliability and accuracy of data; integrity metadata; chain of custody; retention and disposition; transfer and acquisition; intellectual control and access controls. The key products of the overall research, the Preservation as a Service for Trust model and the TrustChain model, result from studies in the control domain but pull together the results of the studies in all domains.
- The **Access** domain investigated open access, open data and open government. Examples of studies: Records Management in Open Government, Patents and Petitions, Trusted Online Access to Distributed Holdings of Digital Public Records, Internet Archives in Russia and Open Government in Sweden.
- The **Legal** domain considered the application of legal privilege (including the issue of extra-territoriality); legal hold; chain of evidence; authentication of evidence offered at trial; certification; and soft laws (in particular UN standard-setting instruments) – mapping, scope, potential impact and constraints. Examples of studies: Policies, Legislation, Standards for RM in the Cloud, Comparison among Legal Issues in the ITrust Regions, Impact of the Italian Legal Framework on Cloud Choices, and a Database of Privacy Case Law.

The cross domains were: Policy, Social, Terminology, Education and Resource:

- The **Policy** cross-domain considered policy issues emerging from studies in the five research domains. Examples of studies: Policy and Plurality, Retention and Disposition in the Cloud, Information Governance Maturity Model and Analysis of Policies for Recordkeeping and Preservation.
- The **Social** cross-domain examined the social change consequent to the use of the internet. Examples of studies: Organizational Culture and Fun in Functional, Social Media and Trust in Government, Social Awareness of Authenticity and Materiality of Records and Attributes of Trust.
- The **Terminology** cross-domain was concerned with the ongoing production of a multilingual glossary, a dictionary and ontologies; it also produced essays as needed, for example on the concept of trust.
- The **Education** cross-domain focused on the development of new models of curricula for transmitting the new knowledge produced by InterPARES Trust.
- Finally, the **Resource** cross-domain took care of the ongoing production of annotated bibliographies, identifying relevant published articles,

books, etc., case law, policies, statutes, standards, blogs and similar grey literature, to support the research in all the domains and cross-domains.

While the original documents, reports, databases and essays are posted and available on the dissemination page of the InterPARES Trust website (www.interparestrust.org), this book aims to convey to anyone who is using or intends to use the cloud for creation, management and/or preservation of information, the most substantial and impactful findings of InterPARES Trust. Because of the breadth of the research team, the book intends to appeal to an international and cross-disciplinary readership of both professionals and lay persons. It will benefit records professionals in exercising their primary functions, such as implementing retention and disposition schedules in the cloud, understanding the role of metadata in cloud services for chain of custody, rethinking issues of appraisal, arrangement and description, and understanding new practices with respect to preservation. Of particular interest to them will be our model for preservation as a series of services that may be implemented by a single Trusted Digital Repository or by a variety of preservation actors.

Our findings in information governance, risk management and authentication practices and technologies will be of interest to organizations considering maintaining their records in the cloud or managing current cloud services. Educators will find guidance for curriculum development. All interested readers will want to learn from the work done in harmonising and understanding relevant terminology, which is often vague or conflicting in definitions and usage. Members of the public at large will want to read this book if they are concerned about their privacy and rights with respect to personal information in the cloud. They will learn about the contracts they must enter into with social media and other service providers and what the risks and remedies are.

Contributors to the book are experts from academia, government and industry. They are all members of the InterPARES Trust international research alliance. Most chapters have several authors or contributors, reflecting the conclusions of various studies undertaken within the InterPARES Trust that relate to the chapter's theme, and one editor who liaised with the researchers, outlined the structure of the chapter and edited it for consistency of language and delivery. The chapters cover all the areas of research, though not all the studies carried out by each regional team. While some of those not included will be covered by forthcoming publications by the teams, all can be accessed on the website.

The book is organized into eleven chapters according to three broad themes: issues and policy; strategies and processes; and roles and competencies. These themes may be broadly interpreted as: Why issues concerning records online matter; What is being (and should be) done; and How should records professionals work and prepare to work in the future. The chapters are supplemented by two appendices.

Issues and policies

Chapter 2 provides an overview of the range of challenges and issues relating to trust and digital records/data in online, networked environments. After a brief introduction to cloud computing, its nature, services and some associated legal issues, McLeod structures the challenges and issues thematically, with reference to further details in the remaining chapters. She organizes her argument around three broad thematic areas: systems and services (e.g. infrastructure and supporting systems and processes), strategies (e.g. records management processes, means of trust), and persons (citizens, organizations, records professionals and educators).

Chapters 3, 4 and 5 establish the nature of open government, citizen engagement, and information governance respectively. Shepherd begins her discourse on open government with some key definitions and then covers critical topics such as access to information, privacy, security and management of classified information in an open government context. She and her contributors present the status of open government initiatives in several countries around the world, based on several InterPARES Trust studies.

In Chapter 4, Foscarini et al. focus on citizen engagement with open government initiatives. The notion of citizen engagement is explored from a socio-cultural and user-centred perspective by drawing on a set of ITrust studies that examined the relationship between records, record systems and the users of both, with an emphasis on human engagement, or participation, that arises from and shapes the relationship.

In Chapter 5, Makhlouf Shabou et al. draw together key InterPARES Trust initiatives on strategies, methods and tools enabling records governance to be applied in a cloud environment. The first section discusses recordkeeping policies in the European Union from the twin perspectives of legislation and cloud service provider solutions. The second and third sections present the role of enterprise architecture for corporate records management and maturity assessment methods and tools.

Strategies and processes

Chapters 6 through 10 address specific processes in the records and archival management workflow as they are applied in cloud environments. In Chapter

6, Franks et al. call upon the findings of four InterPARES Trust studies that explore principles of records retention and disposition in the cloud. Guidance is offered through ten best practices based on the principles.

Chapter 7 discusses the certification of digital records and issues of preserving evidence of their authenticity. This is of particular importance for audit, where auditors require sufficient evidence supporting authenticity of digital records. An equally difficult but critical issue arises with the long-term preservation of digitally signed or sealed records. Stančić proposes a blockchain-based model as a solution to this issue.

In Chapter 8, Intellectual Control, Michetti et al. address challenges for arrangement and description in networked environments. In three sections, the chapter covers the assumptions and opportunities available to archivists faced with making choices about archival description in the context of cloud services, issues of metadata and authenticity, and usability and human-computer interaction in ERMSs.

Distributed services for digital preservation are the subject of Chapter 9. Cunningham et al. discuss how to choose a trusted cloud service for preservation and present Preservation as a Service for Trust (PaaST), which articulates requirements for digital preservation services.

Chapter 10, the final chapter in this section, presents two case studies that deal with the multiple and diverse perspectives pertaining to records of indigenous peoples that are necessary to ensure that national memories do not solely represent dominant or majority perspectives. The Canadian case study interrogates policy and plurality in the context of the National Centre for Truth and Reconciliation (NCTR), investigating how plurality and trust influenced initial steps to make the NCTR records digitally accessible. Researchers in New Zealand explored the attitudes of the Māori to the digitisation of te reo (Māori language) resources by cultural heritage institutions in that country.

Roles and competencies

The final two chapters address the changing roles of records and archives professionals and the competencies required to adapt. A records and archives professional is defined as:

> [A]n individual who is trained in all aspects of managing records and information, including their creation, use, retention, disposition, and preservation, and is familiar with the legal ethical, fiscal, administrative, and governance contexts of recordkeeping.
>
> (Pearce-Moses, 2018, s.v. records professional)

In the era of digital, networked and online records and data, the identity of the records and archives professional is changing and becoming more complex and versatile than the traditional one of trusted custodian. Chapter 11 explores this shift in several contexts of open government in Sweden and the United Kingdom and presents an ontology of functions and activities for the profession.

The role of records and archives professionals is supported by education and this is the subject of Chapter 12. The professional competencies are analysed according to the model of five inter-connected competencies proposed by Cheetham and Chivers (1996, 1998), the DigCurV Curriculum Framework (2013) and Bloom's *Taxonomy* (1956, updated by Anderson and Krathwohl, 2001). Lemieux and Hofman argue that the changes in the characteristics of records and the context of recordkeeping require an updated educational model that draws from diverse knowledge sources.

Finally, two appendices present the InterPARES Trust terminology database – the glossary of definitions used consistently by all research teams – and a list of studies, reports, checklists and guidance documents (annotated), all of which are freely available on the InterPARES Trust website, www.interparestrust.org.

It is our hope that this book will offer not only a significant amount of information derived from original research, a clear and useful guidance to all those who wish to use the cloud environment, a rich resource for students in the records and archives field, and a reliable reference for academics and professionals, but also an interesting and pleasant reading for all those who wish to catch a glimpse of where technology is driving our society and changing the way we behave and perhaps the way we are.

We would like to thank all those who have contributed to the InterPARES project in the course of its 20 years of life, whatever their role in it, as each of them has provided a necessary brick on which everything else rests and without which this book could not have been written.

InterPARES has been funded from 1998–2019 with two MCRI (Major Collaborative Research Initiatives), one CURA (Community-University Research Alliance), and one Partnership grant by the Social Sciences and Humanities Research Council of Canada. Matching funds were provided by the University of British Columbia, and several universities and agencies around the world.

The Education Modules (InterPARES, 2012) and the Multilingual Archival Terminology database (International Council on Archives (ICA) & InterPARES Trust, 2016) were partly funded by the International Council on Archives (ICA). Development of the right to left scripts section of the database was funded by the United Arab Emirates National Archives.

References

Duranti, L. and Preston, R. (eds) (2005) *The Long-term Preservation of Authentic Electronic Records: findings of the InterPARES Project*, San Miniato: Archilab.

Duranti, L. and Preston, R. (eds) (2008) *Research on Permanent Authentic Records in Electronic Systems (InterPARES) 2: Experiential, Interactive and Dynamic Records*, Padova: Associazione Nazionale Archivistica Italiana.

Duranti, L. and Thibodeau, K. (2006) The Concept of Record in Interactive, Experiential and Dynamic Environments: the view of InterPARES, *Archival Science*, **6** (1), 13–68.

International Council on Archives (ICA) and InterPARES Trust (2016) *Multilingual Archival Terminology*, www.ciscra.org

International Council on Archives (ICA) and InterPARES Trust (2012) *Digital Records Pathways: topics in digital preservation*, www.ciscra.org

Pearce-Moses, R. (ed.) (2018) *InterPARES Trust Terminology*, www.interparestrust.org/terminology.

2

The cloud – challenges and issues

Julie McLeod

Introduction

This scene-setting chapter provides an overview of the range of challenges and issues relating to trust and digital records in the cloud. A high-level framework is used as a vehicle for considering those that emerged from the work of the InterPARES Trust undertaken across the range of domains referred to in Chapter 1. Some of the challenges and issues are sufficiently significant and bounded that they are covered in subsequent chapters in their own right, while others feature in a number of chapters or are largely addressed in this chapter (e.g. security, policy models, cloud contracts, legal issues, roles and responsibilities).

Beginning with a brief introduction to cloud computing, including its nature, services and some associated legal issues, the framework is then introduced, followed by a discussion of each thematic group of challenges and issues with reference to further detail in other chapters or other publications.

Issues of trust, including perceptions of trust, run throughout the book.

Cloud computing: an introduction

The 'cloud' is understood in the context of this research as a broad range of infrastructures and services distributed across a network (typically the internet) that are scalable on demand and that are designed to support management of high volumes of digital materials. Because 'cloud' – as a general term – is used in so many contexts and implemented in a variety of ways, its meaning is so broad that it is exceptionally nebulous. To the extent the term has been appropriated by marketing, a specific technical definition may be lost in hype. Often it connotes outsourcing some or all aspects of an organization's information technology services. (Pearce-Moses, 2018, s.v. cloud).

As with many developments, the origins of cloud computing have been credited to various individuals. The computer scientist John McCarthy is thought to have been the first to suggest the concept of using computer time-sharing or 'utility computing' in the late 1950s/early 1960s (Wikipedia, 2018). The term 'cloud computing' is thought to have been used by staff at the Compaq computer company in the late 1960s, with Professor Ramnath Chellappa, at the University of Texas, being the first person to use it more publicly in a 1997 lecture (Madhavaiah, Bashir and Shafi, 2012; Mishra, 2014). However, staff at Oracle are also credited with its development (Bort, 2012).

Whatever the truth about the history of its development, today cloud computing is defined as:

> ...a model for enabling ubiquitous, convenient, on-demand network access to a shared pool of configurable computing resources (e.g. networks, servers, storage, applications, and services) that can be rapidly provisioned and released with minimal management effort or service provider interaction.
>
> (Mell and Grance, 2011)

Three main cloud computing service models exist – Software as a Service (SaaS), Platform as a Service (PaaS) and Infrastructure as a Service (IaaS) – with new ones emerging such as Data as a Service (DaaS) and Preservation as a Service for Trust (PaaST), the latter being a development from the InterPARES research.

It is important to recognise that these service models differ in what they offer; for example, they may simply provide file sharing and storage or back-up and data protection or more complicated long-term preservation (Chapter 6). Four main deployment models exist, namely, private cloud, community cloud, public cloud and hybrid cloud (Mell and Grance, 2011).

The uptake of cloud services has rapidly increased as 'the cloud' is seen as a flexible strategy for technology infrastructure and services. Indeed, Gartner (2016) predicted that 'by 2020, a corporate "no-cloud" policy will be as rare as a "no-internet" policy is today. Cloud-first, and even cloud-only, is replacing the defensive no-cloud stance' that has prevailed in the past. Worldwide expenditure on public cloud services and infrastructure was predicted to be $160 billion in 2018 and, despite an anticipated slowing in growth, a five-year compound annual growth rate of more than 20% is expected over the period 2016–2021, 'with public cloud services spending totaling $277 billion in 2021' (IDC, 2018) across a range of sectors.

Cloud computing is well established, however its very nature, particularly third-party public and hybrid deployment models, raises complex legal issues, such as data protection, information sharing and ownership, data sovereignty and data protection regimes, as well as questions of trust.

A framework for considering the challenges and issues of the cloud

The development of cloud computing offers many benefits and opportunities for individual citizens, organizations and, more broadly, communities and society. With these come new challenges and issues, risks and consequences, some of which are unimagined or unintended. The range of challenges and issues to emerge from the InterPARES Trust research is broad, therefore it is helpful to consider them within a high-level conceptual framework comprising three main elements: systems and services, persons, and strategies (Fig. 2.1).

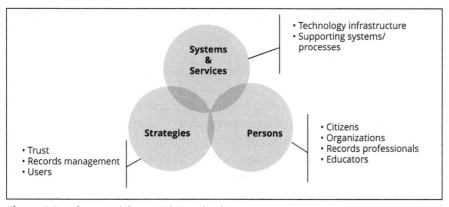

Figure 2.1 *A framework for considering cloud issues*

Systems and services cover not only the digital technologies, systems and services *per se* and their functionality (e.g. IaaS, SaaS, PaaS), but also the systems and processes that enable them to operate properly once deployed. These include interoperability and integration, information security, information sharing and exchange, risk management and sustainability.

Persons are agents, including creators, providers and users of the systems and services. In the context of this book, they are citizens (i.e. members of the public at large) including records professionals and educators and organizations. Organizations may be in any sector – public, private or not-for-profit – and any business within that, for example government, health, education, industry, etc. These persons have different levels of control of the various systems and services.

Strategies are the internal decisions, actions and processes that underpin the adoption, deployment, use and exploitation of cloud services and trust in it. Broadly they cover policies, processes, procedures, models, frameworks and standards, evaluation methods and specific technologies (e.g. blockchain) to address issues of trust, the management of information and records in the cloud and the better understanding and engagement of users.

These three elements are not mutually exclusive as Figure 2.1 illustrates. Persons develop systems, services and strategies; systems and services drive strategies; and strategies are developed by persons to determine system and service use. Some challenges and issues bring all three elements together, however the three main elements form the focus of the chapter with some examples of intersectional issues.

Systems and service issues

Organizations and individual citizens have adopted the cloud deliberately, or by default, for various reasons. These range from access to better hardware/ software infrastructure and services to potential cost savings and new opportunities, e.g. to conduct business in different ways. The key challenges and issues to emerge from the InterPARES Trust research concerned trust, authenticity, reliability and preservation of data/records/information, access and security, integration and interoperability, legal issues around data protection, sharing and ownership because of third party and data protection regimes, and sustainability. These broadly fall into two categories: technology and functionality issues, primarily the concern of service providers and organizations, and non-functional issues such as stakeholder perspectives, issues of trust and the supporting management systems and processes.

Technology infrastructure and functionality

The availability and convenience of obtaining just as much (or more) processing power, storage space and bandwidth by using cloud-based technology infrastructure and services has inclined organizations to use them to support business activities and to offer their services via the internet. This has given rise to e-government, which was the focus of a number of the InterPARES Trust studies. E-government can be simply defined as the use of information technologies, especially the internet, to improve government services for and interactions with citizens (G2C), businesses and industry (G2B) and different divisions of government (G2G) by simplifying processes and by integrating and eliminating redundant systems. (Pearce-Moses, 2018, s.v. e-government).

Although key drivers for e-government are increased efficiency and improved effectiveness (Stančić and Lončarić, 2017), another driver is openness and transparency and the encouragement of citizens to access and use government information through its proactive publication. It is vital that data and records are accurate, reliable, and authentic, that is, trustworthy.

While information flows have always been bi-directional (government to citizen and vice versa), in the e-government and open government context the role of citizens as data/information/records creators is enhanced. Governments can aggregate, search and analyse that data at a much larger scale than was previously possible, to support decision-making about policy, service delivery and development, etc. Data aggregation raises many issues including what should be made available and for how long; who can access it; its quality and accuracy; and the potential impact on the privacy of individuals should it be released (as open data). These and other issues surrounding the access and use of open data from the legal, human and ethical standpoints are discussed in Chapter 3.

Integration and interoperability

Once separate e-services are integrated and provided through a single point of access – a single sign-on (SSO) system – users (both citizens and employees) can log in once and gain access to the various independent services being offered. Not only does the integration of services offer a one-stop-shop experience and 'single source of truth', it also makes them interoperable. In the context of e-government, this enables individuals and businesses to communicate their data only once to governments and public administrations and for that information to be exchanged between the services, providing citizens with access to information and transactions and not requiring any information from them that already exists in any of the interconnected e-services. In Europe, for example, this aligns with the EU's digital single market strategy (European Commission, 2015) and the 'once only principle' (European Commission, 2017). However, this is not yet widespread, either nationally or internationally (Stančić and Lončarić, 2017, 24). Governments and other organizations need to address technical security, interoperability issues and reassure citizens and customers.

How interoperable are government e-services and what is their level of readiness for transborder data exchange? There appears to still be a gap between potential and actual citizen uptake of e-government services, the gap being greater in countries that have not yet developed an SSO. SSO systems interconnection is complex, not only from a technical perspective but also a legal one. Defined and clear legal regulations and frameworks are needed at both national and transnational levels in order to provide fully functional, safe and complete interoperability. The legal framework, wherever the interconnection of SSO systems and/or government e-services is planned, should be proactively developed alongside, or even before, the technical development. However, this is usually not the case and in many situations a technical possibility cannot be fully realised because the law and regulatory developments lag behind (Stančić, Ivanjko et al., 2016).

Security, privacy and access

The Cloud Security Alliance (CSA) has identified 12 critical issues to cloud security based on a survey of its members and industry experts (Cloud Security Alliance, 2017). Ranked top in terms of severity is data breaches, followed by weak identity, credential and access management and insecure APIs. Data loss ranked number eight. According to Gartner Inc. the security challenge lies 'not in the security of the cloud itself, but in the policies and technologies for security and control of the technology. In nearly all cases, it is the user – not the cloud provider – who fails to manage the controls used to protect an organization's data' (Panetta, 2018). In fact, Jay Heiser, a Research Vice President at Gartner Inc. specialising in the cloud, is quoted as saying 'through 2022, at least 95% of cloud security failures will be the customer's fault' (Panetta, 2018). He suggests that organizations should start asking themselves if they are using the cloud securely rather than asking if the cloud is secure. Interestingly, however, Gartner (2016) has predicted that increased security will displace cost savings and agility as the primary driver for government agencies to move to public cloud within their jurisdictions as service providers 'invest heavily in incorporating higher levels of security into their products to continue building confidence that their data is more secure'. They can often invest more than governments or government agencies and hence using cloud services may actually provide greater security.

For cloud users one of the challenges to emerge from the InterPARES research was balancing security, privacy and access, given their various tensions. These include, for example, tensions between privacy and access to data and records; between what is public and what is private data; between managing organizational risk in a public accountability context and protecting personal information while still making data public; and balancing democratic goals with those for business innovation. Cloud-based governmental e-services capture diverse information on citizens. It is important that citizens can trust these to operate securely. They have a right to know how their data is being safeguarded and used and a right to consent to or opt out of their data being shared. Transparency about who is using information and data held in the cloud, why and for what purposes, together with accountability, are required. This is part of good governance and communication. Similarly, organizations need to be confident that cloud service providers are safeguarding the data and information they create and store in the cloud.

Trust in and trustworthiness of systems and services

A number of trust issues arise with the cloud that, though not unique, are increased in this context. For example, access is potentially much wider, data and information sharing much easier, security and privacy more complex to assure and the potential for unintended consequences greater. The issues fall into three broad categories: trust in the digital data/information/records (their accuracy, reliability and authenticity, but especially the latter over the long term); trust in the systems and services; and trust in the parties involved (Borglund, 2015; Duranti and Rogers, 2012; Franks, Poloney and Weck, 2015; Leverich, Nalliah and Suderman, 2015; McLeod and Gormly, 2017; Oliver and Knight, 2015; Stančić, Bursic and Al-Hariri, 2016).

The authenticity of digital data and records is important for many reasons, including to evidence actions and compliance with legal and regulatory requirements, prove ownership, make sound decisions and support business processes and services. In relation to authenticity, one InterPARES Trust project considered people's perceptions of born-digital objects in terms of them being suggested to be the 'real thing' (Bunn et al., 2016) and another explored the notion of trust as a cultural construct shaping and being shaped through social interactions (Oliver, 2018b) (Chapter 5). However, maintaining the authenticity of digital objects over time is complicated (Duranti and Preston, 2005, 2008; Strodl, Petrov and Rauber, 2011).

In relation to systems and services one of the main challenges to have emerged from the InterPARES Trust research is the exchange of sensitive information in a trusted manner. For example, in the transborder exchange of patients' information between e-health e-services of different countries, when a patient of one country needs treatment in another country, could the patient limit what information a foreign doctor is allowed to access? Further, will the established access limitations to certain of the patient's information still be valid when accessing the data using another country's SSO and should there be an access override capability in case of an emergency, for example when the patient is unconscious? Similar situations could arise in transborder communication and data exchange using other e-services interconnected through national SSO systems anywhere (Stančić et al., 2015).

Cloud service providers, and organizations using their services, should provide enough information on the services for users to be able to make informed decisions about trusting them to handle, store, keep and preserve their valuable data. However, a comparative analysis of the security policies of selected cloud infrastructure service providers in Croatia, which sought to identify the information needed for potential customers to view the company as a trusted service provider, highlights that not all service providers perceive the concept of trust in their service as their concern (Stančić, Bursic and Al-Hariri, 2016). Some use disclaimers to place responsibility on the user while others do not understand the special attention required to become a trusted provider. The authors concluded that trust between customers and cloud service providers should be based on providers communicating adequate information and customers negotiating the functionality required. Similarly, SSO systems should also make available as much technical information as possible in order for users to be able to trust that all countries interconnected through such systems comply with the agreed upon requirements and use citizens' data in a trusted manner.

However, a study of the use of mainstream cloud-based social media services such as Facebook, suggests that 'trust in the service provider is a far greater consideration than trust in the technology' (Leverich, Nalliah and Suderman, 2015, 4). This is borne out by McLeod and Gormly (2017) in the context of storing records in the cloud (storage as a service). Their study identified that the primary concerns were the sustainability of the service, its economic viability and its ability to meet records requirements. A subtle additional element is that trust in the service provider does not necessarily translate into trust in the service provided. A user may trust an organization based on the experience of using them for other services and/or technology but if they do not have a positive track record in the particular cloud-based service, a user may still have concerns about the service.

Leverich, Nalliah and Suderman (2015, 4, 8) identify three types of trust particularly applicable in the context of cloud services: cognition, relational and calculated trust. Cognition-based trust is based on judgements, for instance about responsibility and reliability, including (first) impressions of a service or provider. Relational trust is based on direct experience between the parties (trustor and trustee) and includes trust in contractual terms and service sustainability. Calculated trust is a rational economic choice, for example the cost-benefit decision at a point in time. 'Trust should therefore be seen as a combined socio-technical set of requirements, roles and responsibilities, and responsible governance (including rules, policies, procedures and best practices)' (McLeod and Gormly, 2017, 352).

Preservation of information

Cloud services need to be able to preserve data and records safely for as long as it is needed. However, an analysis of twelve Government-to-Citizen and eight Government-to-Business e-services in eight European countries discovered that very little information on the hosting of e-services was available to citizens (Stančić, Brzica et al., 2016). This raises questions about whether there are policies about storage and preservation methods, including for example the preservation of digitally signed records, and whether there are any contingency plans or any long-term service continuity plans. Policies giving information on storage and preservation methods are virtually non-existent or not available online, yet users need to judge whether or not a service will be able to preserve the stored data or records for the legally required period.

In the context of the long-term preservation of digitally signed records, the issue of expiration of signing certificates used in digital signatures also needs to be addressed. E-service providers need to assure users that they will be able to address it or at least that they are aware of the challenge and are actively seeking ways to address it. Lack of information on access to and use of citizen or client data is worrying, as high profile cases, such as Facebook-Cambridge Analytica, have exposed (Cadwalladr and Graham-Harrison, 2018; Rosenberg, Confessore and Cadwalladr, 2018). Users should know how their data will be used and for what purposes. Making short, clear and comprehensible statements about policies and procedures publicly available would greatly improve system operation transparency (Stančić, Brzica et al., 2016). Any person interested in the way an e-service is handling their data should have sufficient and appropriate information available on it to be able to assess how reliable, accurate, secure, transparent and trustworthy it is, and that privacy issues, duties to remember and the right to be forgotten have been considered in its development and operation.

Sustainability and cost

In adopting third-party cloud services, organizations and individuals are, by definition, reliant on the service provider(s) to continue delivering the services for as long as they wish to use them. How sustainable are those services? What (alternative) plans are in place to ensure sustainability, not only business continuity? Can an organization's or an individual's data and records be extracted and transferred to another service and, if so, with what notice period and cost? Are exit and back-up strategies in place?

Part of the sustainability issue is the cost of cloud services, but the modelling of costs appears not yet to be a widespread standard step in the decision-making process. As research by Oliver and Knight highlighted, moving to the cloud means a move from capital to operating expenditure, which is a complicated scenario 'and the financial models aren't there to let you do it' (2015, 7). Models do in fact exist but not all are well known or well used. They are also inadequate for estimating longer term records storage costs, which is very important for records professionals with responsibility for long-term and permanent preservation (McLeod and Gormly, 2018). However, strategies for ensuring the financial sustainability of cloud service adoption and the continued delivery of an economically viable service need to be considered.

Persons

Organizations (including cloud service providers), citizens, records professionals and educators each play a role and have responsibilities and input in the context of entrusting data and records to the cloud. InterPARES Trust research found that some of the roles and responsibilities are changing due to the impact of the digital world on the way we work, live and govern.

For organizations who are not cloud service providers, a key responsibility is to ensure their decision-making processes cover the full range of issues (i.e. systems and services, people, and strategies) and that all key stakeholders are involved. The decisions need to be well informed, risk assessed, and balance short-term business benefits with longer term goals, requirements and obligations, some of which will stretch beyond the organization. Cloud service providers need to understand not only the functional requirements for managing data and records, but the various non-functional requirements such as data ownership and use, security and confidentiality, access and privacy, jurisdictional requirements (e.g. the location of data and records and any cross-border flows), as well as the requirements of different sectors. They need to make it clear, in comprehensible language, if and how their services meet these requirements through policies, terms of service and service level agreements, all of which must then be delivered.

Citizens and organizations need to understand the implications of creating and storing data and records in the cloud, in particular privacy and rights with respect to personal information, including data re-use, but also security, cost and service sustainability. This means understanding the service provider's policies, terms and conditions, making informed risk assessed choices about cloud adoption and any complementary strategies they should consider (Bushey et al., 2016).

In the cloud, some responsibilities, for example controlling the data/records lifecycle, are shared. In theory, the creators (organizations, individuals) maintain responsibility, but in practice they do not have the ability to control the whole lifecycle. For example, preservation of records in the cloud requires not only their guaranteed long-term access but also evidence of their authenticity, that is, identity and integrity. Since the service provider has physical custody of them, they have some responsibility for preservation (e.g. controlling the records' digital components, monitoring technology obsolescence and media fragility, carrying out preservation strategies). The creator has responsibility for specifying the preservation requirements (Chapter 6). Records professionals need to trust third parties as they relinquish some control of custody and they need to be able to properly evaluate options. The question of ownership, for example of the original content and the metadata about its management, is a further complication. All parties therefore have a duty to identify, understand and agree who is responsible for what content, processes and activities, and the parties have a duty to carry out their respective responsibilities.

Shared responsibility calls for collaboration between all stakeholders (i.e. different roles in organizations, service providers, records professionals and citizens); collaboration offers a range of positive outcomes. It enables multiple, sometimes diverse perspectives to be shared and incorporated into needs assessments. Educating service providers about recordkeeping requirements in the context of legal, business and personal needs could lead to better systems and services that meet these and also mitigate risks. Many examples of collaboration between different professionals and stakeholders and citizen engagement were found in the InterPARES research and appear throughout the book.

Records professionals have a central role to play because data and records are being created, captured and stored in the cloud by default, not only by design. They have the capacity to take a holistic perspective that recognises all stakeholders' needs and the broader longer term context and addresses compliance and ethical issues, so that the opportunities of the cloud can be exploited and the risks minimised. To do this they need to assume a strategic and proactive leadership role. An illustration of such an approach is Stockholm City Archives' incorporation of open data into their digital archives strategy, putting the archives at the centre of the information provision in the city (Chapter 11). Horizon scanning needs to be part of records professionals' activities to recognise new and emerging or changing technological, social and regulatory contexts, to identify what knowledge and skills they need and be confident about their contribution and expertise. This is about anticipating, shaping and re-interpreting their role in these landscapes. Some of the 'newer' responsibilities are already recognised in international records management standards and feature in an ontology of functions and activities of records professionals (Gänser and Michetti, 2018).

The cloud opens up many opportunities for records professionals to apply their discipline-specific knowledge and expertise in a more complex environment in collaboration with others. To be successful they will need strong leadership and strategic management skills, up-to-date digital skills, an understanding of the language of other professionals and the ability to communicate their records language. This will require continuing skills development to meet new demands. The future records professional may be very different from the professional of the past. The latter has implications for education and continuing professional and personal development. The dynamic digital landscape offers future records professionals more diverse careers, working contexts and responsibilities. Education programs need to prepare them for this. Chapter 12 discusses this in detail and identifies a broad set of required professional competencies comprising *cognitive competencies* (spanning archival, legal, technological and business knowledge), *functional competencies* (spanning similar areas and additionally research functions) and *social competencies* (covering ethics and relationship management).

Strategies

Each of the four groups of persons needs to develop strategies for managing information in the cloud and trusting both the information and the organizations involved in its creation, provision and use. Depending on the sensitivities and value of the information, individual persons may simply place their trust in the service provider (e.g. Facebook, Google, Amazon, etc.) and the terms and agreements of service use. Where the information is sensitive or valuable (precious) to them, they may be more cautious, seek additional levels of security, access, back-up, preservation and sustainability, etc. The focus here is on organizations and records professionals and their strategies for working with the other persons.

For organizations, the overarching strategy for managing information in the cloud falls within information governance, defined here as:

> … a senior-level administrative structure that establishes roles and respon-
> sibilities, decision-making processes, policies and procedures that promote
> effective decisions regarding the effective and efficient creation, storage, use, and
> disposition of information resources that align with business outcomes.
>
> (Pearce-Moses, 2018, s.v. information governance)

The strategies discussed here offer ways of trusting services providers and trusting that records and data are managed in ways that mitigate risk to the organization or the individual.

Strategies for trusting the cloud

Trust is a question of:

> … confidence of one party in another, based on alignment of value systems
> with respect to specific actions or benefits, and involving a relationship of
> voluntary vulnerability, dependence and reliance, based on risk assessment.
>
> (Pearce-Moses, 2018, s.v. trust)

It is subjective and complex (Nathan, Shaffer and Castor, 2015). For organizations, trust begins with the cloud adoption decision-making process. The process needs to be robust rather than a 'leap of faith' as suggested by Oliver and Knight (2015) in the specific context of cloud storage. McLeod and Gormly (2017) identify a range of factors that contribute to trust in the decision-making process, including having a clear goal, undertaking a thorough analysis of alternatives, service provider reputation and risk assessment. Internal and external policies play an important role here, for example in establishing ownership and use/re-use rights, as discussed in Chapters 3 and 10 in open government and cultural heritage contexts, respectively.

A series of checklists have been developed from the InterPARES Trust research specifically to support organizations, in particular records professionals, to trust in the cloud. A checklist for evaluating cloud contracts covers topics that include data ownership and use; availability, retrieval and use; data storage and preservation; data retention and disposition; security, confidentiality and privacy; data localisation and cross-border data flows; and end of service and contract termination. Other checklists are aimed at trusting specific services and systems: one for Infrastructure-as-a-Service, one for assessing implemented government e-services, and one for assessing implemented single sign-on systems. These and other checklists are outlined in Appendix 2.

In relation to the specific issue of security, different cloud service models (e.g. IaaS and SaaS) each have specific risks and therefore control implications. If, as Gartner suggests (Panetta, 2018), most of the security failures are the user's fault, organizations can help avoid this by implementing an information security management system such as ISO 27001, 2013. Such a system 'preserves the confidentiality, integrity and availability of information by applying a risk management process and gives confidence to interested parties that risks are adequately managed' (ISO, 2013, v). One aspect of an information security management system is the classification of information assets 'to ensure that information receives an appropriate level of protection in accordance with its importance to the organization' (ISO, 2013, clause 8.2).

The InterPARES checklist for developing or revising policies for managing security classified information assets (SCIA) policies can help (Deserno et al., 2017). It includes the question 'Does the policy cover SCIAs not in the physical custody of the organization, but still under the control of the organization, for example SCIAs managed using third-party cloud computing services?', which serves as a reminder to check that a cloud service provider can meet the policy requirements.

Another strategy is to develop data security standards. This has been done in the UK by the National Health Service for public-sector health and care organizations, including other private sector organizations contracted to provide services (NHS England, 2018). These standards were developed in response to a review conducted by the National Data Guardian for Health and Care (2016) in the context of balancing the duty to protect patient confidentiality with the duty to share information in order to realise improvements and opportunities that are in people's interests. Data security is also considered in the Standards of Practice for Archives and Records Management, an overarching framework for what is currently considered as a reasonable and prudent approach to addressing information protection for archives and records management (Cohen, 2015). Security and privacy issues, together with the potential societal impact of sharing digital information, are considered in Chapters 3 and 5.

Strategies for understanding and meeting user needs

In the digital environment, understanding the changing needs and behaviours of information creators and users is critical. Harnessing greater understanding of user information behaviour provides opportunities to develop better systems to meet users' needs. This can be done using technology such as user log analysis and data analytics (Chapter 6) (Schenkolewski-Kroll and Tractinsky, 2015, 2016, 2017), or by involving users either through heuristic evaluation (Chapter 8) or seeking their views. The latter approach was used in a study exploring the attitudes of the indigenous people of New Zealand to the digitisation of resources in their language by cultural heritage institutions (Chapter 10) (Oliver, 2018a).

Strategies for managing information and records

Strategies and principles developed in the physical (paper) world do not always transfer to the cloud in exactly the same way, and possibly not at all. The chain of preservation is one example (Chapter 9). The InterPARES Trust research developed strategies for a number of aspects, including ensuring authenticity and authenticating digital records, intellectual control, appraisal, retention and disposition, and preservation. These will be of particular value to records professionals in exercising their primary functions such as implementing retention and disposition schedules in the cloud, understanding the role of metadata in cloud services for chain of custody, rethinking issues of appraisal, arrangement and description, and understanding new practices with respect to preservation.

Authenticity and authenticating digital records

Assessments of authenticity and reliability (for full definitions see Appendix 1, and Pearce-Moses, 2018) are vital for establishing the trustworthiness of data and records to enable organizations to offer evidence of and defend their actions, prove ownership of physical and intellectual assets, support business processes and demonstrate legislative and regulatory compliance. Different strategies can be adopted to ensure the authenticity of data and records in the cloud; two examples from the InterPARES Trust research are considered here.

The first strategy proposes a framework to certify the trustworthiness of digital records that support an audit process. A framework to authenticate digital records for auditing process comprises profiling records generated in business, recordkeeping or other 'informal' systems and retrieving them in context. It can be applied in different organizational contexts. The checklists for assessing the authenticity and reliability of digital records in each records phase focus on areas such as business process, records management, IT general controls, application controls and record artefacts. The assessment can be used as evidence during an audit (Chapter 7).

The second example relates to aggregated information in a dataset. A records classification scheme can be used to identify candidate records for (open) publication; the context in which they are created and the processes leading to their publication must be captured (Léveillé and Timms, 2015, 173). It must be possible to trace any aggregated open data back to the originating records and, in the case of data 'mashed up' from various sources, the processes used to perform the aggregations should be documented and retained as evidence (McDonald and Léveillé, 2014, 113). Open data licenses are a way to address access, use and re-use rights.

Intellectual control

Two well-established strategies for exercising intellectual control over records are the use of metadata and arrangement and description (Chapter 8). The cloud presents distinct challenges for the former and also opportunities, particularly for automatic metadata capture, which should be exploited.

Recent initiatives are oriented towards systems with semi-structured or semi-automated metadata capture. Metadata that ensures the authenticity, traceability and legal value of information needs to be captured systematically, as descriptive metadata typical of archival processing and essential for access is not sufficient. In the context of e-government homogeneous and transverse practices, rather than local institutional ones, they are needed to support interoperability, both at the technical and organizational levels. The most successful and advanced practices integrate IT, legal, records management and long-term preservation perspectives into information projects. Records professionals should look for opportunities to use technology to enhance existing practice. These can complement, rather than replace, traditional approaches.

Appraisal, retention and disposition

Appraisal is '[t]he process of assessing the value of records for the purpose of determining the length and conditions of their preservation' (InterPARES, 2018). While users and potential users are implicitly considered in the traditional appraisal process, the cloud provides the potential for including human activity as an element in appraisal decisions, for example in relation to websites. By using Google Analytics to understand user behaviour, it is possible to arrive at a formula that may then make it possible to define appraisal metrics that incorporate social value. This is a unique approach to the appraisal of websites and web content (Chapter 6). Of course it is imperative to understand the underlying analytics algorithms in order to trust their meaning.

Retention and disposition are underpinning principles of the lifecycle management of records and information (Chapter 6). Indeed some legislation (specifically data protection laws) requires destruction of records/information after a certain time, but the capacity and apparent economy of digital storage has led to suggestions that we should keep everything. However, there are good reasons for disposing of records and data that are no longer of value to an organization. There is also the important issue of environmental impact, despite the use of machine learning to improve energy efficiency of large data centres, as has been demonstrated by, for example, Google (Google, n.d.; Evans and Gao, 2016).

Retention and disposition are managed via approved retention schedules, applied in ways that are irrespective of the record's format, location or custody, and therefore appropriate in the cloud context. However, since records are in the (physical) custody of the cloud service provider, transparency and responsibility for their disposition must be addressed. A checklist of functional requirements for retention and disposition helps organizations and individuals measure their cloud services against requirements (Franks, 2015, 2016; Appendix 2).

Preservation

Three strategies for managing preservation in the cloud emerged from the research. The first, and simplest, is for the service provider to assume responsibility for preservation. In this case, the preservation policy must demonstrate the existence of robust procedures for maintaining data and records authenticity and accuracy, strategies for monitoring technology, policies for file formats and access control, and a guarantee of service continuity (Chapter 6).

The second strategy builds a framework for preservation and access that can be implemented via a series of interconnected but independent services. Preservation as a Service for Trust (PaaST) is OAIS-compliant, but introduces the concept of a preservation environment, rather than an archival information system, and 'defines a comprehensive set of functional and data requirements that support preservation of digital information regardless of the technologies used or who uses them' (Thibodeau, 2018, 8). The preservation environment is the place where implementation of the require-ments occurs; it can be a single trusted digital repository (see Pearce-Moses, 2018, s.v. trusted digital repository) or a space where a variety of parties are involved in preservation. Although the PaaST model was developed for the cloud context, it can be used in other situations in the preservation of any type of digital material (e.g. in-house preservation and hybrid approaches that use in-house and contracted services). PaaST could be the basis for a new type of service for 'dark' repositories, i.e. offline secure storage infrastructure for digital preservation masters, provided by archival institutions for the trusted storage of external creators' digital records (Chapter 9).

PaaST represents a movement away from in-house preservation (often unsustainable and prone to obsolescence) to more scalable, service-based solutions. Here, multiple competing and/or collaborating service providers can provide flexible, integrated and constantly evolving preservation services for those who are responsible for ensuring the longevity of and access to digital records. The vision is digital archiving as a service. The advantages of this approach are that it avoids the need for expensive in-house investment in equipment and dependence upon (often) scarce digital archiving technical expertise and takes advantage of advances in technology. In addition to the issues of trust discussed earlier, the challenge of this approach is integrating a complex and dynamic set of interconnected services from different suppliers applied to records in distributed physical custody.

The third strategy is to harness emerging blockchain technology that supports the requirement for integrity or immutability 'because everything that is being recorded can no longer be changed or deleted' (Stančić, 2018a, 9). InterPARES Trust research explored its use to address the specific challenge of preserving digitally signed or sealed records. Current preservation strategies for digitally authenticated records rely on the management of digital certificates, which usually have a short life span, to maintain validity. However, the proposed blockchain-based model avoids the need for organizations, especially archival institutions, to periodically re-sign or re-timestamp digitally signed records before their digital certificates expire. The model, called TRUSTER VIP (Validity Information Preservation) Solution: TrustChain, achieves this by:

> ... checking the record's signature validity at ingest and, if valid, writing the signature's hash (and some metadata) in the blockchain. Signature validity is checked by all or, if their number is sufficiently high, some (qualified majority) of the institutions participating in the distributed network of interconnected trusted institutions. If the signature is deemed valid the information is permanently stored in the TrustChain blockchain, i.e. in the distributed ledger.
>
> (Stančić, 2018a, 4)

TRUSTER VIP has been applied to digitally signed medical records, procurement and supplier contracts, minutes of meetings, fund records and e-tax records (Stančić, 2018b, 2018c; Stengård, Almgren and Stančić, 2017), but can be applied more broadly. It is envisioned that the TrustChain solution would be maintained by an international alliance of archival institutions (Chapter 7).

Conclusion

This chapter is not a complete and comprehensive introduction to all the challenges and issues relating to the cloud and management of records and data. Rather, it has presented the key ones that have emerged from the InterPARES Trust research. The cloud offers new opportunities – services 'on demand' and potentially much better services (e.g. preservation, access, storage, etc.). By definition this means a need for trust in the third-party service providers. Trust is complex and goes to the heart of successful adoption and use of the cloud – balancing the range of benefits with the issues and risks. This book explores the detail of many aspects of trust in particular contexts across the world.

The strategies for cloud adoption and trust in cloud services presented here must engage all relevant stakeholders within and outside the organization. They are not restricted solely to records professionals because trustworthy records in the cloud must be considered from the point of creation onwards. Creators, creating organizations and departments and cloud service providers also have responsibilities, which they need to understand. All of these groups can use the various checklists and evaluation/assessment criteria that have been developed. The findings in information governance, risk management and authentication practices and technologies should assist organizations considering putting their records in the cloud or managing existing cloud services and support records professionals in this context. They should also be of interest to educators for curriculum development and individuals who use the cloud.

References

Borglund, E. (2015) What About Trust in the Cloud? Archivists' Views on Trust / La Question de La Confiance Dans Le Nuage: Le Point de Vue Des Archivistes Sur La Question, *Canadian Journal of Information and Library Science*, **39** (2),114–27.

Bort, J. (2012) Here's How Larry Ellison Invented Cloud Computing, *Business Insider*, 2 October 2012, www.businessinsider.com/netsuite-ceo-larry-ellison-invented-cloud-computing-2012-10

Bunn, J., Brimble, S., Obelensky, S. and Wood, N. (2016) *Perceptions of Born Digital Authenticity*. EU28, Final Report, InterPARES Trust, https://interparestrust.org/assets/public/dissemination/EU28_20160718_UserPerceptionsOfAuthenticity_FinalReport.pdf

Bushey, J., Demoulin, M., How, E. and McLelland, R. (2016) *Checklist for Cloud Service Contracts*, NA14. InterPARES Trust, https://interparestrust.org/assets/-public/dissemination/NA14_20160226_CloudServiceProviderContracts_Checklist_Final.pdf

Cadwalladr, C. and Graham-Harrison, E. (2018) Revealed: 50 Million Facebook Profiles Harvested for Cambridge Analytica in Major Data Breach. *The Guardian*, 17 March 2018, News section, www.theguardian.com/news/2018/mar/17/cambridge-analytica-facebook-influence-us-election

Cloud Security Alliance (2017) Top Threats to Cloud Computing Plus: Industry Insights, https://cloudsecurityalliance.org/group/top-threats/

Cloud Security Alliance (n.d.) Cloud Security Alliance – About, https://cloudsecurityalliance.org/about/ [accessed 3 July 2018].

Cohen, F. (2015) *Standard of Practice for Archives and Records Management*, NA03, Final Report. InterPARES Trust, https://interparestrust.org/assets/public/dissemination/NA03_20160202_StandardOfPractice_InternationalPlenary3_FinalReport_Final.pdf

Deserno, I., Sengsavang, E., Shockley, M., Katuu, S. and Kastenhofer, J. (2017) *Checklist for Developing or Revising Policies for Managing Security Classified Information Assets*, TR03. InterPARES Trust, https://interparestrust.org/assets/public/dissemination/TR03-Checklist-2_-final.pdf

Duranti, L. and Preston, R. (eds) (2005) *The Long-Term Preservation of Authentic Electronic Records: findings of the InterPARES Project*, San Miniato, Archilab.

Duranti, L. and Preston, R. (eds) (2008) *Research on Permanent Authentic Records in Electronic Systems (InterPARES) 2: Experiential, Interactive and Dynamic Records*, Padova, Associazione Nazionale Archivistica Italiana.

Duranti, L. and Rogers, C. (2012) Trust in Digital Records: An Increasingly Cloudy Legal Area, *Computer Law & Security Review*, **28** (5), 522–31. https://doi.org/10.1016/j.clsr.2012.07.009

European Commission (2015) EUR-Lex – 52015DC0192: A Digital Single Market Strategy for Europe, https://eur-lex.europa.eu/legal-content/EN/TXT/?uri=celex:52015DC0192

European Commission (2017) EU-Wide Digital Once-Only Principle for Citizens and Businesses – Policy Options and Their Impacts, *Digital Single Market*, https://ec.europa.eu/digital-single-market/en/news/eu-wide-digital-once-only-principle-citizens-and-businesses-policy-options-and-their-impacts

Evans, R. and Gao, J (2016) DeepMind AI Reduces Google Data Centre Cooling Bill by 40%, *DeepMind*, https://deepmind.com/blog/deepmind-ai-reduces-google-data-centre-cooling-bill-40/

Franks, P. (2015) New Technologies, New Challenges: Records Retention and Disposition in a Cloud Environment / Nouvelles Technologies, Nouveaux Défis: Conservation et Déclassement Des Documents Dans Un Environnement de Nuage Informatique, *Canadian Journal of Information and Library Science*, **39** (2), 191–209.

Franks, P. (2016) *Retention and Disposition in a Cloud Environment*, NA06, Final Report. InterPARES Trust, https://interparestrust.org/assets/public/dissemination/NA06_20160902_RetentionDispositionInCloud_FinalReport_Final.pdf

Franks, P., Poloney, K. and Weck, A. (2015) *Executive Summary of Survey Distributed to Members of ARMA International*, InterPARES Trust, https://interparestrust.org/assets/public/dissemination/NA06_20150331_RetentionDispositionClouds_ExecutiveSummary_Report_Final.pdf

Gänser, G. and Michetti, G. (2018) *Ontology of Functional Activities for Archival Systems*, TR05, Final Report.,InterPARES Trust. https://interparestrust.org/assets/public/dissemination/TR05-FinalReport-20180526.pdf

Gartner (2016) Gartner Says Security Will Displace Cost and Agility as Primary Reason Government Agencies Move to Cloud, Press Release, https://www.gartner.com/newsroom/id/3187517

Google (n.d.) DataCenters, *Google Environment*,
https://environment.google/projects/machine-learning/ [accessed 3 July 2018].

IDC (2018) Worldwide Public Cloud Services Spending Forecast to Reach $160
Billion This Year, According to IDC,
https://www.idc.com/getdoc.jsp?containerId=prUS43511618

InterPARES (2018) InterPARES 2 Terminology Database,
www.interpares.org/ip2/display_file.cfm?doc=ip2_glossary.pdf&CFID=
16119752&CFTOKEN=94344076

ISO (2013) ISO/IEC 27001:2013 – Information Technology – Security Techniques –
Information Security Management Systems – Requirements,
https://www.iso.org/standard/54534.html

Léveillé, V. and Timms, K. (2015) Through a Records Management Lens: creating a
framework for trust in open government and open government information/Les
Objectifs Visés Par Les Systèmes de Gestion Documentaires : La Mise En Place
D'un Cadre de Confiance et de La Transparence de L'information Dans Un
Gouvernement Ouvert, *Canadian Journal of Information and Library Science*, **39** (2),
154–90.

Leverich, M., Nalliah, K. and Suderman, J. (2015) *Historical Study of Cloud-Based
Services*, NA11, Final Report, InterPARES Trust,
https://interparestrust.org/trust/research_dissemination

Madhavaiah, C., Bashir, I. and Shafi, S. (2012) Defining Cloud Computing in
Business Perspective: a review of research, *Vision*, **16** (3), 163–73.

McDonald, J. and Léveillé, V. (2014) Whither the Retention Schedule in the Era of
Big Data and Open Data?, edited by Dr Anne Thurston, *Records Management
Journal*, **24** (2), 99–121, https://doi.org/10.1108/RMJ-01-2014-0010

McLeod, J. and Gormly, B. (2017) Using the Cloud for Records Storage: issues of
trust, *Archival Science*, **17** (4), 349–70, https://doi.org/10.1007/s10502-017-9280-5

McLeod, J., and Gormly, B. (2018) Records Storage in the Cloud: are we modelling
the cost?, *Archives and Manuscripts*, March, 1–19,
https://doi.org/10.1080/01576895.2017.1409125

Mell, P. and Grance, T. (2011) SP 800-145, The NIST Definition of Cloud Computing.
NIST, https://csrc.nist.gov/publications/detail/sp/800-145/final

Mishra, D. (2014) Cloud Computing: the era of virtual world opportunities and risks
involved, *International Journal of Computer Science Engineering*, **3** (4), 204–9.

Nathan, L., Shaffer, E. and Castor, M. (2015) Stewarding Collections of Trauma:
plurality, responsibility, and questions of action, *Archivaria*, **80** (40th anniversary
issue), 89–118.

National Data Guardian for Health and Care (2016) Review of Data Security,
Consent and Opt-Outs,
https://assets.publishing.service.gov.uk/government/uploads/system/uploads/
attachment_data/file/535024/data-security-review.PDF

NHS England, Department of Health and Social Care (2018) 2017/18 Data Security and Protection Requirements, https://assets.publishing.service.gov.uk/government/uploads/system/uploads/attachment_data/file/675420/17-18_statement_of_requirements_Branded_template_final_22_11_18-1.pdf

Oliver, G. (2018a) *Kōrero Kitea: Ngā Hua O Te Whakamamatitanga: The Impacts of Digitised Te Reo Archival Collections*, AA08, Final Report, InterPARES Trust.

Oliver, G. (2018b) *User Perceptions of Trust*, AA02, Final Report, InterPARES Trust. https://interparestrust.org/assets/public/dissemination/AA02FinalReport.pdf

Oliver, G. and Knight, S. (2015) Storage is a Strategic Issue: digital preservation in the cloud, *D-Lib Magazine*, **21** (3/4), https://doi.org/10.1045/march2015-oliver

Panetta, K. (2018) Is the Cloud Secure?, *Smarter With Gartner*, https://www.gartner.com/smarterwithgartner/is-the-cloud-secure/

Pearce-Moses, R. (ed.) (2018) *InterPARES Trust Terminology*, InterPARES Trust, www.interparestrust.org/terminology.

Rosenberg, M., Confessore, N. and Cadwalladr, C. (2018) How Trump Consultants Exploited the Facebook Data of Millions, *The New York Times*, 2 April 2018, section U.S. https://www.nytimes.com/2018/03/17/us/politics/cambridge-analytica-trump-campaign.html

Schenkolewski-Kroll, S. and Tractinsky, A. (2015) *Research on Retention and Disposition Processes in an Internet Website of the Government of Israel: The Ministry of Foreign Affairs case study*, EU01, Final Report, InterPARES Trust, https://interparestrust.org/assets/public/dissemination/EU01_20150909_RetentionDispositionProcessesIsraeliForeignAffairs_FinalReport_Final.pdf

Schenkolewski-Kroll, S. and Tractinsky, A. (2016) *Research on Users of the English Website of the Israel Ministry of Foreign Affairs as a Criterion for Appraising Records*. EU25, Final Report, InterPARES Trust, https://interparestrust.org/assets/public/dissemination/EU25_20161001_WebAnalyticsAndAppraisalMinistryForeignAffairsIsrael_FinalReport_Final.pdf

Schenkolewski-Kroll, S. and Tractinsky, A. (2017) *Archival Appraisal, Retention Schedules and Metadata in Web Sites – The Case Study of the Ministry of Foreign Affairs, Israel*, EU36, Final Report, InterPARES Trust, https://interparestrust.org/assets/public/dissemination/EU036_20171120_AppraisalWebsites_FinalReport.pdf

Stančić, H. (2018a) *Model for Preservation of Trustworthiness of the Digitally Signed, Timestamped And/Or Sealed Digital Records (TRUSTER Preservation Model)*, EU31, Final Report, InterPARES Trust, https://interparestrust.org/assets/public/dissemination/TRUSTERPreservationModel(EU31)-Finalreportv_1_3.pdf

Stančić, H. (2018b) *Model for Preservation of Trustworthiness of the Digitally Signed, Timestamped And/Or Sealed Digital Records (TRUSTER Preservation Model) – Case*

Study 1–digitally Signed Retirement Fund Records, EU31, Case Study 1, InterPARES Trust, https://interparestrust.org/assets/public/dissemination/ TRUSTERPreservationModel(EU31)-CaseStudy1v1_2.pdf

Stančić, H. (2018c) *Model for Preservation of Trustworthiness of the Digitally Signed, Timestamped And/Or Sealed Digital Records (TRUSTER Preservation Model) – Case Study 2–digitally Signed E-Tax Records*, EU31, Case Study 2, InterPARES Trust, https://interparestrust.org/assets/public/dissemination/ TRUSTERPreservationModel(EU31)-CaseStudy2v1_2.pdf

Stančić, H., Brzica, H., Adzaga, I., Garic, A., Polijicak Susec, M., Presecki, K. and Stankovic, A. (2016) *Checklist for Comparative Analysis of Implemented Governmental E-Services*, EU09, InterPARES Trust, https://interparestrust.org/assets/public/ dissemination/EU09ComparativeAnalysisofImplementedGovernmentale-Services-Checklistv1.0_.pdf

Stančić, H., Bursic, E. and Al-Hariri, A. (2016) *Checklist for Ensuring Trust in Storage in Infrastructure-as-a-Service*, EU08, InterPARES Trust, https://interparestrust.org/assets/public/dissemination/EU08_IaaS_ Checklistv1.2_.pdf

Stančić, H., Ivanjko, T., Bonic, N., Garic, A., Lončarić, K., Lovasic, A., Presecki, K. and Stankovic, A. (2015) *Analysis of the Interoperability Possibilities of Implemented Governmental E-Services*, EU15, Final Report, InterPARES Trust, https://interparestrust.org/assets/public/dissemination/EU15_20160727_ InteroperabilityGovEServices_FinalReport.pdf

Stančić, H., Ivanjko, T., Bonic, N., Garic, A., Lončarić, K., Lovasic, A., Presecki, K. and Stankovic, A. (2016) *Checklist for Analysis of the Interoperability Possibilities of Implemented Governmental E-Services*, EU15, InterPARES Trust, https://interparestrust.org/assets/public/dissemination/EU15_20160727_SSO_ Checklistv1.2_.pdf

Stančić, H. and Lončarić, K. (2017) Reaching Computational Trust: Requirements for Implementing Trusted E-Government. In Gosternik, N. (ed.) *Digital and Digitized: archives yesterday, today and tomorrow*, 13–25, Pokrajinski arhiv Maribor, www.academia.edu/32397874/Reaching_Computational_Trust_ Requirements_for_Implementing_Trusted_e-Government

Stengård, M., Almgren, H. and Stančić, H. (2017) *Model for Preservation of Trustworthiness of the Digitally Signed, Timestamped And/Or Sealed Digital Records (TRUSTER Preservation Model) – Case Study 3 – Digitally Signed Medical Records, Procurement and Supplier Contracts, Official Political Decisions and Minutes of Meetings*, EU31, Case Study 3, InterPARES Trust, https://interparestrust.org/ assets/public/dissemination/TRUSTERPreservationModel(EU31)-CaseStudy3v1_ 3.pdf

Strodl, S., Petrov, P. and Rauber, A. (2011) Research on Digital Preservation within Projects Co-Funded by the European Union in the ICT Programme, https://pdfs.semanticscholar.org/f48c/b8fc9553633ff6cfe2325c7a1abd82cec8e5.pdf

Thibodeau, K. (2018) *Preservation as a Service for Trust (PaaST)*, NA12, Final Report, InterPARES Trust, https://interparestrust.org/assets/ public/dissemination/PreservationasaServiceforTrust1_0-FINAL.pdf

Wikipedia (2018) John McCarthy (Computer Scientist), https://en.wikipedia.org/w/index.php?title=John_McCarthy_(computer_scientist) &oldid=846909390

3

Open government

Editor: Elizabeth Shepherd
Contributors: Gabriela Andaur, Alicia Barnard,
Ineke Deserno, Carlos Silva Ditadi, Andrew Flinn,
Grant Hurley, Shadrack Katuu, James Lowry,
Julie McLeod, Umi Asma' Mokhtar, Eng Sengsavang,
Anna Sexton and Jim Suderman

Introduction

This chapter seeks to investigate and establish the nature of open government and the role of data, records and archives in promoting and enabling open government around the world. It identifies key issues around open government from the literature reviews and from the research-in-practice undertaken as part of the InterPARES Trust (hereinafter ITrust) project. In its conclusion it draws out some lessons for citizens, public organizations, records professionals and records educators working in the arena of open government to demonstrate the vital role that data and records play in enabling open government activities.

Definitions

This section sets out definitions of the main concepts and terms that will be referred to in the chapter.

The ITrust Terminology Database defines **open government** as:

> ... an approach designed to provide greater access to unrestricted information held by public bodies in order to promote transparency, accountability, and citizen engagement and participation, to accomplish a larger outcome of building and enhancing citizens' trust in their governments.
>
> (Pearce-Moses, 2018, s.v. open government)

Terms used in this definition are also themselves defined in the ITrust Terminology Database. **Accountability** is defined as 'the obligation to answer for actions for which one is responsible'.

Transparency is defined as '(the condition of) timely disclosure of information about an individual's or organization's activities and decisions, especially to support accountability to all stakeholders'.

Citizen engagement is defined as:

> Efforts to actively empower citizens in government decision-making processes through transparent dialog and communication among individual citizens and with the government in order to increase trust in the government and to ensure decisions reflect citizens' interests.
>
> (Pearce-Moses, 2018, s.v. citizen engagement)

Citizen engagement initiatives may make use of technologies to connect with citizens. Synonyms include citizen participation, civic participation, civic engagement and open dialogue. These issues are treated in detail in Chapter 4 and are not discussed here.

In order to deliver open government, public authorities need to proactively release data and information. Two related definitions are, therefore, **open data,** defined as 'data available to anyone that may be used for any purpose and that is in a structure that facilitates its use at little or no charge' (ITrust Terminology) and **open information**, that is, 'the release of government records and published materials for public use, typically in unstructured formats' (Léveillé and Timms, 2015).

The UK study on the role of the records manager identified common elements for the definition of **open government data**, such as 'freely available', 're-usable', and 'machine readable'. The final report suggests that a clear and comprehensive definition of open government data is still needed (Page, Flinn and Shepherd, 2014). The study of open government data in NHS (National Health Service) England observes, however, that defining open government data is difficult, which may account for a lack of consistency in the definitions established to date (Harrison, Shepherd and Flinn, 2015). The ITrust Terminology Database defines it as:

> Data that is created or accumulated in the public sector and is available to anyone, and that may be used for any purpose and is in a structure that facilitates its use at little or no charge.
>
> (Pearce-Moses, 2018, s.v. open government data)

Suderman (2017) identified nine ITrust research projects that pertain to open government. He noted that the definitions of the terms discussed above are better established in Sweden, according to the study of the role of records managers in that jurisdiction (Engvall, Liang and Anderson, 2015). Definitions of open government, open data and open government data as set out by the Open Government Partnership (OGP) (n.d.), opendefinition.org (Open Knowledge International n.d.), the European Parliament's Public Sector Information Directive (2003) and the European Commission's Inspire Directive (2015) have been adopted by Swedish national bodies. The UK studies at local and regional level seem less influenced by the wider EU context than the Swedish study.

The report of the North American study notes the challenge of defining the evolving term 'open government'. The study adopted the four principles of the Open Government Partnership as its definitional scope (McDonald and Léveillé, 2014; Léveillé and Timms, 2015). Variations among definitions of open government, open (government) data and big data illustrate one of the challenges of establishing common record-keeping approaches to supporting open initiatives. The absence of widely adopted definitions of these terms, within individual countries and internationally, presents a challenge to records managers.

Definitions relating to the restriction of access to information are also important since they provide a challenge to the idea of open government. Terms such as 'classified information' are left somewhat ill-defined by current literature. The lack of clarity about what these terms mean and do not mean can cause problems (Hooten, 2011). Classified information is usually secret information with restrictions about who may see it (Aftergood, 2000, 2013). However, in many organizations, restricted information is not confined only to information that is classified for security purposes. For example, personnel information is also restricted, but for privacy purposes. Aftergood (2000) notes that, in the US government, genuine classified information 'pertains to that body of information which, if disclosed, could actually damage national security in some identifiable way'. This mirrors ISO 27002:2013, section 8.2.1, which sets out four levels for information confidentiality classification schemes: (a) disclosure causes no harm; (b) disclosure causes minor embarrassment or minor operation inconvenience; (c) disclosure has a significant short term impact on operations or tactical objectives; (d) disclosure has a serious impact on long term strategic objectives or puts the survival of the organization at risk (International Organization for Standardization (ISO), 2013).

The OGP is an important development that ought to bring these definitions and understandings more in line with each other internationally. The OGP is a multinational organization launched in 2011 with the Open Government Declaration. Eight countries endorsed the Declaration as founding signatories (Brazil, Mexico, South Africa, United States, Philippines, Indonesia, Norway and the United Kingdom) and, since then, over 70 countries have signed. The Declaration had four initial objectives:

- Increase the availability of information about governmental activities
- Support civic participation
- Implement the highest standards of professional integrity throughout our administrations
- Increase access to new technologies for openness and accountability.

Member nations must prepare action plans and report regularly on their progress. For example, Canada has developed three consecutive action plans for 2012 to 2018 (Open Government Partnership, n.d.).

As one of the other co-founding countries, Brazil signed the Open Government Declaration and presented its Action Plan in 2011. Brazil's commitment to OGP was implemented through the Decree of September 15, 2011. Brazil's Action Plan (2016–2018) contains initiatives aligned with the following themes: citizen participation mechanisms, transparency of public funds, open government in states and municipalities, innovation and open government in education, and open data and active transparency in the environment. The mechanisms are implemented with the participation of civil society, public organizations and civilians.

Mexico has presented its Third Action Plan (2016–2018). A main objective is to make <gob.mx> a viable tool for government, in compliance with the OGP Joint Declaration on Open Government for the Implementation of the 2030 Agenda. The Mexican Action Plan has objectives on areas such as human rights and strengthening the rule of law, gender equality, poverty and inequality, public health services, anti-corruption systems, water, public services, natural resources and climate change governance.

Chile formally signed the Open Government Declaration and joined OGP in 2011 and is also implementing its Third Action Plan. The Secretary-General of the Presidency is responsible for Open Government. Initiatives are selected through consultation with public and Civil Society organizations. The Action Plan (2016–2018) describes initiatives in four main areas: neo-extractivism, natural resources and environment; social protection policies and educational policies; modernisation of the State; and integrity and transparency in the public service.

Peru joined the OPG in 2012 and has committed to increasing transparency levels in government, to support and promote citizen participation, to implement high standards of professional integrity in the public administration and to increase access to and use of new technologies. Led by the Presidency of the Ministries Council, the country is implementing its Third Action Plan (2017–2019).

The next two sections outline the development of open government and of open government data and highlight some key themes from the existing literature. These themes are illustrated with practice examples and other regional and country-specific research carried out as part of the ITrust research projects.

Research in practice

Open government is a strategy intended to increase trust in government through access to information and greater citizen involvement in government processes. It brings together the principles of transparency and accountability, which are supported through access to information, with citizen engagement, which is intended to strengthen communication between governments and citizens and open up decision-making processes to active citizen participation. Information access is seen as one way for increasing transparency, accountability and trust in government; fostering a good understanding of the government's decisions; promoting citizen participation in the political process; and increasing government efficiency and integrity (Mendel, 2008; Hazell, Worthy and Glover, 2010). Practices enabling open information, open data and (more recently) citizen engagement are common manifestations of open government.

Open government has evolved as a concept. Clarke and Francoli (2014) argue that it emerged in debates in the 1950s over access to information legislation. Developments in freedom of information legislation in democratic governments included the 1966 Freedom of Information Act in the United States and the 1983 Access to Information Act in Canada (Léveillé and Timms, 2015).

During the late 1990s and early 2000s, the concept of open government embraced the use of new technologies that enabled faster, more personalised dissemination of information by governments (Yu and Robinson, 2012). Open government came to encompass not only the proactive disclosure of information, but also methods to make information more accessible and usable through open data and open information initiatives.

Canada

Open government in Canada has been implemented at the federal, provincial and municipal levels of government. Léveillé and Timms (2015) identified how the principles of open government have been realised by governments in Canada. At the federal level, the government is concerned with implementing the open government action plan in three key areas: open information, open data and open dialogue with citizens (see Chapter 5).

Open information involves making government records and information available, including the results of access to information requests. In the

Canadian federal context, it also includes initiatives such as 'open science' and 'open contracting' to open format-specific types of government information. Open data (information made available through the disclosure of structured datasets) is a subset of open information with emphasis on: accessibility through computer processing-friendly formats or user-friendly web portals; a large quantity of information available; its reusability to allow manipulation and redistribution; and its generally free use. The Canadian government is developing an integrated portal for datasets produced across jurisdictions in Canada, including data and licensing standards.

The UK

Within the EU, the key piece of legislation on the re-use of public sector information is the European Directive 2013/37/EU, transposed in the UK context into the Re-use of Public Sector Information Regulations 2015 (SI 2015, No. 1415). In 2010, the web portal <data.gov.uk> was launched to provide a single access point to open data, from information about school locations, to commuting statistics and public transport timetables. The UK's push towards open data and re-use was developed by the introduction of a 'right to data' by the Protection of Freedoms Act, amending the 2000 Freedom of Information Act to include an obligation for public bodies to publish datasets available for re-use in a re-usable format. Also in the UK, the example of the government health data sharing initiative, <care.data>, was intended to improve access to health services through better shared patient data (McLeod and Childs, 2018).

Malaysia

A study in Malaysia sought to determine the level of citizen's access to government information available through the official government open data portal using a survey of 21 ministries in the government administrative centre, Putrajaya. The focus was on e-government, that is, improved service delivery to citizens and access to government information provided by the use of technology (United Nations, 2014). Different countries promote e-government initiatives for various purposes, depending on the national needs and priorities. In South Africa, the focus is on service delivery, while the UK takes into account strategic objectives. In the US, it increases the efficiency of cross-function service delivery. E-government in Malaysia aims to reduce the digital divide (Delone and McLean, 2003). Petter et al. (2008) identify dimensions of e-government systems which provide measures for the success of government information systems:

- *Quality of system*: ease of use, flexible, reliable and ease of learning
- *Quality of information system*: output features, such as reports and websites that are accurate, concise, complete, current, timely, useful and can be understood
- *Quality of services*: a support service to users that is responsive, accurate, reliable, competent in the technical aspects and empathetic
- *User system*: frequency of use, the prevalence of use, suitability for use, the level of consumption
- *User satisfaction*: of reports, website and support services
- *Advantages*: to individuals, groups, departments, industries and countries by improving the quality of decision-making, productivity, cost reduction and economic development.

The findings of the Malaysia study suggest that Malaysia does not yet have comprehensive access to a government information framework and that proactive release of open government data through the official open data portal is limited. Improvements could include the user friendliness of the portal; providing relevant information according to user needs to improve their quality of life; reliability; comprehensibility; and usefulness of information.

Latin America

The research team in Latin America considered the practices and legislative frameworks which affect open data and open government in that region. The team researched the strategies and objectives of open government through a literature and legislative review, followed by interviews with experts, in a comparative study of Chile, Mexico, Brazil and Peru (Barnard et al., 2017). All these countries have regulations relating to open government and open data, transparency and access to information, although none of them is enshrined in legislation as they are promulgated by decrees, directives, plans and strategies. These regulations do not make a clear connection between open government and records management and the relationship between delivering open government and managing records effectively is not made explicit.

The definitions of open government and open data vary between countries, although similarities include ideas of transparency, accountability, citizen participation and state modernisation in the discussions of open government. In the four countries studied, open government initiatives have been framed by regulations created specifically for that purpose and are closely related with the commitments that each of the four countries has adopted within the OGP framework.

In Mexico, a national plan for 2013–2018 announced the National Digital Strategy to create Mexico's Open Government Strategy and achieve development goals. As a result, a government portal was created <gob.mx>. The main areas of <gob.mx> are Digital Economy, Quality Education, Universal Health and Citizenship Security. It includes links to federal agencies and some state websites and aims to present information of all government procedures to the public. It also incorporates participation mechanisms such as citizen consultations and petitions. The General Transparency, Access of Information and Data Protection Act (Mexico, 2015b) is in force and it regulates the opening of government information.

Open government in Chile was preceded by the Access to Public Information Act and the law on Associations and Citizen Participation in Public Administration (Presidencia, 2008). Actions related to open government were announced in 2012 (Chile, 2012) and included an Open Government portal that integrates transparency, participation and collaboration initiatives, <gobiernoabierto.gob.cl>. The portal provides tools and information to enable public participation (such as public accounts, citizen consultations and civil society councils) and the Open Data portal of the Chilean government.

In Peru, open government is regulated by the Supreme Decree No. 004-2013-PCM, which approved the National Policy on Public Management Modernization. Other initiatives related to open government are in Peru's OGP Action Plans. The Transparency and Access of Information Act is also relevant in the implementation of open government in Peru. Peru has an Open Government website about its participation in OGP (www.gestionpublica.gob.pe/gobierno-abierto) and the open data portal, <datosabiertos.gob.pe>, with information on the main public services of the country.

Brazil's initiatives on open government are also related to its involvement in OGP, although the Federal Constitution of 1988 established the citizen's right to access information held by public agencies. The Brazilian Intergovernmental Open Government Committee (CIGA) is responsible for guiding the implementation and development of the Brazilian Action Plans. CIGA is co-ordinated by the Civil House of the Presidency of the Republic, with the General Comptroller of the Union (CGU) as its executive body. The public monitoring of CIGA's actions take place, among other mechanisms, through the Open Government portal <www.governoaberto.cgu.gov.br>.

Open government data (OGD)

Open government data (OGD) is a concern of current political debate. This section considers the following aspects: privacy and data anonymisation, data quality, open government data and policy-making or governance, technical guidance and evaluation models and methods. Novais, De Albuquerque and Craveiro's (2013) literature review of open government data from 2007 to 2012 is a key work.

According to Bates (2014), the OGD agenda can be defined in the UK as:

> ... an information policy which provides a particular framework for governing the re-use by third parties of datasets that are produced by public institutions. (...) Open Government Data proponents argue that non-personal data that is produced by public bodies should be opened for all to re-use, free of charge and without discrimination.
>
> (Bates, 2014, 390)

Public services generate large volumes of data that is not exploited to its fullest potential. It is argued by Manyika et al. that in the US, for example, the benefits of opening up healthcare datasets 'could run into the hundreds of billions of dollars annually, realised through a combination of re-engineering health services and commercial exploitation' (Manyika et al., 2011, cited in Keen et al., 2013, 229). There is a great deal of interest in the open data community in how open data can facilitate innovation, but this is not reflected in the scholarly literature. Jetzek, Avital and Bjørn-Andersen's (2014) article is one of the few examples of research that considers the value of open data for innovation.

In practice, as a number of writers recognise, exploiting data held in publicly maintained systems through open data initiatives is not free of difficulties. First, the quality of open data is only ever as reliable as the underlying records from which the data is extracted, as Thurston (2012) points out. Secondly, even if the underlying records prove to be authentic and reliable sources of data, the data may not maintain its authenticity and integrity during any process of extraction. Keen et al. (2013) contend that datasets generated from public-sector clinical care records are generally 'chronically incomplete and unquantifiably inaccurate'. Thirdly, one wonders whether the state has the right to decide how and when to open up personal data, given trends in, for example, care of patients being able to control access to their health data (Keen et al., 2013). Proponents of the OGD agenda often frame open data as a direct benefit for the citizen. As taxpayers, citizens should have access to data relating to the services that they help to pay for in order to re-use them with as few restrictions as possible. Yet, positing open data as a 'citizen's right' can be in direct tension to the protection of the citizen's more fundamental rights and freedoms when the data made open derives from personal records.

Privacy and data anonymisation

Privacy and data anonymisation are discussed in Meijer, Conradie and Choenni's (2014) paper and the Open Data Institute's Guides (2015). To be published as wholly 'open data' without any restrictions, datasets must be processed and any personal data removed or anonymised (de-identified). The Article 29 Working Party describe anonymisation as a process that 'prevents all parties from singling out an individual in a dataset, from linking two records within a dataset (or between two separate datasets) and from inferring any information in such a dataset' (European Council, 2014). This is often problematic in practice. Data in an individual level dataset cannot be completely de-identified, because identifiability is context dependent. Controlling the levels of detail (the granularity) in the data is one relatively effective way to manage the risk of identification, but the less detailed the data, the less commercially valuable or useful to researchers the dataset becomes. Keen et al. (2013) suggest that it is 'not clear' if or how 'the circle of data protection and commercially valuable publication can be squared' (238).

Janssen (2011) notes that the EU PSI Directive 2013/37/EU addresses the commercial use of public-sector data by public-sector bodies themselves. If these bodies:

> ... provide added-value information products or services on the market based on their own data, they have to apply the same conditions and charges to their own re-use as to their private sector competitors... Re-use of public sector information has to be open to all potential actors in the market.
>
> (Janssen, 2011, 448)

This reinforces the point that 'openness' is not wholly 'good' for all sections of society all of the time. It is argued by those who see OGD as a form of neo-liberalism (Bates, 2012) that the private sector stands to benefit over and above both the citizen and the public sector. In regards to the citizens, commercial exploitation raises strongly felt privacy and security concerns. Can the private sector be trusted to act in a citizen's best interest?

The fundamental distinction between identifiable and anonymised data made in the European General Data Protection Regulation, as enacted in the UK Data Protection Act (2018), is different from the approach taken in legislation elsewhere. Forgo (2015) points to the US, which has adopted a pragmatic and directly prescriptive approach:

> ... the Health Insurance Portability and Accountability Act of 1996 (HIPAA), for example, on the one hand defines individually identifiable health information and, on the other hand, provides a list of 18 precisely named identifiers that shall

be removed in order to achieve de-identified data. There are no restrictions on the use of de-identified data. If the 18 identifiers are removed, this (purportedly) signifies a negligible risk that the information could be used, alone or in combination with other reasonably available information, by an anticipated recipient to identify an individual who is the subject of the information.

(Forgo, 2015, 57–58)

Even a prescriptive approach such as this cannot completely alleviate the potential risk of identification, however negligible that risk is perceived to be.

Data quality

The primary interest of the open data community has been securing access to government information and distributing it, with increasing attention to the means of delivering information (the raw data or representations of it) to end-users, such as civil society. Relatively little attention was given to issues of data quality in the early enthusiasm for data openness. However, recognition from the open data community that data quality is a significant issue in determining the value and use of open data is demonstrated in, for example, Both's (2012) article, where value to end-users is considered. A correlation between data value and appraisal, as a concept in archival science, suggests possible lines of enquiry that could yield results beneficial to data retention practices and user satisfaction.

Ideas of data quality in relation to data handling – particularly that there is 'no such thing' as raw data – started to emerge in the literature in 2013 with Davies and Frank's (2013) article on the 'socio-technical life of a government dataset'. Denis and Goëta (2014) provide an avenue into the conversation about open data for records managers, whose concern with trustworthiness and authenticity has led to the creation of a body of technical knowledge that could be presented to what is essentially a new user community: open data proponents, analysts and users.

In Mexico, OGD is one of the enablers of the <gob.mx> portal. For the implementation of OGD there are binding regulations with the GTAIA. OGD is carried out in accordance with the Opening Plan established by the Decree of Open Data Regulations (Mexico, 2015b), which set the criteria to define the data to be published based on its value, the responsible agency and its relationship with National Programs, among others. It also established that data should be published in the original format at the time of creation. The required metadata of OGD was also defined and includes an agency catalogue, metadata of the public agency and metadata of the data itself. Under the OGD schema, only the metadata and links to available files are published, as datasets and data resources remain under the responsibility of each agency. Since the guidelines for automatised systems for records management were put in force in 2017, it is not known how the data published in OGD is organized, maintained or preserved, although it is relevant for authenticity and accuracy purposes.

The ITrust study of National Health Service (NHS) England (Harrison, Shepherd and Flinn, 2015) suggested that metadata quality was a significant issue in ensuring data quality. In that research, several different metadata processes were identified, pointing to the need for a spectrum of metadata processes rather than one standardised process. While there are some official and strict processes in place for applying metadata to national data sources and official statistics, for other data there is only guidance and good practice checklists and encouragement. Such approaches will inevitably lead to inconsistent compliance and inconsistencies in data quality, which threatens the viability of re-use of open data. This study also explored the question of how processed open data should be. Some processing, for instance removing personal or identifiable data, is necessary to comply with data protection and privacy legislation, but further processing of data undertaken to make it more understandable or to combine related data before release is often not made transparent and open data may not be traceable back to their source. Such lack of traceability renders open data less reliable and less useful. Much open data is not widely re-used, perhaps because of the ways in which it is rendered, explained and made available technically. Open data is often used by a highly technical specialist audience, not by a more general public. Further research into user groups and user needs would help to develop a deeper understanding of how to enhance open data's contribution to society.

Another study of local government in England (Page, Flinn and Shepherd, 2014) also explored the format and presentation of open data. At local level there is little consistency about what data are made open, unlike at national government level, where <data.gov.uk> provides a central repository for open data and encourages some consistency. Low levels of demand for some data types may lead to better used data being released as a priority, although few public authorities seem to be tracking open data re-use very closely.

OGD and governance

Links between open government data and policy-making, or governance more broadly, are fairly well established in the literature. Napoli and Karaganis (2010) explored the use of 'publicly available data' in US communications policy. Kalampokis, Hausenblas and Tarabanis (2011) explored the use of open data in participatory decision-making and Rajshree and

Srivastava (2012) looked at the use of open government data in fighting corruption, which has long been a focus for thinking about the value of records as evidence. More recently, a number of resources have considered the socio-political implications of open government data. This is epitomised in the work of Bates (2012), which work has raised questions about the UK government's openness agenda and the appropriateness of its tactics in involving civil society in policy-making. Echoing the observations that Darch and Underwood (2010) made about the correlations between Freedom of Information and neoliberal ideas, Bates has asked questions about the political ramifications of open data in the UK (Bates, 2014). In view of some of the current thinking about records and archives in relation to political power, this work could provide a useful means of extending the socio-political line of enquiry between the fields of open data and records and archives.

In Chile, the Presidential Instructions on Open Government (Chile, 2012) declared the Open Data Policy a main component of the Open Government strategy. That policy was implemented through the creation of the Chilean Open Data Portal <datos.gob.cl>, launched in 2011. The Presidential Instructions also specified which institutions were to progressively publish their data in the portal. As in the case of open government, open data policy and related initiatives are under the responsibility of the Modernization and Digital Government Unit of the Office of the Secretary-General of the Presidency.

Another ITrust study of a UK National Health Service (NHS) hospital trust acknowledged the evolving nature of the open government environment in England (Chorley, 2017). Currently a matter of policy rather than legislation, and lacking in formal leadership and direction, policy and practice of the proactive publication of OGD will continue to develop as research is undertaken, challenges are identified and questions are answered. The current infancy of the open government data environment in the public sector in England, however, highlights the complexity of the challenges that lie in its path. The case study hospital trust interviews revealed the extent of unanswered questions especially relating to practical challenges, the lack of clarity about what is meant by 'open government data' and what data would be published, how it would be used and the resource needed to do it. The effect of the loss of public trust in the way the NHS handles data, as highlighted by the failure of the <care.data> programme (McLeod and Childs, 2018), has also had implications for the development of the OGD environment. The distinctions between data sharing and OGD, that is between the proactive publication of open government data and the data sharing of personal and confidential information for medical and treatment purposes need to be made clear. Harrison et al. (2015) described open government data as a fuzzy reality, 'where the technology of open data and the politics of open government cannot be neatly separated'. That study also reflected on the relationship between open data, policy-driven and flexible but open to interpretation, and FOI, a right to access information enshrined in legislation in the UK.

Technical guidance

At a more practical level, there is a body of technical guidance on making government data open, much of it emanating from civil society or from government-funded organizations such as the Open Data Institute (n.d.). An absence of records and archives technical knowledge can be observed in these guides, for example nothing about data preservation over time and web archiving. As the scholarly writing on open government data becomes more diverse, we see broader issues appearing. For instance, people are now thinking about legacy issues: Façanha and Cavalcanti (2014) have written on bringing government legacy system data into the public domain.

Studies of data visualisation, though often found in various fields such as computer science, data management and statistics, are still rare in the scholarly literature on open government data. A notable example is Graves and Hendler (2014). It is interesting to note that the other two principal examples are Kukimoto's (2014) work, which introduces the language of 'evidence' into data visualisation, and Lemieux, Gormly and Rowledge's (2014) work, which appears to be the only one to date that links data visualisation with records management.

The literature review revealed only one example of research into linkages between open data and social media (Alexopoulos et al., 2014). Given ITrust's concern for information integrity in the online, cloud and social media environments, it seems that some of the emerging work on social media could feed into this.

Evaluation models and methods

There is a body of work on models and methods for evaluating open government data. An early example is Kalampokis, Tambouris and Tarabanis' (2011) stage model of open government data, followed by Charalampos et al.'s (2013) 'Evaluation Framework', Parycek, Höchtl and Ginner's (2014) evaluation framework, and Charalabidis, Loukis and Alexopoulos' (2014) Value Models. Following Solar, Concha and Meijueiro's (2012) model for assessing open government data in public agencies, Veljković, Bogdanović-Dinić and Stoimenov (2014) suggested an open data approach and the

International Records Management Trust (IRMT) (2015) proposed bench-marks for open government and trustworthy records. Also in 2015, the Open Data Institute published several guides.

OGD and records and archives management

The intersection between open government data and records and archives management is an under-researched area that warrants much more attention than it is currently receiving.

Following Thurston's 2012 article, the records and archives management discipline generally and ITrust researchers specifically began to engage with open data (Borglund and Engvall, 2014; Lemieux, Gormly and Rowledge, 2014; Lowry, 2015; McDonald and Léveillé, 2014). The role of research data management as a mechanism for implementing open research data was also investigated (Esteve Casellas i Serra, 2014; Childs et al., 2014).

The attention to open data from the records management community continued into 2015 with work from Léveillé and Timms (2015) and Thurston (2015), the latter the result of an in-depth study of openness and information integrity in Estonia, Finland and Norway under the auspices of the World Bank. 2015 also saw the further development of records management guidance in the Open Government Guide, an online resource developed by international civil society organizations to support governments in developing commitments for Open Government Partnership national action plans. Much of this work is concerned with introducing controls to ensure the trustworthiness of data, which had appeared infrequently in the open data literature, with notable exceptions (Ceolin et al., 2013, 2014).

National case studies of open government data exist, including case studies for Albania (Hoxha, Brahaj and Vrandečić, 2011), Brazil (Breitman et al., 2012; Matheus, Ribeiro and Vaz, 2012; Albano and Reinhard, 2014; Brito et al., 2014; Correa et al., 2014), Germany (Datenschutz Datensich, 2012), Greece (Alexopoulos et al., 2014; Galiotou and Fragkou, 2013; Theocharis and Tsihrintzis, 2013), Italy (Viscusi et al., 2014), Latvia (Bojārs and Liepiņš, 2014), Mexico (González et al., 2014), Saudi Arabia (Al-Khalifa, 2013), and Taiwan (Yang et al., 2013). International, comparative studies are far less common, although Murillo (2015) has looked at online data availability in sixteen Latin American countries. These two approaches – national and comparative or international studies – present parameters that could be used in examining records issues in relation to open government data in various jurisdictions. These case studies also suggest various scopes of study that might be useful in research in the records and archives field; some of the case studies are broad overviews of national 'data landscapes' (Bojārs and Liepiņš, 2014) while others are quite specific, looking at issues as particular as sources of data (Alexopoulos et al., 2014).

In Malaysia, agencies like MAMPU (Manpower Planning Unit) act as custodians of information and are responsible for sharing authentic information. MAMPU took an initiative to leverage information sharing and use of data for transforming e-government by creating a people-centric government service system. Since the government embarked on an e-government initiative, digital records have now been given some priority. The lack of sound recordkeeping threatens to undermine the e-government initiative and hinders the delivery of high quality services (Ismail et al., 2013). Moreover, agencies are facing difficulties on how to go about managing records since there are few proper processes and systems (Azimah, 2007). Systems were designed without taking into consideration the records and information management requirement and those designed for managing information are not always appropriate for managing records. For example, a systematic disposal function is not always available in information systems, thus making the system only cater to part of the records lifecycle (creation through maintenance).

Brazil has had rules for records management since 1991, when the Law No. 8159, also known as the Archives Law, was enacted (Brazil, 1991). The law also created the National Archives Council. Later, in 2003, the Archives Management System – SIGA (Sistema de Gestão de Documentos de Arquivo) – of the federal public administration was created (Brazil, 2003). However, even with a normative framework that includes the implementation of both the Open Data Policy and the National Open Data Action Plans, there is no explicit mention of the relationship and relevance of records management.

In Mexico, there are no records and archives regulations related to open government or open government data. Regulations do not require the creation of information or additional metadata that could help manage data as records within record series, which implies that no retention or disposition rule applies and that data is not controlled in a records management system. The required metadata is set out in the guidelines of OGD and is frequently insufficient for records control (Mexico, 2015a). There is a manual of procedures about open government, open data and records management but it does not establish any relation between open government and open data with records management.

In Peru, the Records Management Model was approved by the Legislative Decree 1310 (Peru, 2017). The Decree in Article 8 mandates the interconnection of the records management systems of the Public Administration for the automatic delivery of electronic documents among the agencies through the State Interoperability Platform of Digital Government, managed by the

Presidency of the Ministries Council through the Digital Government Agency. The Records Management Model aims at implementing a reference framework supported by records management standards and good practices to enable public administration agencies to exchange documents through the Interoperability State Platform, whatever their size, nature, complexity or records management maturity level.

Chile does not have a specific piece of legislation to regulate records management. The National Archives was created by the Decree No. 5200 of 1929 (Chile, 1929) and no other norms have been created to regulate the role and responsibilities of the institution regarding the management of current records. Some norms have been published by different public institutions to deal with specific pressing issues, such as Decree No.14 of the Ministry of Economy, Development and Tourism (Chile, 2014), which amends previous regulations regarding electronic records and electronic signatures. For that reason, Chile does not have any type of standard to harmonise records management with Open Data or Open Government strategies or plans.

Data protection, privacy and security classification

In contrast to open government and open data, the development of data protection and privacy legislation across Europe (that is, legislation which keeps information closed) is a complex picture involving the interplay of national and regional approaches and legal systems. Out of this complexity, several writers have sought to categorise the history of data protection legislation into distinct waves (Jori, 2007; Mayer-Schönberger, 1997). 'First-wave' data protection began in the 1970s, when the initial focus was on controlling and regulating the use of technology, and saw the emergence of 'data subject rights' and a 'rights-based' approach. 'Second-wave' data protection law can be characterised by the further embedding of a rights-based approach, attributed to a landmark German Constitutional Court ruling in 1983 that cemented the concept of 'informational self-determination' as a doctrinal cornerstone.

'Third-wave' data protection law, in the wake of the 1995 European Directive, marked the continued adherence to a rights-based approach alongside an acceptance of the need for specific sectorial regulation and codes of conduct. The introduction of the General Data Protection Regulation (GDPR) at the European level is a 'fourth wave'. The GDPR came into effect on 25 May 2018. The GDPR defines personal data in Article 4 (1) as information relating to an identifiable natural person ('data subject'). Article 4 (5) defines 'pseudonymization' as the processing of personal data in such a manner that the personal data can no longer be attributed to a specific data subject.

In an era of 'social networking sites, cloud computing, location-based services and smart cards', a new 'robust set of rules' is needed to ensure that 'people's right to personal data protection – recognised by Article 8 of the EU's Charter of Fundamental Rights – remains effective in the digital age' (European Commission, 2015). It was argued that a single pan-European law for data protection, replacing the inconsistent patchwork of national laws, was required so that companies could deal 'with one law, not 28' (European Commission, 2015).

An alternative view on the closure of data and records is provided by the ITrust study that researched the security classifications of records in organizations, particularly international organizations, handling security classified information (Deserno et al., 2017). The research aimed to identify best practice in security classified information management in a framework that supports the preservation of reliable, authentic and usable records. It considers how security classified information is distinct from other kinds of information and how it sits alongside standards of open governance, such as accountability and transparency, within a records management framework. It also considers the digital transition and the changes that arise in copying, transferring and transforming security classified information. The level of granularity to which classifications are applied is addressed: a single information asset, a group of information assets or a cluster such as a database? The preservation of metadata relating to security classification and the criteria, timeframes and methods for reclassification and declassification were investigated. The questions were whether, at the end of the process, there was a mechanism for public disclosure of previously classified information and how was such information transferred from the security environment into a more accessible environment.

The ever-present tension between the right to information and the need for security – and therefore secrecy – is one of the defining issues within the literature. Hitchens (1997) observes that accountability and public involvement are democratic expectations. Although access to information does not guarantee citizen involvement, there can be no discourse without it; as such, 'the provision of information is the first step in the process of consultation, openness and accountability' (Hitchens, 1997, 145). He argues that this is true not only at the state level, but also in the context of IGOs, because access to IGO information is 'essential to discourse and accountability at the global level'. At the same time, an appearance of transparency should not exclude a critical approach (Roberts, 2004). Several authors discuss the often invisible barriers to access to information, more often in a national context, but also in an IGO context. Efforts at transparency at the policy and/or legislative level do not necessarily equal access to information in reality.

There is a need for more literature on best practices and strategies for managing classified information, especially from a records and information management perspective. Organizations could benefit from the expertise of records professionals in addressing the substantial challenges of classification and declassification in order to increase efficiency, transparency and the security of classified information.

Conclusion

A key goal of open government is to encourage citizens to access and use government information. Citizen access is enabled by a patchwork of regulation and legislation in each jurisdiction: national and public archives have to provide proactive access to permanently retained records; systems for freedom of information requests should seek to balance the need for security and privacy with rights to access; and privacy and data protection laws are designed to keep personal data closed. Open government, with its emphasis on rapid information access, does not always align with archives and freedom of information processes and are often organizationally separate. Privacy can be seen as the opposition to openness. All have much in common: an interest in providing accurate, reliable and authentic information to citizens while protecting privacy.

Key differences relate to access timelines and the scale of aggregation. Government data can be made available soon after creation. Data aggregation means that information in datasets can be easily queried, analysed and re-used in ways that access to original individual records could not have supported. But the processes of aggregation obscure links back to original records, leading to doubts about the data accuracy and authenticity. Releasing information may affect the privacy of individuals. How to strike the balance between privacy and openness? What information should be made available? For how long should it be made available? How can its quality and accuracy be verified? And how can open government data be made accessible and usable from a legal standpoint and a human standpoint? These questions need to be addressed by records professionals and by their employers to establish policy, procedural and technical responses to ensure that citizens are able to exercise their information rights.

Open government is usually driven by government and political policy, without statutory requirements. Open government programmes are vulnerable to rollbacks in commitments. Public archives and access to information and privacy legislation, on the other hand, have a statutory basis which makes them less likely to change in the medium term. As the final report of ITrust's study on open government concluded, 'record keeping policy and practice was weak or absent in relation to aspects of Open Government, and particularly in relation to citizen engagement initiatives' (Suderman and Timms, 2016). Few measures of success were identified for engagement initiatives nor did any criteria seem to be well established within or across jurisdictions reviewed. The research undertaken by ITrust provides an opportunity to develop international responses to these challenges.

References

Aftergood, S. (2000) Secrecy is Back in Fashion, *Bulletin of the Atomic Scientists*, **56** (6), 25–30, https://doi.org/10.1080/00963402.2000.11457006.

Aftergood, S. (2013) An Inquiry into the Dynamics of Government Secrecy, *Harvard Law Review*, **48** (2), 511–30.

Albano, C. S. and Reinhard, N. (2014) Open Government Data: facilitating and motivating factors for coping with potential barriers in the Brazilian context. In Janssen, M., Scholl, H., Wimmer, M. A. and Bannister, F. (eds), *Electronic Government*, 8653:181–93. Berlin, Heidelberg, Springer Berlin Heidelberg, https://doi.org/10.1007/978-3-662-44426-9_15

Alexopoulos, C., Zuiderwijk, A., Charapabidis, Y., Loukis, E. and Janssen, M. (2014) Designing a Second Generation of Open Data Platforms: integrating open data and social media. In Janssen, M., Scholl, H. J., Wimmer, M. A. and Bannister, F. (eds), *Electronic Government*, 8653, 230–41, Berlin, Heidelberg, Springer Berlin Heidelberg, https://doi.org/10.1007/978-3-662-44426-9_19

Al-Khalifa, H. S. (2013) A Lightweight Approach to Semantify Saudi Open Government Data. In *2013 16th International Conference on Network-Based Information Systems*, 594–96, IEEE, https://doi.org/10.1109/NBiS.2013.99

Azimah, Mohd Ali (2007) Taming the Wild Frontier: improving systems and processes in creating digital records in government, Digital Futures International Forum, 18-19 September, 2007, Australia. https://slideplayer.com/slide/4464631/.

Barnard, A., Mendoza, A., Andaur Gómez, G., and Augusto Silva Ditadi, C. (2017) Gobierno Abierto, Datos Abiertos ¿Existe Una Relación Con La Gestión Documental? Análisis En Cuatro Países de Latinoamérica, *Boletín Del Archivo General de La Nación*, 13, www.h-mexico.unam.mx/node/20755

Bates, J. (2012) 'This Is What Modern Deregulation Looks Like': co-optation and contestation in the shaping of the UK's Open Government Data Initiative, *The Journal of Community Informatics*, **8** (2), http://ci-journal.net/index.php/ ciej/article/view/845

Bates, J. (2014) The Strategic Importance of Information Policy for the Contemporary Neoliberal State: the case of open government data in the United Kingdom, *Government Information Quarterly*, **31** (3), 388–95, https://doi.org/10.1016/j.giq.2014.02.009

Bojārs, U. and Liepinš, R. (2014) The State of Open Data in Latvia: 2014, *Modern Computing*, **2** (3), 160–70.

Borglund, E. and Engvall, T. (2014) Open Data?: data, information, document or record?, *Records Management Journal*, **24** (2), 163–80, https://doi.org/10.1108/RMJ-01-2014-0012

Both, W. (2012) Open Data – What the Citizens Really Want, *The Journal of Community Informatics*, **8** (2).

Brazil (1991) Lei No 8.159, de 8 de Janeiro de 1991 (Archives Law), www.planalto.gov.br/ccivil_03/leis/L8159.htm

Brazil (2003) Decreto Nº 4.915 de 12 DE Dezembro de 2003. www.planalto.gov.br/ccivil_03/decreto/2003/d4915.htm

Breitman, K., Salas, P., Casanova, M. A., Saraiva, D., Gama, V., Viterbo, J., Magalhaes, R. P., Franzosi, E. and Chaves, M. (2012) Open Government Data in Brazil, *IEEE Intelligent Systems*, **27** (3), 45–49, https://doi.org/10.1109/MIS.2012.25

Brito, Kellyton dos Santos, Marcos Antonio Silva Costa, Vinicius Cardoso Garcia, and Silvio Romero de Lemos Meira (2014) Experiences Integrating Heterogeneous Government Open Data Sources to Deliver Services and Promote Transparency in Brazil. In *2014 IEEE 38th Annual Computer Software and Applications Conference*, 606–7, IEEE, https://doi.org/10.1109/COMPSAC.2014.87

Ceolin, D., Moreau, L., O'Hara, K., Fokkink, W., Van Hage, W. R., Maccatrozzo, V., Sackley, A., Schreiber, G., and Shadbolt, N. (2014) Two Procedures for Analyzing the Reliability of Open Government Data. In Laurent, A., Strauss, O. Bouchon-Meunier, B. and Yager, R. R. (eds), *Information Processing and Management of Uncertainty in Knowledge-Based Systems*, 442, 15–24, Cham, Springer International Publishing, https://doi.org/10.1007/978-3-319-08795-5_3

Ceolin, D., Moreau, L., O'Hara, K., Schreiber, G., Sackley, A., Fokkink, W., Van Hage, W. R. and Shadbolt, N. (2013) Reliability Analyses of Open Government Data. In *CEUR Workshop Proceedings*, 1073, 34–39, www.scopus.com/inward/record.url?eid=2-s2.0-84924742944&partnerID=40&md5=36af14737da954db53dbbde67cb1ff96

Charalabidis, Y., Loukis, E. and Alexopoulos, C. (2014) Evaluating Second Generation Open Government Data Infrastructures Using Value Models. In *2014 47th Hawaii International Conference on System Sciences*, 2114–26, IEEE, https://doi.org/10.1109/HICSS.2014.267

Charalampos, A., Loukis, E., Charalabidis, Y. and Zuiderwijk, A. (2013) An Evaluation Framework for Traditional and Advanced Open Public Data E-Infrastructures. In Castelnovo, W. and Ferrari, E. (eds), *Proceedings of the 13th European Conference on Egovernment*, 102–11, ACPIL.

Childs, S., McLeod, J., Lomas, E. and Cook, G. (2014) Opening Research Data: issues and opportunities, edited by Dr Anne Thurston, *Records Management Journal*, **24** (2), 142–62, https://doi.org/10.1108/RMJ-01-2014-0005

Chile (1929) DFL 5200 (1929) (National Archives Act),
https://www.leychile.cl/Navegar?idNorma=129136

Chile (2012) Instructivo Presidencial N° 005 – 2012 Sobre Gobierno Abierto,
https://transparenciaactiva.presidencia.cl/Otros%20Antecedentes/
Gab%20Pres.%20N°%20005.pdf

Chile (2014) Decreto 14 Del Ministerio de Economía, Fomento Y Turismo (2014)
(Decree N°14 of the Ministry of Economy, Development and Tourism),
https://www.leychile.cl/Navegar?idNorma=105977

Chorley, K. (2017) The Challenges Presented to Records Management by Open
Government Data in the Public Sector in England: a case study, *Records
Management Journal*, **27** (2), 149–58, https://doi.org/10.1108/RMJ-09-2016-0034

Clarke, A. and Francoli, M. (2014) What's in a Name? A Comparison of 'Open
Government' Definitions across Seven Open Government Partnership Members,
JeDEM – eJournal of eDemocracy and Open Government, **6** (3), 248–66,
https://jedem.org/index.php/jedem/article/view/227

Correa, A. S., Correa, P. L. P., Silva, D. L. and Correa Da Silva, F. S. (2014) Really
Opened Government Data: a collaborative transparency at sight. In *2014 IEEE
International Congress on Big Data*, 806–7, IEEE,
https://doi.org/10.1109/BigData.Congress.2014.131

Darch, C. and Underwood, P. G. (2010) *Freedom of Information and the Developing
World: the citizen, the state and models of openness*, Oxford, Chandos.

Datenschutz und Datensicherheit (2012) BMI: Studie, 'Open Government Data
Deutschland', *Datenschutz und Datensicherheit*, **36** (10), 779,
https://doi.org/10.1007/s11623-012-0255-7

Davies, T. and Frank, M. (2013) 'There's No Such Thing as Raw Data': exploring the
socio-technical life of a government dataset. In *Proceedings of the 5th Annual ACM
Web Science Conference*, 75–8, ACM Press, https://doi.org/10.1145/2464464.2464472

Delone, W. and McLean, E. (2003) The DeLone and McLean Model of Information
Systems Success: a ten-year update, *Journal of Management Information Systems*, **19**
(4), 9–30, https://doi.org/10.1080/07421222.2003.11045748

Denis, J. and Goëta, S. (2014) Exploration, Extraction and Ratification. The Shaping
of Transparency in the Back Rooms of Open Data, *SSRN Electronic Journal*,
https://doi.org/10.2139/ssrn.2403069

Deserno, I., Sengsavang, E., Shockley, M., Katuu, S. and Kastenhofer, J. (2017)
*Checklist for Developing or Revising Policies for Managing Security Classified
Information Assets*, TR03, InterPARES Trust.
https://interparestrust.org/assets/public/dissemination/TR03-Checklist-2_-final.pdf

Engvall, T., Liang, V. and Anderson, K. (2015) *The Role of the Archivist and Records
Manager in an Open Government Environment in Sweden*, EU11, Final Report,
InterPARES Trust,
https://interparestrust.org/assets/public/dissemination/EU11_20150707_

RoleRMOpenGovSweden_EUWorkshop5_FinalReport_Final.pdf

Esteve Casellas, Serra, L. (2014) The Mapping, Selecting and Opening of Data: the records management contribution to the Open Data Project in Girona City Council, edited by Dr Anne Thurston, *Records Management Journal*, **24** (2), 87–98, https://doi.org/10.1108/RMJ-01-2014-0008

European Commission (2014) Article 29 Data Protection Working Party. Opinion 05/2014 on Anonymisation Techniques, https://www.dataprotection.ro/servlet/ViewDocument?id=1085

European Commission Press Release (2015) EU Data Protection Reform on Track: Commission Proposal on New Data Protection Rules in Law Enforcement Area Backed by Justice Ministers, http://europa.eu/rapid/press-release_IP-15-5812_en.htm

European Parliament (2003) Directive 2003/98/EC of the European Parliament and of the Council of 17 November 2003 on the Re-Use of Public Sector Information, http://data.europa.eu/eli/dir/2003/98/oj

Façanha, R. L. and Cavalcanti, M. C. (2014) On the Road to Bring Government Legacy Systems Data Schemas to Public Access. In *CEUR Workshop Proceedings*, Vol. 1301, www.scopus.com/inward/record.url?eid=2-s2.0-84916232274&partnerID=40&md5=6878b127273b81dbcf32953af645e0be

Forgo, N. (2015) My Health Data – Your Research: some preliminary thoughts on different values in the General Data Protection Regulation, *International Data Privacy Law*, **5** (1), 54–63, https://doi.org/10.1093/idpl/ipu028

Galiotou, E. and Fragkou, P. (2013) Applying Linked Data Technologies to Greek Open Government Data: A Case Study, *Procedia – Social and Behavioral Sciences*, **73** (February), 479–86, https://doi.org/10.1016/j.sbspro.2013.02.080

González, J. C., Garcia, J., Cortés, F. and Carpy, D. (2014) Government 2.0: a conceptual framework and a case study using Mexican data for assessing the evolution towards open governments. In *Proceedings of the 15th Annual International Conference on Digital Government Research*, 124–36, ACM Press, https://doi.org/10.1145/2612733.2612742

Graves, M. and Hendler, J. (2014) A Study on the Use of Visualizations for Open Government Data, *Information Polity*, **1** (2), 73–91, https://doi.org/10.3233/IP-140333

Harrison, E., Shepherd, E. and Flinn, A. (2015) *A Research Report into Open Government Data in NHS England*, EU19, Final Report, InterPARES Trust, https://interparestrust.org/assets/public/dissemination/EU19_20150421_UKNationalHealthService_FinalReport.pdf

Hazell, R., Worthy, B. and Glover, M. (2010) *The Impact of the Freedom of Information Act on Central Government in the UK*, London, Palgrave Macmillan UK, https://doi.org/10.1057/9780230281998

Hitchens, A. (1997) A Call for IGO Policies on Public Access to Information,

Government Information Quarterly, **14** (2), 143–54.

Hooten, B.T. (2011) How Many Ways Can 'Classified' Be Said? http://members.rimpa.com.au/lib/StaticContent/StaticPages/pubs/nat/ inForum2011/HootenPaper.pdf.

Hoxha, J., Brahaj, A. and Vrandečić, D. (2011) Open.data.al: increasing the utilization of government data in Albania. In *Proceedings of the 7th International Conference on Semantic Systems.* ACM Press, https://doi.org/10.1145/2063518.2063558

International Organization for Standardization (ISO) (2013) *ISO/IEC 27002:2013 – Information Technology – Security Techniques – Code of Practice for Information Security Controls,* https://www.iso.org/standard/54533.html

International Records Management Trust (IRMT) (2015) Benchmarks for Open Government and Trustworthy Records, www.irmt.org/portfolio/ open-government-trustworthy-records/attachment/benchmarks-for-open-government-and-trustworthy-records-final-2

Ismail, M. B., Yusof, Z. M., Ahmad, K. and Yusof, M. M. (2013) *Pengurusan Dan Perkongsian Pengetahuan Sektor Awam (Management and Knowledge Sharing in Public Sector),* Bangi, UKM.

Janssen, K. (2011) The Influence of the PSI Directive on Open Government Data: an overview of recent developments, *Government Information Quarterly,* **28** (4), 446–56, https://doi.org/10.1016/j.giq.2011.01.004

Jetzek, T., Avital, M., and Bjørn-Andersen, N. (2014) Data-Driven Innovation through Open Government Data, *Journal of Theoretical and Applied Electronic Commerce Research,* **9** (2), 100–20.

Jori, A. (2007) Data Protection in Europe, *SecondGeneration,* 23 October 2007, http://web.archive.org/web/20071023201818/www.dataprotection.eu/ pmwiki/pmwiki.php?n=Main.SecondGeneration

Kalampokis, E., Hausenblas, M. and Tarabanis, K. (2011) Combining social and government open data for participatory decision-making. In Proceedings of the Third IFIP WG 8.5 international conference on Electronic participation. Springer-Verlag, 36–47.

Kalampokis, E., Tambouris, E. and Tarabanis, K. (2011) Open Government Data: a stage model. In Janssen, M., Scholl, H. J., Wimmer, M. A. and Tan, Y. (eds), *Electronic Government,* 6846, 235–46, Berlin, Heidelberg, Springer Berlin Heidelberg, https://doi.org/10.1007/978-3-642-22878-0_20

Keen, J., Calinescu, R., Paige, R. and Rooksby, J. (2013) Big Data + Politics = Open Data: the case of health care data in England, *Policy and Internet,* **5** (2), 228–43, https://doi.org/10.1002/1944-2866.POI330

Kukimoto, N. (2014) Open Government Data Visualization System to Facilitate Evidence-Based Debate Using a Large-Scale Interactive Display. In *2014 IEEE 28th International Conference on Advanced Information Networking and Applications,*

955–60, IEEE, https://doi.org/10.1109/AINA.2014.116

Lemieux, V., Gormly, B. and Rowledge, L. (2014) Meeting Big Data Challenges with Visual Analytics: the role of records management, edited by Dr Anne Thurston, *Records Management Journal*, **24** (2), 122–41, https://doi.org/10.1108/RMJ-01-2014-0009

Léveillé, V. and Timms, K. (2015) Through a Records Management Lens: creating a framework for trust in open government and open government information / Les Objectifs Visés Par Les Systèmes de Gestion Documentaires: La Mise En Place D'un Cadre de Confiance et de La Transparence de L'information Dans Un Gouvernement Ouvert, *Canadian Journal of Information and Library Science*, **39** (2), 154–90.

Lowry, J. (2015) *Open Government Data Literature Review*. EU02, InterPARES Trust, https://interparestrust.org/assets/public/dissemination/EU02_20151210_OpenGovernmentDataLiteratureReview_FinalReport.pdf

Matheus, R., Ribeiro, M. M. and Vaz, J. C. (2012) New Perspectives for Electronic Government in Brazil: the adoption of open government data in national and subnational governments of Brazil. In *Proceedings of the 6th International Conference on Theory and Practice of Electronic Governance*, 22, ACM Press, https://doi.org/10.1145/2463728.2463734

Mayer-Schönberger, V. (1997) Generational Development of Data Protection in Europe. In Agre, P. and Rotenberg, M. (eds), *Technology and Privacy: The New Landscape*, 219–41, Cambridge, Mass, MIT Press.

McDonald, J. and Léveillé, V. (2014) Whither the Retention Schedule in the Era of Big Data and Open Data?, edited by Dr Anne Thurston, *Records Management Journal*, **24** (2), 99–121, https://doi.org/10.1108/RMJ-01-2014-0010

McLeod, J. and Childs, S. (2018) Public Trust in Online Records. In Anderson, K., Becker, I. C. and Duranti, L. (eds), *Born Digital in the Cloud: challenges and solutions, Contributions to the 21. Archival Sciences Colloquium, International Symposium of the Archives School Marburg*, Veröffentlichungen Der Archivschule Marburg, Hochschule Für Archivwissenschaft, Nr. 65, Marburg, Archivschule Marburg.

Meijer, R., Conradie, P. and Choenni, S. (2014) Reconciling Contradictions of Open Data Regarding Transparency, Privacy, Security and Trust, *Journal of Theoretical and Applied Electronic Commerce Research*, **9** (3), 32–44, https://doi.org/10.4067/S0718-18762014000300004

Mendel, T. (2008) *Freedom of Information: a comparative legal survey*, 2nd edn, Paris, UNESCO, www.unesco.org/new/en/communication-and-information/resources/publications-and-communication-materials/publications/full-list/freedom-of-information-a-comparative-legal-survey-2nd-edition/

Mexico (2015a) Decreto Por El Que Se Establece La Regulación En Materia de Datos Abiertos (Decree of Open Data Regulations).

Mexico (2015b) Ley General de Transparencia Y Acceso a La Información Pública

(General Transparency, Access of Information and Data Protection Act (GTAIA)).

Ministerio Secretaría General de la Presidencia (2008) LEY-20285 20-AGO-2008 Ministerio Secretaría General de la Presidencia. Ley Chile – Biblioteca Del Congreso Nacional, 20 August 2008, https://www.leychile.cl/Navegar?idNorma=276363&idParte=

Murillo, M. J. (2015) Evaluating the Role of Online Data Availability: the case of economic and institutional transparency in sixteen Latin American nations, *International Political Science Review*, **36** (1), 42–59, https://doi.org/10.1177/0192512114541163

Napoli, P. M. and Karaganis, J. (2010) On Making Public Policy with Publicly Available Data: the case of U.S. communications policymaking, *Government Information Quarterly*, **27** (4), 384–91, https://doi.org/10.1016/j.giq.2010.06.005

Novais, T., De Albuquerque, J. P. and Craveiro, G. S. (2013) An Account of Research on Open Government Data (2007–2012): a systematic literature review. In Wimmer, M. A. (ed.), *Electronic Government and Electronic Participation: Joint Proceedings of Ongoing Research of IFIP EGOV and IFIP ePart 2013, 16-19 September 2013 in Koblenz, Germany*, GI Edition Proceedings 221, Bonn, Ges. für Informatik, www.scopus.com/inward/record.url?eid=2-s2.0-84918551984&partnerID=40&md5=8b722dd21af1f1c3743202eaeaae389d

Open Data Institute (2015) Guides – The ODI, https://theodi.org/knowledge-opinion/guides/

Open Government Partnership (n.d.) Open Government Partnership, https://www.opengovpartnership.org/ [accessed 10 July 2018].

Open Knowledge International (n.d.) The Open Definition – Open Definition – Defining Open in Open Data, Open Content and Open Knowledge, https://opendefinition.org/ [accessed 10 July 2018].

Page, J., Flinn, A. and Shepherd, E. (2014) *The Role of the Records Manager in an Open Government Environment in the UK*. EU03, Final Report. InterPARES Trust, https://interparestrust.org/assets/public/dissemination/EU03_20141105_RoleRMOpenGovUK_FinalReport.pdf

Parycek, P., Höchtl, J. and Ginner, M. (2014) Open Government Data Implementation Evaluation, *Journal of Theoretical and Applied Electronic Commerce Research*, **9** (2), 13–14, https://doi.org/10.4067/S0718-18762014000200007.

Pearce-Moses, R. (ed.) (2018) *InterPARES Trust Terminology*, InterPARES Trust, www.interparestrust.org/terminology/.

Peru (2017) Decreto Legislativo N°1310 (Legislative Decree 1310), https://www.scribd.com/document/335533186/Decreto-Legislativo-N-1310

Petter, S., DeLone, W. and McLean, E. (2008) Measuring Information Systems Success: models, dimensions, measures, and interrelationships, *European Journal of Information Systems*, **17** (3), 236–63, https://doi.org/10.1057/ejis.2008.15

Rajshree, N. and Srivastava, B. (2012) Open Government Data for Tackling

Corruption – A Perspective. In *Semantic Cities: Papers from the 2012 AAAI Workshop*, Technical Report/Association for the Advancement of Artificial Intelligence WS, 2012,13, Palo Alto, Calif, AAAI Press.

Roberts, A. (2004) A Partial Revolution: the diplomatic ethos and transparency in intergovernmental organizations, *Public Administration Review*, **64** (4), 410–24.

Solar, M., Concha, G. and Meijueiro, L. (2012) A Model to Assess Open Government Data in Public Agencies. In Scholl, H. J., Janssen, M., Wimmer, M. A., Moe, C. E. and Flak, L. S. (eds), *Electronic Government*, 7443, 210–21, Berlin, Heidelberg, Springer Berlin Heidelberg, https://doi.org/10.1007/978-3-642-33489-4_18

Suderman, J. (2017) *Summary of Open Government Studies Conducted in InterPARES Trust*. InterPARES Trust, https://interparestrust.org/assets/public/dissemination/SummaryofOpenGovernmentstudies_Final_14Oct2017.pdf

Suderman, J. and Timms, K. (2016) *The Implications of Open Government, Open Data, and Big Data on the Management of Digital Records in an Online Environment*, NA08, Final Report, InterPARES Trust, https://interparestrust.org/assets/public/dissemination/IPTITRUST_NA08_FinalReport_1Oct2016_fordistribution_.pdf

Theocharis, S. A. and Tsihrintzis, G. A. (2013) Open Data for E-Government: the Greek Case. In *IISA 2013*, 1–6, IEEE, https://doi.org/10.1109/IISA.2013.6623722

Thurston, A. (2012) Trustworthy Records and Open Data, *The Journal of Community Informatics*, **8** (2). http://ci-journal.org/index.php/ciej/article/view/951

Thurston, A. (2015) Managing Records and Information for Transparent, Accountable, and Inclusive Governance in the Digital Environment: lessons from Nordic countries, 98723, The World Bank, http://documents.worldbank.org/curated/en/222041468189536195/Managing-records-and-information-for-transparent-accountable-and-inclusive-governance-in-the-digital-environment-lessons-from-Nordic-Countries

United Kingdom (2018) Data Protection Act 2018. www.legislation.gov.uk/ukpga/2018/12

United Nations (2014) UN E-Government Survey 2014. https://publicadministration.un.org/egovkb/en-us/reports/un-e-government-survey-2014

Veljković, N., Bogdanović-Dinić, S. and Stoimenov, L. (2014) Benchmarking Open Government: an open data perspective, *Government Information Quarterly*, **31** (2), 278–90, https://doi.org/10.1016/j.giq.2013.10.011

Viscusi, G., Spajiu, B., Maurino, A. and Batini, C. (2014) Compliance with Open Government Data Policies: an empirical assessment of Italian local public administrations, *Information Polity*, **3** (4), 263–75, https://doi.org/10.3233/IP-140338

Yang, T.-M., Lo, J., Wang, H.-J. and Shiang, J. (2013) Open Data Development and Value-Added Government Information: case studies of Taiwan e-government. In

Proceedings of the 7th International Conference on Theory and Practice of Electronic Governance, 238–41, ACM Press, https://doi.org/10.1145/2591888.2591932

Yu, H. and Robinson, D. G. (2012) The New Ambiguity of 'Open Government', *SSRN Electronic Journal*, https://doi.org/10.2139/ssrn.2012489

4

Citizen engagement

Editor: Fiorella Foscarini
Contributors: Jenny Bunn, Laura Dymock,
Lois Evans, Fiorella Foscarini, Paige Hohmann,
Silvia Schenkolewski-Kroll, Elizabeth Shepherd
and Assaf Tractinsky

Introduction

This chapter explores the notion of 'citizen engagement' from a socio-cultural and user-centred perspective. It does so by drawing on a set of InterPARES Trust (hereinafter ITrust) studies which looked at the relationship between records (understood both in a specific sense and as information objects), record systems (including any technologies used to manage all kinds of data and information) and the users of such records and systems (e.g. creators, subjects, administrators, curators, end-users) with an emphasis on the kind of human engagement, or participation, that arises from, and gives shape to, such a relationship. The contributions gathered in this chapter try to answer questions such as:

- How do people perceive born-digital objects? What makes them trust the records and the institutions in charge of them? (Questions addressed in EU27 User Perceptions of Born-Digital Authenticity (Bunn et al., 2016));
- How has citizens' communication with the government changed over time? Has the nature of patents and petitions – two very common legal genres enabling the interaction between people and institutions – shifted in the digital age? (Questions addressed in NA13 Patents, Petitions, and Trust (Hohmann, 2016; Foscarini, 2019);
- How are open government initiatives and civic technologies changing society and the way citizens participate in public matters? Questions addressed by NA08 The Implications of Open Government, Open Data, and Big Data on the Management of Digital Records in an Online Environment (Suderman and Timms, 2016); and EU05 Models for Monitoring and Auditing of Compliance in the Flow from Registration to

Archive in e-Register (Strahonja, 2018);
- Can social media be used by local governments to increase citizen trust? What can we learn about the administration of social media that results in an increase in trust in government? (Questions addressed in NA05 Social Media and Trust in Government (Franks, 2016));
- Are the users taken into account when appraising an institutional website? What can we learn about citizen engagement through measuring visitor interactions with such websites? (Questions addressed in EU25 Using Web Analytics in Appraisal of Records on the Foreign Ministry of Israel Website (Schenkolewski-Kroll and Tractinsky, 2016)).

Perceptions of authenticity
Jenny Bunn

Study EU27 User Perceptions of Born-Digital Authenticity sought to explore people's perceptions of born-digital records in terms of their being suggested to be the real thing. The interaction that it investigated, therefore, was that between an individual and a record. Interviews were carried out in which participants were directed to four different records and asked whether or not they thought the record in question was the real thing or not and why they held that opinion.

The majority of the participants were in the 18–24 age group, but there were also individuals in older age groups, with the oldest interviewee being in the 40–49 age group. This participant reported that they had first regularly used a computer or other digital device in early adulthood, while the others reported that they had done so either at primary school (aged 5–11) or secondary school (aged 12–18). All the nine participants were either archives and records management practitioners or postgraduate students enrolled in courses in either archives and records management, library and information studies, information science or digital humanities.

The records under consideration were located in a variety of different 'archives', two of which were associated with traditional physically located memory institutions, namely The National Archives and the British Library, in the case of the UK Web Archive, and two of which were not – the 911 Digital Archive and WikiLeaks. Two of the records were born-digital versions of traditional physical analogues (a memo and a press release – although the memo also included the 'tracked changes' of a word-processed record betraying its born-digital origins and the press release was accompanied by a page of metadata detailing its born-digital origins) and two were not – an e-mail conversation and a website. Finally, two of the considered items were administrative records (the memo and the press release) and two were personal records, generated as a result of traumatic events (the e-mail conversation and the website, which formed part of the Web Archive's collection around the London terrorist attack on 7 July 2005).

Transcriptions from the interviews were coded against a framework adapted from an article by K. F. Latham (2015), entitled 'What is "the real thing" in the museum? An interpretative phenomenological study'. Latham's study aimed to understand how museum visitors understood their experience of the real thing and was based on interviews with 21 visitors from five museums who were asked to walk through their visit to an exhibit and consider questions such as: *What does 'the real thing' mean to you?* and *What if museums went completely online?* (Latham, 2015, 4, original italics).

The framework used Latham's main finding of 'four qualitatively different ways of understanding "TRT" in the museum'. In coding against this framework, attention came to rest on the following ideas against which to conduct the analysis:

- Self: The terms in which people expressed themselves when explaining their judgements on the degree to which the records were the real thing or not
- Surround: The sense in which these records seemed not to be seen as sharing an environment with the participants, but nonetheless had presence somewhere
- Presence: The nature of the presence of these records, more somewhere than here and in relation to time
- Relation: The people, imagined or known, who were discussed in relation to the individual records and the roles they were assigned.

These foci were then grouped under two thematic headings: judgements of authenticity, where the point in question seemed to be the degree of confidence the participants had, not so much in the records themselves, as in the version of events being portrayed in them; and digital presence, where the point in question was more around the way in which the records were perceived to be things and to have a presence in their own right.

For the purposes of this chapter, we will concentrate on only the first of these themes, because it is in this question of confidence, of judgements of authenticity, that the findings start to intersect with ideas of trust, defined as:

> Confidence of one party in another, based on alignment of value systems with respect to specific actions or benefits, and involving a relationship of voluntary vulnerability, dependence and reliance, based on risk assessment.
>
> (Pearce-Moses, 2018, s.v. trust)

In the participants' interactions with the records, there were no other parties as such, and yet, when the question of the real thing was being seen in terms of judgements of authenticity, it was noticeable that other parties became implicated in the discussion, imagined and conjured up by the participants.

These other parties sometimes remained anonymous – 'they' or 'people' – and where they remained so, they were sometimes assumed to be similar to the participants – 'it is created by someone like you or me'. Imagining these others, and perhaps both explicitly and implicitly imagining them to be similar to oneself, opened up questions of personal agendas, including the desire to present oneself in a positive light – 'I guess not necessarily authentic if people are sort of presenting a different online persona to what they think in real life'.

In some cases, however, the other parties were more of a known quantity to the participants. In these cases, the other parties might be known just by name, for example Roger Maxell (in the metadata accompanying the press release) or Sean, Chris, etc. (in the posts on the website), but they could also be known in the additional sense of that name conveying something more. For example, where the party was named as, for example, The National Archives, or the WikiLeaks organization, many participants already held a view in terms of the party's motivation and agenda, for example: 'I guess it's interesting that it's on the WikiLeaks page because *they* are known for digging up the truth, so it makes me sort of think it's authentic'.

In analysing the data, it was also noticeable that these other parties were conjured up in certain roles more than others. The more common roles were those of the author/creator and the current holder or publisher of the document, while the less common ones were previous users of the same documents and also any kind of intermediary between the creator and the current holder or publisher. From a record-keeping perspective, the absence from imagination of these sorts of parties is troubling, because the use of records by others implies some kind of reliance on them, a weaving into further events that could support a judgement of authenticity. Then again, it is in the period and space of the intermediary that a record is most at risk of intentional or unintentional alteration or loss.

Perhaps then, in the context of trust and of individuals' interactions with born-digital records, the role of the record-keeper becomes about expanding that interaction beyond the parties most obvious in the encounter with a record – its author and current holder/publisher – to an interaction with both the others who have used and acted on its basis and also with those through whose actions it has passed through space and time.

Legal genres as tools to engage with the government

This section reports on a two-part study, NA13 Patents, Petitions, and Trust, where the starting point for both investigations was a specific genre, or 'typified social action' (Miller, 1984): patents for the first part and petitions for the second part of the study. Legal genres, that is, recurrent typologies of records and situations whose form, function and any other discursive dimensions are enabled and constrained by means of some legal framework, are more 'stable' in their intrinsic and extrinsic characteristics than less structured genres (e.g. personal diaries, love letters), although legal genres do change over time too. As rhetorical genre scholar Bazerman (1994) put it, 'legal systems are relatively stable, but they are not ossified'. Analysing human activities that are structured through highly articulated social systems, such as the legal system, has the advantage of not requiring a large sample of texts, people and situations to be able to recognise patterns. Also, the evolution of forms and circumstances within a legal context tends to be slower and less dramatic than in other domains of life. The following subsections will focus on those findings of the two genre studies that more directly speak to issues of engagement with the legal entity responsible for the genres (e.g. the patent office, the patent database or any institution to which a petition is addressed).

Accessing patents in the archives and online
Fiorella Foscarini and Laura Dymock

The patents that are the subject of the first part of Study NA13 are legal instruments used by public authorities to grant exclusive rights to an inventor or assignee for a limited period of time in exchange for the public disclosure of the invention. They are descendants of the *letters patent* (from Latin *litterae patentes* for 'open letters'), which were published written orders issued by a king or other head of state generally granting an office, right, monopoly, title or status to a person or corporation. As dispositive acts aiming to protect intellectual property, patents started to be granted in England as Crown privileges as early as the 16th century. In North America, the US government set up an office responsible for managing this kind of matters in 1790, while Canada's first federal Patent Act came into force in 1869 (Duy, 2001).

Study NA13 focused on one particularly illustrious example of an early patent, granted in 1923 to Banting, Best, Collip and Macleod for the discovery of insulin. By using diplomatics and rhetorical genre studies to reveal the socio-historical circumstances in which a team of medical doctors sought a legal instrument with an apparent commercial orientation to protect their discovery, two goals were accomplished. First, light was shed on the complex negotiations behind the patenting of a medical product and process and the communities involved in such negotiations. Second, a thorough understanding was gained of the identity and nature of this specific patent. The latter understanding allowed the researchers to compare the representation of the patent within the University of Toronto's Insulin Committee papers (1920–25) – a fonds which is listed on the UNESCO's Memory of the World Register because of its global significance – and the digital copies of the insulin patent available through the Patents Database of the Canadian Intellectual Property Office (CIPO).

The historical investigation of the insulin patent is beyond the scope of this chapter. However, by examining how the medical community dealt with the misalignment between its ethical stance (where any personal benefit of commercial monopoly is seen as incompatible with the greater good that medical innovation aims to accomplish) and the mercantile nature of the patents genre, something important was learned about citizen engagement in a broad sense. The genre analysis of the social intentions embedded in a patent shows that there are various entities involved in the patent genre system (e.g. applicants, lawyers, judges, patent examiner and record-keepers). Therefore, what one tends to frame as 'citizen-state' interaction in reality involves multiple communities, each having specific motives, objectives and concerns, which may be in conflict with one another.

Seeking out and acquiring context for the patenting of insulin across the large body of paper records that make up the Insulin Committee fonds kept in the Archives of the University of Toronto is a very different experience from that of accessing any available digital versions. The CIPO database is a primary example of the contrasting analogue and digital experiences. These findings will be discussed in some detail, given the centrality of the notion of access to that of engagement.

First, there is no surrounding documentation included from the paper-based Insulin Committee fonds in the CIPO database, which only contains pages from original patent applications and relevant metadata. In the case of the insulin patent, searching for it on the database is particularly challenging as the word 'insulin' appears nowhere in CIPO's digital version. If a site visitor attempts to retrieve the record for this patent using the obvious keywords 'insulin' and 'Banting', no results are returned. 'Insulin' alone returns too many results to sift through, nonetheless the Banting and Best patent is not among the first pages where one would rightly expect it. A simple search using only 'Banting' finally brings up the desired patent as the fifth search result with a match score of 80%. What is the title of this patent that made it somewhat hard to retrieve? Its name: 'Extract Obtainable from the Mammalian Pancreas or from Related Glands of Fishes'. It can be confirmed this is the correct patent by noting that the inventors (Banting and Best), the owners (Governors of the UofT) and the date issued (18 September 1923) are in line with the researchers' informational expectations, but there is still other missing or clearly incorrect information in the metadata on the site. This includes 'Unknown' countries of citizenship/residency for the inventors, citing the owners' country as 'Afghanistan' and indicating 'NA' for the patent agent when anyone interacting with the physical fonds would know that individual was Charles H. Riches, a Toronto patent and trademark lawyer. These kinds of metadata issues are especially problematic because they are the only way to retrieve these older records. For those patents filed after 1978, it is possible to also search text of the documents themselves in addition to their CIPO metadata record, but this capability has not been extended to earlier applications.

For pre-1978 records, the CIPO Patents Database has scanned images of many of those patent applications. However, these scans of the original records are not guaranteed to be complete or to maintain the original order. This is at least partly attributable to CIPO's establishment of a fixed six-part template for the online database. The 1923 Banting and Best insulin patent, as we might expect, does not naturally follow this template and so it has been reconfigured to make it conform. Not only has re-ordering taken place, but other distortions of the original form have occurred. This is most noticeable in the 'Drawings' section, where a scanned page that says 'Substitute – Section is not Present' is provided. The intended meaning here is unclear: drawings are an optional part of the Canadian patent application process, but other sections that were not mandatory or commonly used in 1923 are simply marked 'N/A'. It is unknown at present whether there was a drawing for the first insulin patent – there are drawings associated with some of the patent records in the fonds at the University of Toronto, but there are also many without one. In any case, there is no way for the online reader to know what the original structure of this patent was because the form of the original record is simply lost or obscured in this digital representation.

In returning to the problematic keyword search described earlier, part of the less-than-intuitive nature of the CIPO Patents Database may lie in for whom it is intended. While, in line with open government principles, greater dissemination of patent information was a primary reason for creating the database, it can be argued that patent professionals rather than ordinary citizens have been more heavily identified as the 'designated community' because of the specialised way the patents are presented. At the very least, members of the lay public looking to obtain patent information would have to spend some time familiarising themselves with the terminology used in the database as well as its structural components. Fortunately, there are resources available to the end-user for this very purpose, including a glossary and help section. If lay persons were themselves looking to patent something for the first time, the CIPO website is a boon not only because it allows them to verify whether their idea has already been patented – assuming they can conjure up the right keywords – but also for the educational resources it provides, including information on how to file a patent application in the current system.

In contrast to the novice's experience, examiners within the CIPO office, patent agents and other patent professionals can utilise the variety of specialised information that is available through the database (e.g. International Patent Classification Number, Patent Cooperation Treaty, Application Priority Data) to establish a degree of institutional context for a patent that is possibly often lost on the lay person. This context will largely be institutional or legal, but it does not shed much light on the wider social context of creation for the patent in the first place. Since that information falls outside the purview of a patent professional's duties it is likely no great loss to them, but for someone wanting to understand why a patent was obtained, they will undoubtedly have to search elsewhere.

Petitions: an evolving genre
Fiorella Foscarini and Paige Hohmann

The second part of Study NA13, dedicated to petitions, was triggered by the observation that, in the last few years, this legal genre has been undergoing a remarkable metamorphosis from purely physical instantiations to hybrid and/or purely digital instantiations. The researchers' main goal was to build a solid conceptual framework for the understanding of petitions and what they 'do'. Corresponding with the elucidation of the petition as a socio-political and legal instrument, they sought to enhance understandings of trust in digitally represented petitions.

The most substantial contribution of the study may be found in a comprehensive literature review and in the theoretical framework applied, which involved a combination of diplomatics and rhetorical genre studies (Foscarini, 2012). This approach allowed the researchers to develop a multi-faceted and fluid definition of petition based on a thorough survey of some of the historical, rhetorical and social baggage carried by the genre.

The etymology of the word 'petition' (from the Latin *petere*, 'to request') describes generally any type of formally articulated demand originating outside of a governance structure, or an impulse travelling from inferior to superior power (Hoad, 1996). In a study of the role of petitions in the Middle Ages – a time when this genre was primarily meant to fulfil expectations of decorum and social status – Held (2010) identifies the following key issues, which explain why this genre is a rich site for analysis for archival research and for this study in particular:

- Petitions are speech acts carried out in an asymmetric interpersonal relationship; thus *power* is nearly always the constituting feature and as such the most important variable from a historical view
- Petitions are *ritualised public interactions* where individual aspects are subordinated to coercive social constraints
- Petitions are part of the epistolary genre and thus *fruit of their own rhetorical tradition and instructive literature*
- Petitions are *ubiquitous and timeless political instruments* that yield cross-cultural data for comparative analysis in which similarities, differences and changes can be pointed out. [All italics added for emphasis.]

As van Voss (2002) put it, 'petitions are demands for a favour, or for the redressing of an injustice, directed to some established authority'. The tone and tenor of the petition reflects existing power dynamics but does not explicitly seek to subvert them. As for how petitions were (and arguably, still are) used, governments have the prerogative of acting or not acting, but the subtext implicit in the petition suggests a tacit threat of revolt or democratic ousting.

Several sources agree that petitions have a secondary use by governments as an indicator of popular sentiment and of the issues of import to citizens. For example, the Hansard Society (2012) refers derisively to digital petitioning in the current e-petitioning platform in the United Kingdom as amounting to merely 'a finger in the wind'. Van Voss (2002) confirms that this is nothing new, as even in the 19th century and earlier, petitions were used to feel the 'temperature' of the relationship between the citizens and the state.

Another interesting point in relation to the theme of this chapter is that petitions, in addition to being generally valuable from a historical perspective in as much as there are many and they are well preserved, also shed rare light on the 'silent masses of history' as a consequence of the fact that the genre exacts ritualised communication from commoners to the elite. That is to say, petitions allow us to study ordinary people (Wuergler, 2002).

Based on our review of the literature on the nature of power dynamics as present in legal, legislative and political discourse, the following elements were added to our developing definition of 'petition' for the purposes of this study:

- To build on a previous note that the petition does not seek to subvert power structures, the petition has an explicit convention, as a genre, to *ask, not demand* (Dodd, 2007)

- A petition benefits from *communicative competence* on the part of the petitioners; an expert or professional writer may be enlisted to enhance this competence for stronger grounding when addressing power (Longe, 1985)
- When a collective accepts participating in the petition transaction, that *collective accepts the prevailing power dynamic* and performs work to perpetuate it (Baker, 1999)
- The orientation of a petitioning group can be described in terms of *positioning theory*, which posits a 'cluster of rights, obligations, and duties' (Barrault-Méthy, 2015). [All italics added for emphasis.]

The petition genre has been subject to modifications even before the transition from paper to digital. It is not therefore unexpected that considerable changes have taken place concurrent with the introduction of e-petitions, which is a development closely related to the rise of the internet as a medium of mass communication. Lindner and Riehm (2009) suggest that one of the main differences between traditional paper-based petitions and e-petitions is the 'point of contact between the principal petitioner and the receiving institution'. They explain:

> The internet-based procedure ... requires the petitioner to contact the administration prior to the signature phase. ... On the one hand, the early contact with the experts in the administration opens the opportunity to improve the petition text, and the petitioner may receive useful tactical advice on how to promote the e-petition. On the other hand, it cannot be ruled out that the petitioner's genuine request might be distorted in this process. By comparison, paper petitions, submitted after the signatory phase, are – at least theoretically – more likely to be rejected on formal grounds.
>
> (Lindner and Riehm, 2009, 6)

Regardless of how e-petitions get disseminated (e-mail, third-party platform or government platform), it is noted that the introduction of e-petitions has not been a silver bullet for diversifying citizen political engagement (Hersh and Schaffner, 2017). Our review of the most recent literature on this subject confirms that many of the assumptions about the democratisation of society through this and other online means of civic engagement are nothing more than 'digital folklore'. E-petitioning, despite its low barriers to participation, does actually very little to engage those groups not already poised to be civically active. Hersh and Schaffner's (2017) article supports the notion that 'slacktivism' is indeed an empirically provable phenomenon; it also suggests that it is not a function of laziness, but a consequence of our narrative-driven consciousness.

Our study concluded that in the electronic environment, the focus of petitions appears to be shifting from 'requesting' to merely 'expressing'. Thus, the kind of citizen engagement that this genre enables is also changing. We also hypothesised that the electronic petition is actually not identical to or even a simple descendant of the paper petition; rather, it is a 'hybrid genre' (Yates and Orlikowski, 1992) which only resembles the traditional petition in its form and very much less so in its rhetorical force and purpose.

Citizen engagement and civic technologies
Elizabeth Shepherd

Open government as an instrument for citizen engagement
Study NA08, The Implications of Open Government, Open Data, and Big Data on the Management of Digital Records in an Online Environment, started from the assumption that citizen engagement is a communicative, interactive and iterative process or initiative that actively involves citizens in policy or program development at any level of government and as such is more complex than simple provision of open data. The level of engagement and flow of information can range from simply making information available, to gathering feedback and ideas, and on to more complex relationships where individuals and groups are transferred greater decision-making power and authority to deliberate issues and their solutions (Hurley, 2017). Though many citizen engagement initiatives originate in government, other instances may involve citizen-originated initiatives that are designed to engage government.

When more complex, two-way engagement initiatives are in play, citizen engagement processes and initiatives may share or transfer decision-making power from governments to citizens by using 'collective problem-solving and prioritization' (Sheedy et al., 2008, 5). In many other cases, citizens may submit feedback or ideas but governments will take authority over final decision-making power. Successful citizen engagement programs are grounded in transparent, trusted information and mutual respect between all involved participants. Individuals are given an equal chance to speak or contribute and their contributions are treated with respect. These principles do not assume that citizens have adversarial interests in an engagement initiative either between each other or with governments, but that in order for the results of initiatives to be trustworthy, the process has to take place in an environment of trust. As is clear from the difficulties in establishing definitional boundaries for the concept of citizen engagement, it is highly context-dependent: each initiative will differ in its rationale, intentions, participants and methods of determining success.

The benefits of citizen engagement are manifold: strong citizen engagement initiatives can help remedy the power inequities between citizens and governments, boost the value of government leadership through creating stronger governance and policy and help citizens cultivate a better understanding of the issues their communities face (Nabatchi, 2012). Critics of citizen engagement point to the inefficiencies created by the time, money and effort used to consult citizens, both on the part of governments' and citizens' lost time. Citizen engagement initiatives may also be criticised as merely token measures to make governments appear more accountable and transparent without necessarily acting on the results of an initiative. The question remains for these critics whether citizen contributions have a meaningful or lasting impact on decisions or actions.

However, the field has changed to develop into an aspect of the open government movement and the broader field of participatory democracy, which actively solicits citizen involvement at the beginning of a decision-making process rather than working to reactively respond to citizen feedback after a decision has been made. Prior to the 1990s, governments had attempted to learn from private sector practices and to manage government as a business, but the 'new public service' was motivated to 'place citizens at the center' (Denhardt and Denhardt, 2000). These concepts are connected to current ideas around citizen engagement initiatives that make use of technologies for interaction with governments, including social media platforms for creating input and processing technologies to analyse this input. For example, the British Columbia government produced a plan called *Citizens at the Centre: Government 2.0* (Canada, 2010) to communicate its plans for open government technology as a means of delivering government information and services to citizens and supporting greater participation and industry innovation. The plan emphasises the key role that technology will play 'to deliver services that better support citizens and help them meet their needs', with the expectation that citizens will increasingly turn to web-based venues to interact with their government directly (Canada, 2010, 8).

The emphasis on data and information is symptomatic of the maturity of citizen engagement in Canada. Provincial and municipal jurisdictions are beginning to explore this aspect of open government more fully through consultation initiatives that address public policy, legislation and decision-making. For example, the City of Toronto has created a space for ongoing, smaller scale consultations. In 2014–15, the City piloted a citizen engagement tool called IdeaSpaceTo where questions were posed by City representatives and citizens were encouraged to submit ideas and solutions. These are all noteworthy examples of open dialogue-type initiatives, but most governments in Canada, including the federal government, are still at the learning stage when it comes to designing and conducting citizen engagement initiatives.

Civic technologies

Civic technologies take government data and present it to users in visual or interactive ways for the purpose of effecting social change. Broadly defined, civic technology is technology that intersects with public life, enabling engagement or participation of the public with the government for a variety of purposes, from making government more transparent and accountable, to enhancing civic communities and impacting policy decisions.

The Knight Foundation has identified two specific strands of civic technology: open government and community action. From this, civic technology can be further divided into five streams: public data access and transparency; social causes and civic engagement; place-based networks and community forums; funding for projects enhancing public services and spaces; and peer-to-peer sharing of resident-owned goods and services (Knight Foundation, 2015). Civic technology can be embodied through a variety of initiatives (e.g. FixMyStreet www.fixmystreet.com; They Work For You www.theyworkforyou.com). Applications that enable residents to share goods and skills and a website allowing resident feedback on environmental issues posited by local government are both examples of civic technology. However, a common thread is a foregrounding of the user-citizen, with a focus on their empowerment and engagement within the community, and therefore the political process, through technological means.

Civic technologies provide opportunities for case studies of the data management and handling practices into which records management could feed. For example, Gurstein's (2012) article on the use of data for addressing problems with public toilets in India, an often-cited example of the positive potential social impact of open data, and Hayakawa, Imi and Ito's (2014) work on the OpenStreetMap community in Japan following the Tohoku earthquake, invite critical review from the records management community. For instance, what is the impact on citizens and data users when data is not drawn from records? How can data from records work with or against crowdsourced data to produce an accurate picture of events or circumstances?

In Peru, the National Strategy of Open Data promotes the opening and re-use of open data by society, aimed at increasing the involvement of the citizenship in public matters and improving public services by creating value from the collaboration and the innovation. The Strategy has established the following lines of action in Peru:

- The establishment of the institutional regulatory framework, as well as the implementation of the regulatory framework for re-opening and re-use of Government Open Data in accordance with the Transparency and Access to Public Information regulations, among other topics
- Development of the Technological Infrastructure of Open Data: Implementation of the Open Data Service Portal and development of the required ICT infrastructure
- Promotion of participatory and collaborative initiatives and instances for data opening and re-use.

Scholars in the area of e-government approach open government data from their own perspective. Examples include Ngwenya, Lubbe and Klopper's (2012) thinking about openness and e-government in the developing world; Milić, Veljković and Stoimenov's (2012) framework for data mining; and Misuraca and Viscusi's (2014) questions about the usefulness of raw data, which has synergies with questions coming out of the records and archives management discipline.

Data flows: from government to citizen and back again

One potential assumption of a records or archives manager working to support open government is that the flow of information always runs from government to citizen. Governments create information, package it for consumption and citizens access it. And while citizens have long been the subject of government information, it is less often the case they actively create it. Citizen engagement processes, particularly ones that encourage uses of civic technologies, are in the position to reverse this condition. Through citizen engagement processes, citizens create records that governments are in a position to receive, analyse, store and manage, potentially for the long term. This is not to say that aspects of this two-way relationship have not always been present: elections, town hall meetings and letters and depositions submitted to officials have all been common forms of citizen engagement with long legacies in governments. Similarly, citizens often have the opportunity to submit complaints or requests regarding government services. Rather, citizen engagement may create new forms and sources of data that touch upon a much wider array of services and functions than previously, and citizen-derived information, as in open government data, may be aggregated and analysed on a much larger scale.

Governments that use citizen information to provide for decision-making must be able to demonstrate the trustworthiness and transparency of the processes taken to make those decisions. A useful method for examining how these flows of information might impact records creation is through the IAP2 Public Participation Spectrum, which describes the qualities of different kinds of citizen-government interactions at different levels. In *Managing Records of Citizen Engagement: a primer* (Hurley, Léveillé and McDonald 2016), the different levels of the IAP2 Spectrum are mapped to different records contexts as a method of identifying issues and strategies for records management.

Records and information professionals have to be aware of the ways in which data can flow between governments and citizens, a flow that creates records that may be unanticipated by the usual records schedules. The first is instances in which governments directly seek feedback from citizens as part of a citizen engagement initiative. Such initiatives may seek information in various forms: e-mail submissions, social media comments, structured surveys, opportunities to edit or provide commentary on documents, or more conversational, discourse-based platforms. In consultation-based projects, these processes are intended to end up in some kind of decision or action on a particular issue. The feedback must be analysed and packaged in such a way to inform decisions, which are then theoretically implemented by a government.

At other levels of the IAP2, feedback may actually constitute the decision itself, such as in a vote on an issue, or decision-making processes may be created by back-and-forth discourse and problem-solving. All these events create information that must be managed and audit trails that attest to how records created by citizens were used and acted on. In many cases, governments are now using sophisticated data analysis methods such as natural language processing software to summarise the opinions from a large corpus of submissions. As in 'Your Comments Here: contextualizing technologies, seeking records and supporting transparency for citizen engagement':

> … transparency of the whole engagement process, and how different
> information technologies for input and analysis were used to get from the
> beginning to the end, is a crucial contributor to establishing trust in the system
> itself through the availability of evidence.
>
> (Hurley, 2017, 18)

Citizens themselves may also create data independently of governments that has an impact on government services. Websites such as FixMyStreet (www.fixmystreet.com) or other crowdsourced data collected by third parties could be used to inform governments of a variety of issues, from infrastructure to policy. Governments could potentially take in this data, but it must be verified and packaged in such a way that a government could act upon it. The appropriate rights over the use and ownership of this data would have to be worked out between the creators and governments; if governments receive such data, it is conceivable that that may wish to use it for their own purposes and will have to manage its retention and disposition accordingly.

E-registers: a Croatian civic information system

Research work in Croatia examined the function of e-registers as a form of open public register (Strahonja, 2018). A public register is a register under the authority and direction of a public body, including government agencies and international organizations, established and maintained manually or now usually by computer in accordance with a certain statutory regulation or other act and open fully or partially for public inspection, searching, printing and copying data according to certain rules. A public register is a collection of data on individuals, legal entities, documents, assets and other items of registration, which is operated by the registration body in accordance with a prescribed procedure. The concept of the public register is similar to some other concepts and the study researched similarities and differences with other entities, such as an index of cases and the register of actions in case management and workflow management systems and an index of documents in document management systems.

Terminology surrounding registries was developed at the time of manually created registers in book format and it is still used today. So a register typically consists of the general ledger (main book) which contains data on the state and the status of subjects of registration; the register of changes (register of action) which contains information on the contents and status of proposals for change of the data related to the subject of registration; and a collection of authentic records on which entries in the register are made and other records related to the subject of registration, such as auxiliary materials, e.g. indexes, catalogues and delivery records. Because of the ubiquitous use of ICT to deliver the register, registration bodies must pay more attention to the semi-structured or unstructured information and records, which include e-mail, instant messages, spreadsheets and images, etc. Good practice in these areas is a prerequisite for standardisation of information in public e-registers.

Contemporary public registers are civic information systems. In addition to registration, they provide services to public agencies, citizens and businesses by mediation of information and communication technologies. The internet is the main channel of delivery, but mobile phones, public kiosks and other channels are also considered. Thus, public registers reflect the main properties of e-services (Rowley, 2006) and may be described as e-registers. Operational risk management, legal compliance and ease of discovery using role-based permissions have become key business imperatives. Thinking about the e-service component of e registers, an objective of project EU05 was an analysis of the applicability of service quality models. One of the quality models is SERVQUAL, developed in the mid-1980s, and RATER (an acronym of the e-register's five attributes: Reliability, Assurance, Tangibles, Empathy, Responsiveness) a few years later (Zeithaml, Parasuraman and Berry, 2009).

Participation in local government through social media
Lois Evans

Study NA05, Social Media and Trust in Government, began in 2013, the year in which WikiLeaks (2006–7) and the Snowden disclosure (2013) had a significant impact on the levels of trust in government. According to the Edelman Trust Barometer, levels of trust fell to 42% in the US and 54% in Canada, although the levels of trust among the informed public were higher, at 49% in the US and 60% in Canada (Edelman, 2014, 3). Trust in government is believed to be supported by demonstrations of equality and honesty by government (Uslaner and Brown, 2005) and to be built upon 'a foundation of at least some measure of information' (Burkert, 1999).

In addition, there were residual expectations that social media would be a transformative source for democracy, based on the Obama election campaigns (2008, 2012) and the Arab Spring (2011). The researchers' attention focused on local government, where social media was adopted at amazing rates: an estimated 86% of US cities had adopted social media by 2010 and 93.5% by 2012 (Norris and Reddick, 2013, 173). Social media was expected to lead to greater transparency, participation and collaboration (Mergel, 2013, 33), based on a tradition of direct citizen involvement at this level of governance (Mossberger, Wu, and Crawford, 2013, 351). It was expected to foster two-way communication between governments and citizens, with co-creation of content providing 'great potential for enhanced democratization of information exchange' (Graham, 2014, 363). The study, which was conducted from late 2013 to early 2016, examined what part social media as records played in open government and the government-citizen trust relationship in local government in the United States and Canada.

Tying the research to the ITrust project's theme of trust, the researchers focused on two questions: can social media be used by local governments to increase citizen trust? And, what can we learn about the administration of social media that results in an increase in trust? The research design was exploratory and process-oriented, with two overlapping phases. Since trust involves a relationship between two parties, the researchers first looked at the government perspective using a qualitative approach leveraging interviews and content analysis. In the second phase, they took a quantitative approach, collecting Twitter data and using sentiment analysis. They also planned to conduct an online citizen survey which, although unsuccessful, provided an important insight into local governments' use of social media.

The study investigated ten American and ten Canadian cities that were selected on the basis of having successful social media programs. The researchers looked for demographic and geographic diversity. The US cities included: Atlanta, Austin, Boston, Honolulu, Kansas City, Mesa, New York, Raleigh, Riverside and Seattle. The Canadian cities included: Calgary, Edmonton, Fredericton, Halifax, Ottawa, Regina, Surrey, Toronto, Vancouver and Winnipeg. Reviewing their selection, the researchers found that over half were capital cities and almost all were among the top 50 cities in the US by population or the top 25 in Canada.

As the research team included an archivist, a record manager and a data scientist, it was consistently focused on the trustworthiness of records. However, in this study, its position shifted to thinking about how records support trust in government, noting that trust is always based to some degree on information (Burkert, 1999). However, there are many theories of how trust works, four of which were examined in a literature review and a short paper on social media and trust in law enforcement (Franks and Evans, 2015): trust as a component of social capital (social capital theory); trust as found in social relationships (social networking theory); trust based on operational choices (behavioural trust theory); and trust based on leveraging components to achieve maximum profit (resource-based trust). In the end, it was found that trust is largely viewed as a form of social capital, along with obligations, expectations of reciprocity and knowledge provision.

Social capital refers to the resources embedded in one's social networks that can be accessed for collective action (Skoric et al., 2016, 1820). However, what researchers were most interested in learning was whether social media impacts social capital in a way that results in participation or action (Boulianne, 2015; Skoric et al., 2016). In thinking about how trust is created, scholars talk about trust as a progression, from personality based, to a societal tie, to emergent through mutual relationships and as a feature of a community as a whole. They also talk about process-based trust, which is associated with the provision of goods and services: people trust institutions because the institutions provide something to them (Franks and Weck, 2015).

In the study, these themes of trust influenced the researchers' views of open government. In the ITrust terminology database, trust is defined as:

... an approach designed to provide greater access to unrestricted information held by public bodies in order to promote transparency, accountability, and citizen engagement and participation, to accomplish a larger outcome of building and enhancing citizens' trust in their governments.

(Pearce-Moses, 2018, s.v. trust)

This definition emphasises the role information plays in building trust, presenting a ground-level view of open government. In disciplines such as public administration, the next-level version sees open government as involving citizens in decisions that affect them in their daily lives. Further, open government can be operationalised through three streams: open information (which includes freedom of information, protection of privacy and proactive release); open data (which is provided through data portals and datasets); and open dialogue (which includes social media) (Treasury Board of Canada, 2014). These streams operationalise the three components most associated with open government: transparency, through open information; accountability, through open data; and participation, through open dialogue. An important differentiation is to be made here between citizen engagement, which refers to people being involved in their community (e.g. volunteering, attending events, supporting neighbourhood initiatives) and public participation, which refers to people being involved in the political process (e.g. voting, attending Council meetings, taking part in consultations). A significant amount of research has been completed on social media and participation, which is summarised by two meta-analytic reviews by Boulianne (2015) (36 studies) and Skoric et al. (2016) (22 studies). Both found that the relationship between social media use and participation is clearly positive but not necessarily statistically significant and that the question of causation remains unanswered.

Returning to the study research, the researchers contacted staff at all 20 of the US and Canadian cities and interviewed social media staff at 17 of the 20 cities. They also completed content analysis of social media and record policies, guidelines and terms of use, web pages and social media account home pages, and reports for a total of 348 documents (Evans, Franks, and Chen, 2018). In terms of results, it was found that the administration of social media programs is quite similar in the US and Canada:

- *Adoption*: Social media was adopted between 2008 and 2010, mainly in response to an emergency or major weather event in Canada and at the request of Council or in the course of business in the US. Adoption was rapid, with business units adopting various platforms and launching many accounts – the range in number was between 15 to 130 social media accounts per city.

- *Structure*: Social media was administered by the Communications departments, which considered it secondary and auxiliary to their websites as the primary place where the cities engaged citizens and where city business was conducted. The social media administration structure was described as hub-and-spoke, with Communications directly managing the main city accounts and controlling which platforms could be adopted by business units, whether or not they could have accounts and which staff could have administrative rights. However, neither the Council members nor the police accounts were considered to be within Communications' area of responsibility.
- *Policy*: Communications' control over social media was enshrined in social media policies, where high concern over the cities' reputations and possible liability was demonstrated. The policies included directives to employees around appropriate use, consistent messaging and confidentiality and privacy. There were also terms of use directed at social media audiences, focused on appropriate content tone and language, and stating that contravening material could be removed.
- *Use*: In terms of use, the focus was on providing information about initiatives and events in a one-way, broadcast fashion. Two-way use was limited to issue management and responding to the odd service request.
- *Monitoring*: In the US, the social media team only monitored the city's main accounts while in Canada they also monitored the accounts managed by the business units. In both countries, inappropriate content was removed at a rate of two or three posts per account per month. In Canada, users were occasionally banned if they consistently broke the terms of use.
- *Reporting*: Both measurement and reporting of social media results were sporadic. In the US, only one city provided regular reports to senior teams, while in Canada about half produced reports at varying intervals. The teams said this was due to a lack of staff resources, funding for tools and expertise. The teams did not know much about their audiences beyond basic demographics.

In terms of the relationship with citizens, social media teams thought about trust in terms of their own trustworthiness as agents of the cities. They saw the city accounts as the official voice of the city, particularly around contentious issues and in times of emergency. In this, social media provided an advantage over traditional media as there was no filtering by the press and they could speak directly to their audiences. They noted that they were non-partisan and at arm's length from the elected officials, who had their own accounts and their own staff. They emphasised their own professionalism and the fact that they provided factual, corrected and updated content and were very careful about removing or responding to negative feedback. Given their concerns around reputation, they were surprisingly risk tolerant: issues included parody accounts, hacked accounts, viruses introduced through analytic software and mistakes made by employees. They focused on prevention and then just fixed things that went wrong.

This tolerance extended to their treatment of social media as records. Although they knew that social media content included records subject to state laws and management and, although most had responded to FIPPA (Freedom of Information and Protection of Privacy Act, a Canadian provincial law) or legal requests involving social media, only a small minority had formalised procedures for managing social media as records. Instead, they were comfortable relying on whatever facilities were provided by the social media platforms, noting that it was difficult to provide records after the fact and that business units making requests were advised to do so as early as possible. Finally, the social media teams did not appear to give much thought to the social media platform's role in how their messaging was distributed.

In the second phase of the study, the researchers used sentiment analysis to examine the citizen side of the trust relationship. Sentiment analysis is a technique that uses natural language processing, statistics or machine learning methods to extract or characterise the sentiment content of a text unit in terms of feelings, attitudes, emotions and/or opinions (Chen, Franks, and Evans, 2016, 291). The use of sentiment analysis in this study is important because it is based on actual content and extends previous work which is as much based on self-reporting surveys or panels (Boulianne, 2015; Skoric et al., 2016) as it is based on analysis of actual content. For the study, the researchers collected Twitter data from all 20 cities for the city, mayor and police accounts (60 accounts in total). The data were collected retrospectively for a 20-month period, extending from 1 January 2013 to 25 August 2014. Essentially, the researchers captured the data, cleaned it, ran it through processing and then finalised the analysis using three different tools. In organizing the data, they were impressed by the sheer quantity of tweets sent and received over the 20-month period, with the number of tweets sent through each of the main city accounts ranging from 2,000 to 18,000 and the number of tweets received by the cities' social media teams ranging from 1,000 to 70,000. Since the cities run anywhere from 15 to 130 accounts, the volume of content is significant and may explain some of the ambivalence expressed by the team with respect to managing social media as records.

In terms of analysis, the researchers found no significant difference between the US and Canadian city accounts in terms of longevity, number of followers, number of tweets and number of audience tweets. Beyond this, the study's main result concurred with findings from previous studies: researchers found a positive, significant relationship between social media use by cities and positive sentiment, where positive sentiment is associated with emotions such as joy, surprise and trust (as compared to negative sentiment associated with emotions like anger, disgust, fear and sadness) (Pengate and Delen, 2014, 5). In terms of administration, however, it appeared that the four available measures of account longevity (i.e. the number of days the account had been running), number of followers, number of city tweets and number of audience tweets did not impact positive sentiment. There was an insignificant negative relationship between longevity of accounts and positive sentiment, and an insignificant positive relationship among number of followers, number of city tweets and number of audience tweets.

However, there was a significant difference in positive sentiment by account type. The mayors' accounts had a mean of 34% positive sentiment, the cities had 28% and the police had 23%, which may suggest that the audiences may be expressing different levels of trust for the different roles. The researchers were told by some of the social media teams that their audiences were aware of the operational nature of city accounts and directed their more political comments to Council members. Beyond this, the researchers observed different uses by mayors, who sought ongoing contacts with voters, city staff, who broadcasted information about initiatives and events, and the police, who were responding to incidents and emergencies.

As noted, the researchers planned to partner with four of the sample cities to run an online questionnaire. The cities would run notices about the survey on their social media accounts and the researchers would run the survey. Although cities seemed to be interested in the survey phase, most said they were too busy with other initiatives to participate. One of two Canadian cities agreed after airing a general concern around reputation and specific concerns regarding questions on the survey that compared levels of trust with regards to elected officials, police and staff. Significantly, the team noted that social media audiences were not representative of the population, stressing that findings drawn from a survey of these audiences would be of limited value.

Through this, researchers came to understand the impact of non-representativeness which, combined with difficulties around collecting data, contributed to the cities' one-way use of social media platforms. Given the limitations of the platforms, the cities had begun to launch their own consultation portals where citizens could sign up as forum members and provide feedback through surveys, discussions and other online mechanisms, with their responses tied to their locations within their city and relevant demographic data. Evidently, the cities responded to third-party platform controls by not playing the game, that is by creating their own fora to collect data for use in political decisions and by using social media to broadcast information about their initiatives. In fact, the consultation portals do provide a level of real participation, where audience feedback is collected, reported and published as reports and tied to government decisions (e.g. TalkVancouver, 2018). Consultation portals appear to be gaining popularity in Canada and there is evidence of ad hoc use in the US.

In conclusion, the case studies revealed that the cities' social media teams were committed to gaining the trust of their audience by creating an official voice, taking a non-partisan approach, acting ethically in administering accounts and taking care in monitoring content. In terms of open government, the study found that social media is used by the cities to broadcast information about opportunities to engage and participate but not as a forum for engagement and participation, due to the non-representative nature of the audiences and the challenges associated with third-party platform reporting. Turning to the sentiment analysis, in response to the study's first research question, it was found that there was a positive relationship between social media use and citizen trust in government. Regarding the second research question as to what can be learned about the administration of social media that might result in an increase in trust, it was found that it was not account longevity, number of followers, number of tweets or number of audience tweets that determines positive sentiment but who is doing the tweeting, and, likely, what they are tweeting about.

The role of users in the appraisal of a government website

Silvia Schenkolewski-Kroll and Assaf Tractinsky

This section discusses some of the major findings of a case study that was carried out through three successive ITrust projects:

- EU01 Research on Retention and Disposition Processes in an Internet Website of the Government of Israel: The Ministry of Foreign Affairs Case Study
- EU25 Using Web Analytics in Appraisal of Records on the Foreign Ministry of Israel Website
- EU36 Archival Appraisal, Retention Schedules and Metadata in Web Sites: The Case Study of the Ministry of Foreign Affairs, Israel.

The research objective was to examine the process of archival retention and disposition on the English website of the Israeli Ministry of Foreign Affairs and to create a set of procedures and guidelines by which the organization would be able to choose which documents should be permanently preserved and transferred to another repository or archival institution, and which should be disposed of, in compliance with the regulations included in the Israel Archives Law.

The study focused on the question: Have users ever served as a parameter for the appraisal of archival material? The archival appraisal literature does include expressions of interest in the users, especially when appraisal moves from its basic focus – administrative and legal values – to an emphasis on research values and the values for society. Following Hans Booms (1987), one may say that the social value that can be attributed to a website is mainly based on the opinion of citizens who will determine which records will remain for future generations. Leaving aside a total representation of citizens as proposed by Booms' theoretical approach, it appears to be possible to apply the social criterion to the appraisal of a website. The main evaluative element for a website is in fact the number of visitors and its implications, returning visitors or the time visitors spend on the site.

The informative or public relations nature of a website places the issue of visitors in a preferred position in the parameter scale for appraisal and may even give it exclusive rights. In records of this nature, the quantity and repeated time on a page are indicators of interest, that is, a sign of success in achieving the goal that the institution owning the site set for itself when creating the site and operating it.

The results of the first part of this study focusing on the Israel Ministry of Foreign Affairs website showed that, when comparing the two sections 'MASHAV' (Agency for International Development Cooperation) and 'Foreign Policy' with the control section 'About Israel', there are more visits to the informative sections but less time spent there. The MASHAV section, due to its operational nature, has fewer users, but more time is spent there. Thus, each one of the sections required a process of study and analysis of its internal organization and of its content and the diplomatic form of the records. Accordingly, the researchers recommended scheduling the retention of the content of each section separately (Schenkolewski-Kroll and Tractinsky, 2015).

The second part of the study used Google Analytics (GA) to enable a total analysis of the website. In the field of interest, GA makes it possible for webmasters to see quantitative values, including estimates, which are the result of the activities such as counting pages by the number of page views (including details of how visitors reached the site) and listing from where in the country or abroad the visitors come, etc. The online tool also makes it possible to know the length of time spent by users on the various pages; the bounce rate on any page and exits from the site; the number of returning visitors to the site; and what the main landing pages and exit pages of the site are. GA provides a great amount of information, which is displayed in the form of graphs. This allows checking for rises in numbers, drops or no change and makes it easier for webmasters to decide how to become more efficient and what can be done to improve and optimise the site (Schenkolewski-Kroll and Tractinsky, 2016).

As suggested, one of the basic units of measurement of content on GA is the number of views. Two methods of measurement exist; one is by Session and a second one is by Page View. A session is the period of time a user is actively engaged with the website or application. All usage data (Screen Views, Events, E-commerce, etc.) is associated with a session. In other words, the measurement of views on the site is done from the moment the users enter it until they apparently exit it, in the unit of time during which they are active on the site. In contrast, the Page View is defined as the total number of pages viewed. Repeated views of a single page are counted; in other words, the number of user's views on a page is counted.

A measurement unit is composed of data on the user's activities on the page, and not on the session. A session is an artificial unit, in which measurements are relatively inaccurate, due to the technical structure of the site and the depth of the embedding of GA within it (as detailed above). There is no practical way of knowing how the users are counted during the approximately half hour from the moment they actually leave the site and the end of their being attributed to the session, because only then does the system disconnect itself, when there is no further activity. In contrast, a measurement unit based on activity on the pages themselves is more accurate, because it gives a record of leaving the pages. Therefore, on the Foreign Ministry website, it is better to consider the viewing of data on the pages and the average time period of activity on the page, rather than the average time period of a session.

GA allows distinguishing the types of visitors between new visitors – those who appear on the site for the first time – and returning visitors – those who return to the site more than once. The study had a special focus on users who return to the site and their activities, because they know the site and are interested in the information on it.

The exit data represents the percentage of exits from the group of pages attributed to a section and which – according to the Google definition – can be measured; in contrast to the Bounce Rate, in which – according to the Google definition – the variable does not include the possibility of measurement at this level (there is no set of pages). These metrics are not intended to result in the sum of 100% because they are used only in relation to the pages in the section; as a specific page is found in a specific section, the exits also accumulate at the section level, not just at the level of a single page. According to the Google definition, the state of exit exists not only at the level of a single page, but also at the section level, as well as on the entire site.

The study examined the behaviour of users according to their countries of origin. A small number of countries from the comprehensive list of countries present in Google Analytics was selected. Data regarding the users' origin was examined in relation to the sections researchers were working on.

In light of the above, the study developed a formula that would determine a parameter for users, in which:

> The number of page views by returning visitors
>
> x
>
> Average time spent on a page by returning visitors x (1-%Exit)
>
> =
>
> Appraisal metric

The formula differentiates between new and returning visitors and uses the data of returning visitors because they show more interest in the information found in the section. In order to reach a result, the study took the number of page views by returning visitors multiplied by average time spent on a page by returning visitors. The last part of the formula consists of the %Exit, which represents those leaving the page; then, 1-%Exit means those remaining on the page and the product gives the estimated total number of hours spent by returning visitors on a specific section during a specific period of time.

The higher the resulting figure, the higher the level of interest. Thus, this formula may serve as a parameter for appraisal. It may then be possible to determine a minimum threshold of the metric and if this minimum threshold is not met, the material would not be retained permanently.

The parameters by which users can be measured are:

- The number of page views in a given period of time, both in absolute numbers and in percentages – this is done by the number of new and/or returning visitors to the various sections
- The average time of users on a page in each one of them, while being in each one of the two states mentioned above
- Percentages of exit (%Exit) from a section
- Total hours in a section.

In addition, the same criteria can be used by country. Taking into consideration all these elements, the study arrived at a formula that could be used to define appraisal metrics.

According to the results of the tests mentioned above, it is possible to check and reach conclusions related to the level of interest users have in each one of the sections that were studied. The level of interest itself may serve as a parameter for appraisal when the main objective of a website is the distribution of information and public relations. That is why the returning visits of the users and their time in specific sections were considered significant. Small number of entries and longer time periods on pages were taken as signs of interest in a particular section.

The results of the analysis should be taken into account in appraising each section separately, and no overall appraisal of the site should be made. For, as has been proven above, each section has a different nature in terms of content, goals, method of presenting the materials and periods of change.

In order to try to identify some additional appraisal criteria, the researchers examined the following parameters: Page, Unique Page Views, Average Time on Page, Views, Total Hours in Section and %Exit during the period 1 September 2015 to 29 April 2016. The parameters were examined at the section level and at that level new visitors were differentiated from returning visitors. Those data were also examined according to the countries from which the users entered the site.

They found that most of the new visitors entering the site exited it immediately after their entry. The number of returning visitors was low compared to the total number of users of the site. Most of the sections on the site are of a public relations nature. On such informative sections, the average time on a page is not high. In contrast, for the sections with a more administrative nature, there are fewer entries but the average time on page rises. A clear example of that is the MASHAV section, which has few entries the first time and even fewer repeat users, but the time on the pages is high.

More research is needed to arrive at an appraisal of the behaviour of users on the site by country and section. Google Analytics does not provide all the information required to do so. An in-depth study should be made of the ratio of the number of returning users on the site from a specific country and the time they spend on a specific section. This data may give us an indication of the preferences of users from various regions. Also, the mathematical formula created by this study should be tested. This empirical test will enable the researchers to define the significance of the suggested metric as a criterion for appraisal (Schenkolewski-Kroll and Tractinsky, 2017).

Conclusion

A common theme that emerges from all the ITrust studies included in this chapter is that an engaged, global citizenry requires active, co-ordinated efforts from governments in different jurisdictions, so that citizens are put in a position to participate meaningfully in public affairs. Technology itself, even when designed to promote openness and participation (see e-petitions and other civic technologies), is not enough to make the government more open and inclusive or the citizens more aware and effective. As a prerequisite for engagement, trust needs to be part of the equation. Government officials, technology developers and us, the citizens, are all called upon to reflect on what trust means to each of us and what makes each of us trustworthy. This chapter offers a few starting points for this discussion.

References

Baker, B. K. (1999) Traditional Issues of Professional Responsibility and a Transformative Ethic of Client Empowerment for Legal Discourse, *New England Law Review*, **34** (4), 809–906.

Barrault-Méthy, A. M. (2015) Obscurity in the Micropolitics of English for Legal Purposes: towards an anthropological framework, *Sustainable Multilingualism*, 6, 60–88.

Bazerman, C. (1994) Systems of Genres and the Enactment of Social Intentions. In Freedman, A. and Medway, P. (eds), *Genre and the New Rhetoric*, 79–101. Taylor & Francis.

Booms, H. (1987) Society and the Formation of Documentary Heritage: issues in the appraisal of archival sources, *Archivaria*, **24** (Summer 1987), 69–107.

Boulianne, S. (2015) Social Media Use and Participation: a meta-analysis of current research, *Information, Communication and Society*, **18** (5), 524–38.

Bunn, J., Brimble, S., Obelensky, S. and Wood, N. (2016) *Perceptions of Born Digital Authenticity*, EU28, Final Report, InterPARES Trust, https://interparestrust.org/assets/public/dissemination/EU28_20160718_ UserPerceptionsOfAuthenticity_FinalReport.pdf

Burkert, S. (1999) Trust and Information, *Hume Papers on Public Policy*, **7** (3), 26–32.

Canada, Province of British Columbia (2010) Citizens @ the Centre: B.C. Government 2.0. Victoria, BC, Province of British Columbia, www.gov.bc.ca/citz/citizens_engagement/gov20.pdf

Chen, M., Franks, P. and Evans, L. (2016) Exploring Government Uses of Social Media through Twitter Sentiment Analysis, *Journal of Digital Information Management*, **14** (5), 290–301.

Denhardt, R. B. and Denhardt, J. V. (2000) The New Public Service: serving rather than steering, *Public Administration Review*, **60** (6), 549–59, https://doi.org/10.1111/0033-3352.00117

Dodd, G. (2007) *Justice and Grace: private petitioning and the English Parliament in the late Middle Ages*. Oxford University Press.

Duy, V. (2001) *A Brief History of the Canadian Patent System: executive summary*. CBAC.

Edelman, R. (2014) *Edelman Trust Barometer 2014: annual global study*, New York,

Endelman Intelligence. https://www.edelman.com/2014-edelman-trust-barometer/

Evans, L., Franks, P. and Chen, H. M. (2018) Voices in the cloud: social media and trust in Canadian and US local governments, *Records Management Journal*, **28** (1), 18–46. https://doi.org/10.1108/RMJ-11-2016-0041

Foscarini, F. (2012) Diplomatics and Genre Theory as Complementary Approaches. *Archival Science*, **12** (4). 389–409. https://doi.org/10.1007/s10502-012-9173-6

Foscarini, F. (2019) The Patent Genre: between stability and change, *Archivaria* **87** (Spring 2019).

Franks, P. (2016) *Social Media and Trust in Government.* NA05, Final Report, InterPARES Trust, https://interparestrust.org/assets/public/dissemination/ NA05_20161209_SocialMediaTrust_Phase1_FinalReport.pdf

Franks, P. and Evans, L. (2015) Social Media and Trust in North American Local Government Law Enforcement. In Sarmento, A. and Peres, P. (eds), *Proceedings of the 2nd European Conference on Social Media*. England: ACPIL.

Franks, P. and Weck, A. (2015) *Social Media and Trust in Government Literature Review.* NA05. InterPARES Trust. https://interparestrust.org/assets/public/ dissemination/NA05_20151013_SocialMediaResearch_LiteratureReview_v2.pdf

Graham, M. (2014) Government Communication in the Digital Age: social media's effect on local government public relations, *Public Relations Inquiry*, **3** (3), 361–76.

Gurstein, M. (2012) Two Worlds of Open Government Data: getting the lowdown on public toilets in Chennai and other matters, *The Journal of Community Informatics*, **8** (2). http://ci-journal.net/index.php/ciej/article/view/927

Hansard Society (2012) What Next for E-Petitions?, Hansard Society, https://www.hansardsociety.org.uk/publications/briefings/ what-next-for-e-petitions

Hayakawa, T., Imi, Y. and Ito, T. (2014) Towards a Sustainable Volunteered Community: an analysis of the OpenStreetMap community in Japan and its activity after the 2011 Tohoku earthquake. In Kocaoglu, D. F. (ed.), *2014 Portland International Conference on Management of Engineering and Technology (PICMET 2014)*, Portland International Center for Management of Engineering and Technology, and Portland State University. Piscataway, NJ: IEEE.

Held, G. (2010) 'Supplica La Mia Parvidade…' – Petitions in Medieval Society – A Matter of Ritualised or First Reflexive Politeness?, *Journal of Historical Pragmatics*, **11**, 194–218.

Hersh, E. D. and Schaffner, B. F. (2017) Post-Materialist Particularism: what petitions can tell us about biases in the policy agenda, *American Politics Research*, **46** (3), 434–64.

Hoad, T. F. (1996) Petition. *The Concise Oxford Dictionary of English Etymology*. Oxford University Press.

Hohmann, P. (2016) *Petitions, Rhetorical Genre, and Archival Diplomatics: A Literature Review*. InterPARES Trust.

https://interparestrust.org/assets/public/dissemination/NA13_20160229_
PatentsPetitionsTrust_LiteratureReview_Final.pdf

Hurley, G. (2017) Your Comments Here: contextualizing technologies, seeking records and supporting transparency for citizen engagement, *Tidsskriftet Arkiv*, **8** (1). https://doi.org/10.7577/ta.1956

Hurley, G., Léveillé, V. and McDonald, J. (2016) Managing Records of Citizen Engagement: a primer, NA08. InterPARES Trust. https://interparestrust.org/assets/public/dissemination/NA08_20161001_ManagingRecordsCitizenEngagement_Primer_Final.pdf

InterPARES Trust (2018) Terminology Database. https://interparestrust.org/terminology/term/reliability%20~paL~record~paR~

Knight Foundation (2015) Assessing Civic Tech: case studies and resources for tracking outcomes. https://knightfoundation.org/reports/assessing-civic-tech-case-studies-and-resources-tr

Latham, K. F. (2015) What Is 'the Real Thing' in the Museum? An Interpretative Phenomenological Study, *Museum Management and Curatorship*, **30** (1), 2–20.

Lindner, R. and Riehm, U. (2009) Electronic Petitions and Institutional Modernization. International Parliamentary E-Petition Systems in Comparative Perspective, *JeDEM-eJournal of eDemocracy and Open Government*, **1** (1).

Longe, V. U. (1985) Aspects of the Textual Features of Officialese: the register of public administration, *International Review of Applied Linguistics in Language Teaching*, **23** (4).

Mergel, I. (2013) A Framework for Interpreting Social Media Interactions in the Public Sector, *Government Information Quarterly*, **30** (4), 327–34.

Milić, P., Veljković, N. and Stoimenov, L. (2012) Framework for Open Data Mining in E-Government. In *Proceedings of the Fifth Balkan Conference in Informatics*, 255–58, ACM Press, https://doi.org/10.1145/2371316.2371369

Miller, C.R. (1984) Genre as Social Action, *Quarterly Journal of Speech*, **70** (2), 151–67.

Misuraca, G. and Viscusi, G. (2014) Is Open Data Enough?: e-governance challenges for open government, *International Journal of Electronic Government Research*, **10** (1), 18–34. https://doi.org/10.4018/ijegr.2014010102

Mossberger, K., Wu, Y. and Crawford, J. (2013) Connecting Citizens and Local Governments? Social Media and Interactivity in Major U.S. Cities, *Government Information Quarterly*, **30** (4), 351–8.

Nabatchi, T. (2012) An Introduction to Deliberative Civic Engagement. In Nabatchi, T., Gastil, J., Weiksner, G. M. and Leighninger, M. (eds) *Democracy in Motion: evaluating the practice and impact of deliberative civic engagement*, London, Oxford University Press.

Ngwenya, B., Lubbe, S. and Klopper, R. (2012) Institutionalisation, Framing, and Diffusion: the logic of openness in egovernment and implementation decisions – a lesson for developing countries. In Bwalya, K. J. and Zulu, S. F. C (eds),

Handbook of Research on E-Government in Emerging Economies: adoption, e-participation, and legal frameworks, IGI Global, https://doi.org/10.4018/978-1-4666-0324-0

Norris, D. and Reddick, C. G. (2013) Local E-Government in the United States: transformation or incremental change?, *Public Administration Review*, **73** (1), 165–75.

Pearce-Moses, R. (ed.) (2018) InterPARES Trust Terminology, InterPARES Trust, http://www.interparestrust.org/terminology/

Pengate, S. and Delen, D. (2014) Evaluating Emotions in Mobile Application Descriptions: sentiment analysis approach. In Twentieth Americas Conference on Information Systems, https://pdfs.semanticscholar.org/459d/ 0cfbd88bd6ce67272a3d6ee7f356275d540f.pdf

Rowley, J. (2006) An Analysis of the E-Service Literature: towards a research agenda, *Internet Research*, **16** (3), 339.

Sheedy, A., MacKinnon, M., Pitre, S. and Watling, J. (2008) *Handbook on Citizen Engagement: beyond consultation*, Ottawa, Canadian Policy Research Networks, www.cprn.org/documents/49583_EN.pdf

Schenkolewski-Kroll, S. and Tractinsky, A. (2015) *Research on Retention and Disposition Processes in an Internet Website of the Government of Israel: the Ministry of Foreign Affairs case study*, EU01, Final Report, InterPARES Trust, https://interparestrust.org/assets/public/dissemination/EU01_20150909_ RetentionDispositionProcessesIsraeliForeignAffairs_FinalReport_Final.pdf

Schenkolewski-Kroll, S. and Tractinsky, A. (2016) *Research on Users of the English Website of the Israel Ministry of Foreign Affairs as a Criterion for Appraising Records*, EU25, Final Report, InterPARES Trust, https://interparestrust.org/assets/public/dissemination/EU25_20161001_ WebAnalyticsAndAppraisalMinistryForeignAffairsIsrael_FinalReport_Final.pdf

Schenkolewski-Kroll, S. and Tractinsky, A. (2017) *Archival Appraisal, Retention Schedules and Metadata in Web Sites – the case study of the Ministry of Foreign Affairs, Israel*, EU36, Final Report, InterPARES Trust, https://interparestrust.org/assets/public/dissemination/EU036_20171120_ AppraisalWebsites_FinalReport.pdf

Skoric, M. M., Zhu, Q., Goh, D. and Pang, M. (2016) Social Media and Citizen Engagement: a meta-analytic review, *New Media and Society*, **18** (9), 1817–39.

Strahonja, V. (2018) Models for Monitoring and Auditing of Compliance in the Flow from Registration to Archive in E-Register, Croatia and Mid Sweden, InterPARES Trust, https://interparestrust.org/assets/public/dissemination/EU05IPTFinalReport.pdf

Suderman, J. and Timms, K. (2016) *The Implications of Open Government, Open Data, and Big Data on the Management of Digital Records in an Online Environment*, NA08, Final Report, InterPARES Trust, https://interparestrust.org/assets/public/ dissemination/IPTITRUST_NA08_FinalReport_1Oct2016_fordistribution_.pdf

TalkVancouver (2018) Chinatown Development Policies Review Talk Vancouver Survey, Summary of Feedback, https://vancouver.ca/files/cov/survey-results-summary-2018.pdf.

Treasury Board of Canada (2014) *Canada's Action Plan on Open Government 2014-16*, www.deslibris.ca/ID/244793

Uslaner, E. M. and Brown, M. (2005) Inequality, Trust, and Civic Engagement, *American Politics Research*, **33** (6), 868–94.

van Voss, L. H. (ed.) (2002) *Petitions in Social History*, Cambridge University Press.

Wuergler, A. (2002) Voices from Among the 'Silent Masses': humble petitions and social conflicts in early modern Central Europe. In van Voss, L. H. (ed.), *Petitions in Social History*. Cambridge University Press.

Yates, J. and Orlikowski, W. J. (1992) Genres of Organizational Communication: a structurational approach to studying communication and media, *The Academy of Management Review*, **17** (2), 299–326, https://doi.org/10.2307/258774

Zeithaml, V. A., Parasuraman, A. and Berry, L. L. (2009) *Delivering Quality Service: balancing customer perceptions and expectations*, New York, Free Press.

5

Strategies, methods and tools enabling records governance in a cloud environment

Editor: Basma Makhlouf Shabou
Contributors: Basma Makhlouf Shabou, Maria Guercio,
Shadrack Katuu, Elizabeth Lomas and Arina Grazhenskaya

Introduction

Cloud computing is currently at a very rapid stage of development. The option to outsource various aspects of informational processing is becoming standard for business and personal computing. This interest in existing cloud solutions is greater than some years ago, particularly in the context of public institutions. The diversity of services and offerings is fuelling this development, with options for cloud usage including hybrid and open source solutions. Recent studies show that cloud solutions may help institutions to optimise management of their informational resources and maximise efficiency (Makhlouf Shabou and Léveillé, 2014). McLeod and Gormly's (2017) InterPARES Trust (hereinafter ITrust) study concluded that few organizations can avoid working in the cloud.

The most appealing factor for consumers is the potential savings resulting from reduced data management and IT costs. Unlike an internal IT infrastructure, purchasing cloud options and services means that the cost of hardware and software – which would otherwise be managed by the user – is absorbed by the cloud provider; the user does not have to worry about managing infrastructure. In addition, the cloud provides economies by operating at a larger scale. This facility can also be seen as problematic as it gives an external entity/service the ability to control corporate data and records and their availability and security. However, proper records management and information governance can counterbalance this with a range of options in terms of how the institution maintains control of its data and records. It is important to recognise that key risks are not transferred from the records creator to the service provider; for example, data protection responsibilities in an EU context remain the responsibility of the creator. A

Service Level Agreement (SLA) should be tailored to consider the best conditions to favour appropriate corporate records governance that fits to business needs and priorities.

This chapter draws together key ITrust initiatives on strategies, methods and tools enabling records governance to be applied in a cloud environment. The first section presents the role and quality of recordkeeping policies in the context of the European Union, considering on the one hand recent legislative evolutions and, on the other, the cloud solutions. The second section presents the leveraging of enterprise architecture for efficient management of complex records corporate realities. The third section compares records governance and maturity assessment methods and tools and offers some practical answers.

Role and quality of policies for recordkeeping
Maria Guercio

The role and the quality of policies for recordkeeping systems are analysed here with reference to their increasing relevance in the current complex digital environment, characterised by the use of internet networking systems, including those implemented as cloud services. The analysis takes into account policies and practices mostly developed by the European Union, particularly in Italy and Spain, but it also considers the evolution of European Commission legislation and international standards (Allegrezza et al., 2016, 2018; Bushey et al., 2016).

Role and positive consequences of policies

Policies may be defined as formal statements of principles and strategic decisions aimed at pursuing long-term goals. In the archival field, they affect the planning and development of records and archives systems and their management, both organizational and technical. Records management policies are recognised as a crucial tool due to their ability to improve its practices, as well as the quality of electronic records management tools, including software procurement. This is especially evident in those countries where public agencies have a legal obligation to implement records man-agement systems, including the definition of their procedures. Also, the standardisation of documentation for records management and preservation processes (records management manual, preservation manual, submission reports, formal delegation of responsibilities) increases the professionalism of records and archives practitioners and promotes a better definition and distinction of responsibilities for each phase of the digital records' life cycle. In the case of long-term preservation of digital records, policies are key elements for mitigating risks of technological obsolescence and supporting digital heritage access and system interoperability in complex environments.

In the case of electronic recordkeeping and digital preservation systems implemented in the current environment of the internet and the cloud, the risks for the management of reliable digital resources are higher and more difficult to control than in an in-house environment. They relate to data and records accuracy, authenticity, security, availability, retrieval and use, confidentiality and privacy, storage and location, retention and disposition and long-term preservation. Most of these risks derive from the lack of control over data and records entrusted to third parties. In addition, the creators are not aware that ensuring authenticity, for example, cannot be delegated only to technological solutions, such as digital signatures and seals. This implies a lack of adequate investment in organizational infrastructure. These challenges should be addressed through:

- A co-ordinated set of instructions and rules designed through co-operation among working groups of experts, institutions and technology suppliers
- The definition of flexible tools for interoperability in the exchange of digital information among different recordkeeping and preservation systems
- An accreditation process and a certification service for both the suppliers of private services and the public institutions which intend to be trusted third parties for long-term digital preservation (including preservation implemented as cloud services), to ensure and verify the quality of related processes (according to the guidelines for auditing digital repositories identified by ISO 16363) (International Organization for Standardization (ISO), 2012b).

In the specific case of cloud services, guidelines addressing relevant records and archives issues are required to assist legal departments of organizations in the drafting of contracts with cloud providers. Usually, the commercial interest of the service provider prevails in standard non-negotiated contracts and aspects that may have repercussions in recordkeeping practices, such as metadata, data storage and preservation, are undefined.

Role of policies and risks of fragmentation in national legislations

In many laws and recommendations for the preservation of digital resources (not only records but also data and documents), policies are not explicitly recognised for their relevance and effectiveness, even if national legal frameworks have developed where policies play a crucial role in balancing rigid technological requirements and flexible solutions for supporting and documenting institutional and individual responsibilities.

With reference to digital records creation, transmission and maintenance, legal requirements have implied more consistency and detailed specifications in terms of action plans and definition of responsibilities and controls, due to the need to ensure the juridical function of records persistency. Therefore, the recordkeeping domain has developed, more than other sectors, robust principles and comprehensive frameworks for the creation, management and preservation of digital records. Usually, these policies are recognised in the national legislation and in international standards and could provide meaningful examples for other domains (such as digital libraries). However, they still present ambiguities and inconsistencies (also at the terminological level) that prove the need for further efforts in the definition of tools able to guide and normalise recordkeeping and digital preservation, especially in a networked environment. There is a delay in recognising the main risks posed by the new environment for digital records, with specific reference to the complex dimension and the challenges involved in cloud computing.

In Europe, despite efforts to enhance co-operation and co-ordination on records and archives policies and practices among the member countries of the European Union, the existing regulations are insufficient and fragmented. Records management and digital preservation have not been prioritised by the European Union. In fact, developments in this sector have responded to initiatives or strategies that deal indirectly with records-related issues, such as the release of directives on e-government aimed at improving the relationship between public administration and citizens and to contribute to democracy; or directives on information and communications technology (ICT) to ensure free movement of information society services among member states, including cloud computing strategies to encourage productivity.

The alignment with these European directives, especially e-government, has meant that the European Union countries have incorporated digital records management and preservation policies in their legislation. This is important because member states have autonomy to define their strategies, procedures and systems according to their specific traditions and practices. Furthermore, the development of regulations at national levels may not have been the result of co-operative work, mostly in those countries in which competencies for records and archives management are decentralised and assumed by autonomous regions (such as Spain). These factors have led in the past to duplication and lack of consistency, even in Italy, which has one of the most comprehensive legal frameworks for records management and digital preservation.

In the specific case of Italy – similarly to other European examples – an updated set of directives and detailed rules is currently in place for the public administrations with the aim of enabling the implementation of integrated digital records management and record-keeping systems. However, some contradictions have characterised these regulations, specifically with respect to legislation for the digitisation and preservation processes. The main reason for the delay in defining a satisfactory solution concerns the fact that efforts for approving these regulations are not part of a common interdisciplinary work but are fragmentary and not co-ordinated over time. The most relevant consequence is a lack of convergence and consistency for entire legislative frameworks.

Records management has been incorporated in the legislation of Spain in the last 10–15 years. This presence and recognition goes hand in hand with the introduction of ICTs in the public administration. In general, Spanish legislation on records management and digital preservation provides generic provisions and even if legislation is in the process of further development, the implementation of electronic records management at the public administration level is delayed due to organizational and technical issues, such as the lack of co-ordination and co-operation at all levels to adopt shared services and infrastructures that improve rationalisation and efficiency; the lack of technical instructions to implement policies; the selection of adequate management tools and their integration with existing ones; and the need for investment and personnel training.

Conclusions

Even if not completely current with respect to the integration of cloud services and recordkeeping systems and in spite of the still open challenges in records management implementation and digital preservation, national policies offer a good and practical basis to support reliable digital records management systems, as well as provide preservation models based on international standards and flexible and sustainable principles. Legislation for governance of cloud systems is not yet in place in Europe, but in jurisdictions such as Italy, in which the general framework for digital record-keeping systems and digital preservation systems is consistent, the risks posed by the cloud environment are better supported.

ITrust research findings show from many points of view the need for a more precise and detailed analysis aimed at reinforcing the role and quality of policies when cloud services are in place. They also confirm the importance of shared checklists, such as the checklist for evaluating cloud service contracts developed by ITrust (Bushey et al., 2016) to analyse how complex functions would be carried out by a third party. The international nature of the checklist allows for it to be easily applied to national environments and supports the consistency and completeness of controls to be implemented by digital records creators or preservers.

Leveraging enterprise architecture in the management of records in complex environments
Shadrack Katuu

Modern institutions invest significant resources to build technology platforms and business applications that will support organizational activities in fulfilling their institutional mandate (Riempp and Gieffers-Ankel, 2007, 359). Over time, institutions build complex technology ecosystems that are difficult even for ICT professionals to manage. For many such institutions, creating an inventory of systems or applications is just the beginning of the process of managing them.

Effective management has necessitated the development of portfolio management techniques and models that can be used to map out the complete ICT ecosystem within institutions. For the most part, these efforts have been inward looking, serving the ICT professionals and not necessarily reflecting the wider governance and operational objectives of the institution. Therefore, for records professionals in an institution with a complex technological environment, the challenge is how to best understand the complexity so that their professional mandate, the identification, capture and management of records for as long as they are required can be fulfilled.

Records professionals need to make sense of a vast array of business applications as well as technological infrastructure and understand how they are connected in supporting the institution's functions and activities. This is necessary in order to establish a lifecycle management for records generated by these business applications. For this reason, a study titled 'Template of Analysis (TOA)' was conceived in 2015 under the auspices of the ITrust Project (Katuu, 2018). The TOA study has identified Enterprise Architecture (EA) within the IT field as a discipline that could provide models to assist records professionals in better understanding technological complexity within modern institutions.

Enterprise Architecture
Enterprise Architecture (EA) emerged in the 1980s as a way to deal with institutional complexity in an increasingly sophisticated organizational environment (Ahlemann et al., 2012, 3). Over time, EA emerged as an approach to improve:

... the alignment between the organization's business and their information technologies. It attempts to capture the status of the organization's business architecture, information resources, information systems, and technologies so that the gaps and weaknesses in their processes and infrastructures can be identified, and development directions planned.

(Dang and Pekkola, 2017, 130)

According to Iyamu and Mphahlele (2014, 2), one of the premises of EA deployment is to address institution-wide integration through coherent principles, methods and models. EA deployment provides holistic views, which are sometimes used to address the organizational structure, business processes, information flow, information systems and infrastructure (Iyamu and Mphahlele 2014, 2). EA models differ from pure business process models as they holistically describe related enterprise capabilities and different layers' assets, as illustrated in Figure 5.1.

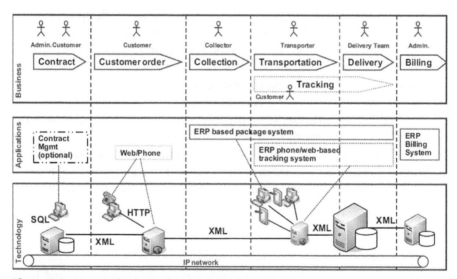

Figure 5.1 *An example of a simple Enterprise Architecture* (Basten and Brons, 2012, 216)

Since the mid-1980s, EA practitioners have developed more than two dozen frameworks, the most commonly used of which are the Zachman Framework, the Open Group Architectural Framework (TOGAF) and the Federal Enterprise Architecture (FEA) framework. These frameworks are popular because of their maturity, with Zachman being the oldest and TOGAF and FEA allowing free access to resources and information (Basten and Brons, 2012, 209). The TOA study chose to use TOGAF as the basis for developing a model that would assist records professionals in assessing business applications and technology platforms.

The Open Group Architectural Framework (TOGAF)

TOGAF is a prominent framework in the EA domain that has a well-defined method for designing an information system in terms of a set of building blocks and for showing how the building blocks fit together and interact (Raj and Periasamy, 2011, 72). TOGAF has three main pillars: Enterprise Architecture Domains (EAD), Architecture Development Method (ADM) and Enterprise Continuum (EC). Within EAD are four interrelated areas of specialisation called architecture domains:

- Business architecture: the processes that the business uses to meet its goals, including the business strategy, governance, organization and key business processes of the organization.
- Applications architecture: how specific applications are designed and how they interact with each other. This provides a blueprint for the individual systems to be developed, showing their relationships to the core business processes of the organization with the frameworks for services to be exposed as business functions for integration.
- Data architecture: how the enterprise data stores are organized and accessed, i.e. the structure of an organization's logical and physical data assets and the associated data management resources.
- Technical architecture or technology architecture: the hardware, software and network infrastructure needed to support the deployment of core, mission-critical applications and their interactions (Raj and Periasamy, 2011, 72).

The records profession contributing to TOGAF architecture domains

TOGAF has been described as a flexible toolkit that can be tailored to fit numerous situations and organizations (Kotusev, 2016). The TOA study adopted the TOGAF architecture domains by abstracting how capabilities, applications and technologies could be mapped out in an institution. It mapped out business and technology components related to the management of enterprise content within a typical large institution using an information management lifecycle model (Maldony and Katuu, 2016). The resultant architecture, with anonymised names for applications and technologies, addressed the business, architecture and technology layers. However, the data layer did not have any content in the institutional abstraction. Therefore, the study reached out to a previous phase of the InterPARES Project that had developed a framework for identifying authenticity metadata that could be adapted for the data layer of the EA model (Rogers and Tennis, 2016).

Once the data layer adaptations were incorporated into the larger model, it offered a number of benefits. For institutional stakeholders, the data layer provides an objective and consistent method for assessing metadata requirements implemented in the business applications and technology platforms in the other layers of the framework (Katuu, 2018). Overall, the EA model provides an overview of how individual layers, as well as individual business capabilities, applications, technology platforms and data aspects, are connected to each other.

The use of TOGAF greatly enhances records professionals' understanding of the complex technology ecosystem leveraging the benefits brought about by EA. This provides the opportunity to create synergies and ensure that knowledge of lifecycle management of records over time supports institutional functions and activities.

Information and records governance and maturity assessment methods and tools: some practical answers

Basma Makhlouf Shabou, Elizabeth Lomas and Arina Grazhenskaya

This section gives an overview of two studies on information governance EU29 and EU30 (Makhlouf Shabou, Grazhenskaya and Lomas, 2017), a Master thesis of Grazhenskaya (2017) and the Master research performed by Anderfuhren and Romagnoli (2018) under the direction of Makhlouf Shabou at the Information Sciences Department of HEG/HESSO in Geneva, Switzerland.

Holistic approaches to records management are required in the context of the cloud. Information governance (IG) is broader than records management (RM), which is primarily responsible for the management of records during the active and semi-active phase of their lifecycle, with focus on their evidentiary function (International Organization for Standardization (ISO), 2016) and adopts a wider global vision. It provides a general framework that favours the optimisation of all information resources, including organizational knowledge (GlassIG, 2016; Perrein, 2012), and their use to adequately meet the organization's strategic and functional objectives (ARMA International, 2016). It is also based on a multidimensional approach (archival, legal, technical, technological, economic, etc.) to managing information resources. Several authors have highlighted this integrated and encompassing strategic aspect of IG (Corbier, 2017, 2018; Garde, 2014; Iron Mountain, 2014; Surrey Health Borough Council, 2015; Wildhaber et al., 2015). Saffady (2015) explained that RM focuses primarily on the operational aspect of records management, while IG focuses on the strategic level of information management.

In order to effectively assume this strategic role, IG needs a number of processes and tools including policies and guidelines (Garde, 2014; Larrivee, n.d.; Pearce-Moses, 2018). While the need for establishing an IG approach when cloud solutions are deployed may be readily accepted, the reality of delivering this into practice is challenging. What to maintain, improve upon and invest in needs to be carefully defined. At the heart of the IG process are ethical considerations that inform risk management. These concerns suggest that an IG maturity model would help in developing IG frameworks. The ITrust IG studies developed the main dimensions, methods and tool for assessment of information and records governance in the context of cloud practices.

IG perception

Governance is defined as the process of co-ordinating and organizing power at the head of an organization through arrangements and rules for the conduct and control of business (Iron Mountain, 2014; Wildhaber et al., 2015) in accordance with the organization's objectives and interests (Canadian Institute of Chartered Accountants, 2006; Quebec, 2015). IG is a multidisciplinary approach to managing information which draws together information and records management, compliance, information security, ICT and ethics. IG grew out of the rising emphasis on corporate governance in the latter half of the twentieth century, which in part relied on information to deliver key corporate governance goals, including transparency and accountability (Willis, 2005). As an appreciation of the value of information as an asset has grown, with new technologies giving rise to new opportunities, dangers, laws and the regulations, the need to more actively manage information has shaped the information governance agenda (Lomas, 2010).

Why do we need an IG maturity assessment in cloud solutions practices and choices?

> A maturity model consists of a sequence of maturity levels for a class of objects.
> It represents an anticipated, desired, or typical evolution path of these objects
> shaped as discrete stages. Typically, these objects are organizations or processes.
> (Becker, Knackstedt and Pöppelbuß, 2009)

Applying maturity models supports institutions and public-sector organizations to optimise their efficiency and development. Undertaking such an assessment provides a clear overview of the corporate information landscape and an accurate characterisation of the weaknesses and main gaps to be addressed when considering adopting cloud services.

Synthesis of existing IG maturity models

Proença et al. (2017) have compared maturity models based on attributes and maturity levels (Table 5.1).

Table 5.1 *An overview of existing maturity models* (adapted from Proença et al., 2017)

Maturity Model	Attributes		Maturity levels	
	Name	Number	Name	Number
Asset Management Maturity Model (Lei, Ligtvoet, Volker, Herder, 2011)	Dimensions/ Category	4	Initial; Repeatable; Defined; Managed; Optimising	5
Digital Asset Management (DAM) Maturity Model (Real Story Group, DAM Foundation, 2017)	Categories/ Dimensions	4/15	Ad Hoc; Incipient; Formative; Operational; Optimal	5
Information Governance Maturity Model (ARMA International, 2017)	Principles	8	Sub-standard; In Development; Essential; Proactive; Transformational	5
Digital Preservation Capability Maturity Model (DPCMM) (Dollar, Ashley, 2014)	Domains/ Components	3/15	Nominal; Minimal; Intermediate; Advanced; Optimal	5
Brown Digital Preservation Maturity Model (Brown, 2013)	Process Perspective	10	No Awareness; Awareness; Roadmap; Basic Process; Managed Process; Optimised Process	6
Preservica Digital Preservation Maturity Model (Preservica, 2014)	-	-	Safe Storage; Storage Management; Storage Validation; Inform-ation Organization; Information Processes; Inform-ation Preservation	6
ECM Maturity Model (Pelz et al., 2010)	Categories/ Dimensions	3/13	Unmanaged; Incipient; Formative; Operational; Pro-Active	5
Gartner Enterprise Information Management Maturity Model (Newman, Logan, 2008)	-	-	Unaware; Aware; Reactive; Proactive; Managed; Effective	6

(Continued)

Table 5.1 *Continued*

Maturity Model	Attributes		Maturity Levels	
	Name	Number	Name	Number
Capability Maturity Model for Research Data Management (CMM for RDM) (Croston, Qin, 2010)	Key Process Areas	5	Initial; Managed; Defined; Quantitatively Managed; Optimising	5
Stanford Data Governance Maturity Model (Stanford University, 2011)	Dimensions/ components	3/6	5 criteria unnamed	5
Data Management Maturity (DMM) Model (CMMI Institute, 2018)	Categories / Process Areas	6/25	Performed; Managed; Defined; Measured; Optimised	5
JISC Records Management Maturity Model (JISC InfoNet, 2013)	Sections	9	Absent; Aware; Defined; Embedded	4

Based on the analysis in Table 5.1, some trends are identified:

- Existing models propose to cross diverse axes (area/domains dimensions) through different levels that indicate their development and their progression towards reaching the optimised level
- Dimensions and sub-dimensions are used to target progressively different aspects to assess in informational practices
- Most studied maturity models use 5 levels of development
- To enable the use and the assessment of a given corporate information practice a qualitative data collection is applied (interviews, observation, etc.).

ITrust IG maturity models

This work provides an IG maturity model mainly for a public-sector context. However, it could be adapted to the context of other sectors.

Main IG dimensions

Based on the literature reviewed, two dimensions can be identified: those related to corporate business and those related to corporate IT (Wildhaber et al., 2015). However, this distinction is difficult to apply, particularly when an element could be considered as belonging to each dimension, such as rights management. Ten dimensions are proposed (Grazhenskaya, 2017; Makhlouf Shabou, Grazhenskaya and Lomas, 2017; Wildhaber et al., 2015):

- **Responsibilities and roles**: explicit definition of the roles and rules governing information users, producers and managers' practices (Mêgnigbêto, 2010; Scott, 2013)
- **Stakeholder engagement**: explicit connection to all those with a vested interest in the information in order to deliver social justice agendas
- **Framework and policy, including risk management**: strategic documents that define the information resources and their specific context, embedding risk management frameworks to navigate uncertainty to seize opportunities and mitigate threats/vulnerabilities (Desroches, 2015; International Organization for Standardization (ISO), 2018, n.d.; Léger, 2015a, 2015b; Lemieux, 2004; Lemieux and Krumwied, 2011; Smallwood, 2014)
- **Information asset identification, creation and ownership**: consideration of the creation, co-creation and citizen ownership of information (Adesemowo, Von Solms and Botha, 2016)
- **Information value, quality and delivery**: tools, standards and rules to provide reliable data, efficiency, transparency, audit, sharing, use (including proper understanding and digital literacy) and reuse through time (International Organization for Standardization (ISO), 2016; Makhlouf Shabou, 2011, 2014, 2015)
- **Rights management**: to ensure the protection of privacy, confidentiality, individual and societal rights (Confédération Suisse, 2014; Information & Privacy Commissioner of Ontario, 2013; Shepherd and Yeo, 2003)
- **Records management**: tools, standards and rules for data and records retention and disposition schedules and processes and classification plan. It includes the quality of data and records (International Organization for Standardization (ISO), 2011; International Organization for Standardization (ISO), 2016)
- **Information security and resilience**: to provide information availability and protections to ensure the maintenance of information for operational and compliance delivery, vital records management and business continuity (Agence Nationale de la Sécurité des Systèmes d'Information (ANSSI), 2004; eCH Cloud Computing Group, 2012)
- **Long-term preservation**: infrastructures, tools, standards and directives guaranteeing the durable access to organisational records and archives where they are deemed to have enduring value (International Organization for Standardization (ISO), 2012a)
- **Monitoring and change**: activities and actions supporting changes and developments to ensure the system remains up-to-date and relevant, responding to new challenges and opportunities.

IG delivery levels

The assessment involves in general the identification of criteria clearly defined and objectively applied with defensible choices and reproducible methods. The maturity levels indicate the organizational level against the criteria as: (L1) Not existent; (L2) Developing; (L3) Minimum standards; (L4) Aspirational standards; and (L5) Transformational. To reach the highest transformational standards it is key to ensure that ethical considerations underpin all aspects of the model.

Criteria for IG dimension assessment

Maturity levels are measured against dimensions and additional criteria related to:

- People (P) – Criteria including leadership, professional expertise, citizen inclusion, etc.
- System (S) – Criteria including framework design, process development, software and tools, buildings and infrastructures, training, etc.
- Ethics (E) – Criteria including different compliance such as laws, regulations, directives and standards, and includes specific (related to domain/sector) and general structures.

Individual stakeholder and participant needs span this delivery but must be balanced and determined in terms of ethical considerations, such as environmental and wider societal needs. The systems in place leverage the success of the delivery.

Grid as a tool

The ITrust IG maturity model incorporates the dimensions, levels and criteria presented in Table 5.2 opposite. It can be used to assess general IG maturity or evaluate readiness for cloud adoption.

Delivering across all the dimensions in a balanced and proportionate way in line with resource requirements is a complex process. The grid enables a general visualisation for consideration. As shown in Table 5.2, the assessment should be carried out by addressing the maturity of all ten dimensions evaluated with respect to the three criteria (people, systems, ethics). This method may be applied partially to target some dimensions if needed. For each dimension, specific objectives and accurate recommendations may be defined to target what should be performed to reach more efficiency.

Table 5.2 *IG maturity model: assessment grid*

Dimension	Criteria	Maturity Levels					General/Cloud practices and choices
		1	2	3	4	5	Objectives, recommendations and deadlines
Responsibilities and roles	P S E						
Stakeholder engagement	P S E						
Framework and policy, including risk management	P S E						
Information assets identification, creation and ownership	P S E						
Information value and delivery	P S E						
Rights management	P S E						
Information security	P S E						
Records management	P S E						
Long-term preservation	P S E						
Monitoring and change	P S E						

Conclusion

Each section of this chapter has demonstrated different aspects of records management and information governance with respect to cloud service delivery. There is no one way to choose proper cloud solutions and good practices for records governance.

In the first section an illustrative example from the European context highlighted the importance of tailoring recordkeeping policies, taking into account the particular juridical context. These policies should support high quality and rigorous records processing over the entire lifecycle to preserve information assets and mitigate associated risks.

The second section proposed a relevant framework to support good records management in a complex and modern environment.

The third section focused on information and records governance and proposed an information maturity assessment model to control corporate information and records. Based on a simple and practical method and grid, records may be well managed to support quality, security and relevance, particularly when cloud solutions are used.

References

Adesemowo, A. K., Von Solms, R. and Botha, R. A. (2016) Safeguarding Information as an Asset: Do We Need a Redefinition in the Knowledge Economy and Beyond?, *South African Journal of Information Management*, **18** (1). https://doi.org/10.4102/sajim.v18i1.706

Agence Nationale de la Sécurité des Systèmes d'Information (ANSSI) (2004) PSSI – Guide d'Élaboration de Politiques de Sécurité des Systèmes d'Information. https://www.ssi.gouv.fr/guide/pssi-guide-delaboration-de-politiques-de-securite-des-systemes-dinformation/ [accessed 12 July 2018].

Ahlemann, F., Stettiner, E., Messerschmidt, M. and Legner, C. (eds) (2012) *Strategic Enterprise Architecture Management: challenges, best practices, and future developments*, Berlin Heidelberg, Springer-Verlag.

Allegrezza, S., Bezzi, G., Caravaca, M., Guercio, M., Leo, L., Monte, M., Pescini, I., Tommasi, B. (2016) *Policies for recordkeeping and digital preservation: Recommendations for analysis and assessment services*, EU04, InterPARES Trust, https://interparestrust.org/assets/public/dissemination/EU04_20170330_PoliciesRecordkeepingDigitalPreservation_FinalReport.pdf.

Allegrezza, S., Bezzi, G., Caravaca, M., Guercio, M., Pescini, I., Tommasi, B. (2018) *The impact of the Italian legal framework for cloud computing on electronic recordkeeping and digital preservation system*, EU35, InterPARES Trust, https://interparestrust.org/assets/public/dissemination/EU04_20170330_PoliciesRecordkeepingDigitalPreservation_FinalReport.pdf.

Anderfuhren, S. and Romagnoli, P. (2018) *La Maturité de la Gouvernance de l'Information dans les Administrations Publiques Européennes: la perception de la gouvernance de l'information dans l'administration publique genevoise*, Geneva, Haute école de gestion.

ARMA International (2016) *Glossary of Records Management and Information Governance Terms*, 5th edn, Overland Park, KS, ARMA International.

Basten, D. and Brons, D. (2012) EA Frameworks, Modelling and Tools. In Ahlemann, F., Stettiner, E., Messerschmidt, M. and Legner, C. (eds), *Strategic Enterprise Architecture Management: challenges, best practices, and future developments*, 201–27, Berlin Heidelberg, Springer-Verlag.

Becker, J., Knackstedt, R. and Pöppelbuß, J. (2009) Developing Maturity Models for IT Management: a procedure model and its application, *Business & Information Systems Engineering*, **1** (3), 213–22, https://doi.org/10.1007/s12599-009-0044-5

Bushey, J., Demoulin, M., How, E. and McLelland, R. (2016) *Checklist for Cloud Service Contracts*, NA14, InterPARES Trust, https://interparestrust.org/assets/public/dissemination/NA14_20160226_CloudServiceProviderContracts_Checklist_Final.pdf

Canadian Institute of Chartered Accountants (2006) Governance. Retrieved from http://gdt.oqlf.gouv.qc.ca/ficheOqlf.aspx?Id_Fiche=501580

Confédération suisse (2014) Loi fédérale sur la protection des données (LPD) du 19 juin 1992 (État le 1er janvier 2014). Retrieved from https://www.admin.ch/opc/fr/classified-compilation/19920153/index.html

Corbier, A. (2017) Rapport Annuel Gouvernance 2017 – Partie 3 [Text], www.serda.com/content/rapport-annuel-gouvernance-2017-partie-3 [accessed 12 July 2018].

Corbier, A. (2018). Rapport Annuel Gouvernance 2018 – Partie 1 [Text], www.serda.com/content/rapport-annuel-gouvernance-2018-partie-1 [accessed 12 July 2018].

Dang, D. D. and Pekkola, S. (2017) Review on Enterprise Architecture in the Public Sector, *Electronic Journal of E-Government*, **15** (2), 57–154.

Desroches, C. (2015) *La gestion des risques informationnels dans l'entreprise privée: perspective des gestionnaires de la sécurité*. École de criminologie de l'université de Montréal, https://papyrus.bib.umontreal.ca/xmlui/handle/1866/11469

eCH Cloud Computing Group (2012) Swiss Strategy on Cloud Computing – www.egovernment.ch, https://www.egovernment.ch/en/umsetzung/e-government-schweiz-2008-2015/cloud-computing-schweiz/ [accessed 12 July 2018].

Garde, J. (2014) Information Governance with MoReq. In *Proceedings of the DLM Forum—7th Triennial Conference* (99), Lisbon, Portugal, National Library of Portugal.

GlassIG (2016) The Rise and Rise of Information Governance, http://web.archive.org/web/20170406205938/ [accessed 12 July 2018], http://glassig.com/2016/02/24/rise-rise-information-governance/

Grazhenskaya, A. (2017) *Information Governance: nature and implementation from the European public administrations' perspective*, Haute école de gestion, Geneva, http://doc.rero.ch/record/306588?ln=en

Information and Privacy Commissioner of Ontario (2013) *Privacy by Design*. Toronto: Information & Privacy Commissioner of Ontario, https://www.ipc.on.ca/wp-content/uploads/2013/09/pbd-primer.pdf

International Organization for Standardization (ISO) (2011) *ISO 30300:2011 – Information and Documentation — Management Systems for Records — Fundamentals and Vocabulary*, https://www.iso.org/standard/53732.html [accessed 12 July 2018].

International Organization for Standardization (ISO) (2012a) *ISO 14721:2012 – Space Data and Information Transfer Systems – Open Archival Information System (OAIS) Reference Model*, https://www.iso.org/standard/57284.html [accessed 8 July 2018].

International Organization for Standardization (ISO) (2012b) *ISO 16363:2012 – Space Data and Information Transfer Systems — Audit and Certification of Trustworthy Digital Repositories*, https://www.iso.org/standard/56510.html [accessed 8 July 2018].

International Organization for Standardization (ISO) (2016) *ISO 15489-1 Information and Documentation – Records Management, Part 1 Concepts and Principles*. Geneva: ISO. Retrieved from https://www.iso.org/standard/62542.html.

International Organization for Standardization (ISO) (2018) *ISO 31000:2018 – Risk Management*, https://www.iso.org/iso-31000-risk-management.html [accessed 12 July 2018].

International Organization for Standardization (ISO) (n.d.) *ISO/TR 18128:2014 – Information and Documentation — Risk Assessment for Records Processes and Systems*, https://www.iso.org/standard/61521.html [accessed 12 July 2018].

Iron Mountain (2014) *A Practical Guide To Information Governance*, www.ironmountain.com/resources/whitepapers/a/a-practical-guide-to-information-governance

Iyamu, T. and Mphahlele, L. (2014) The Impact of Organisational Structure on Enterprise Architecture Deployment, *Journal of Systems and Information Technology*, **16** (1), 2–19, https://doi.org/10.1108/JSIT-04-2013-0010

Katuu, S. (2018) *Assessing Information Systems: a template for analysis*, TR04, Final Report, InterPARES Trust, https://interparestrust.org/assets/public/dissemination/TR04FinalReportJuly2018.pdf

Kotusev, S. (2016) The Critical Scrutiny of TOGAF [BCF: The Chartered Institute for IT], https://www.bcs.org/content/conWebDoc/55892 [accessed 12 July 2018].

Larrivee, B. (n.d.). Time for Organizations to Get Serious about Governance, *Credit Control*, **38** (1).

Léger, M.-A. (2015a) Pour une Définition du Risque Informationnel, www.leger.ca/2015/10/02/pour-une-definition-du-risque-informationnel/

Léger, M.-A. (2015b) Typologie des Risques Informationnels, www.leger.ca/2015/10/23/typologie-des-risques-informationnels/

Lemieux, V. (2004) Two Approaches to Managing Information Risks, *The Information Management Journal*, **38** (5), 56–62.

Lemieux, V. and Krumwied, E. (2011) Managing Records Risks in Global Financial Institutions. In Coleman, L., Lemieux, V., Stone, R. and Yeo, G. (eds), *Managing Records in Global Financial Markets: ensuring compliance and mitigating risk*, London: Facet Publishing, 91–105.

Lomas, E. (2010) Information Governance: Information Security and Access within a

UK Context, *Records Management Journal*, **20** (2), 182–98,
https://doi.org/10.1108/09565691011064322

Makhlouf Shabou, B. (2011) *Étude sur la définition et la mesure des qualités des archives définitives issues d'une évaluation* (Doctoral Dissertation). École de bibliothéconomie et des sciences de l'information, Montreal,
https://papyrus.bib.umontreal.ca/xmlui/handle/1866/4955

Makhlouf Shabou, B. (2014) Le Projet QADEPs: un outil au service de la pérennisation des archives publiques. In Hiraux, F. and Mirguet, F. (eds), *De la Préservation à la Conservation: stratégies pratiques d'archivage*, Louvain-la-Neuve, Academia l'Harmattan, 87–98.

Makhlouf Shabou, B. (2015) Digital Diplomatics and Measurement of Electronic Public Data Qualities: what lessons should be learned?, *Records Management Journal*, **25** (1), 56–77, https://doi.org/10.1108/RMJ-01-2015-0006

Makhlouf Shabou, B., Grazhenskaya, A. and Lomas, E. (2017) Information Governance in European Public Administrations. Presented at the ALA-ICA Annual Conference 2017 *Archives, Citizenship and Interculturalism*, Mexico City, www.alaarchivos.org/wp-content/uploads/2017/12/4.-Basma-Arina-Granzhenskaya.pdf

Makhlouf Shabou, B. and Léveillé, V. (2014) Records in the Cloud. Presented at the 43e Congrès de l'Association des Archivistes du Québec (AAQ), Montreal, http://arodes.hes-so.ch/record/586/files/Texte%20int%C3%A9gral.pdf

Maldony, M. and Katuu, S. (2016) Assessing Information Systems: a template for analysis (TR04). Presented at the Sixth Transnational Team Research Workshop, Vienna, Austria.

McLeod, J. and Gormly, B. (2017) Using the Cloud for Records Storage: issues of trust, *Archival Science*, **17** (4), 349–70, https://doi.org/10.1007/s10502-017-9280-5

Mêgnigbêto, E. (2010) Information Policy: content and challenges for an effective knowledge society, *The International Information and Library Review*, **42** (3), 144–8, https://doi.org/10.1016/j.iilr.2010.07.008

Pearce-Moses, R. (ed.) (2018) *InterPARES Trust Terminology*, InterPARES Trust, www.interparestrust.org/terminology/

Perrein, J. P. (2012) Le risque informationnel, une menace ou une opportunité, https://www.gouvinfo.org/IAI/le-risque-informationnel-une-menace-ou-une-opportunite/ [accessed 12 July 2018].

Proença, D., Vieira, R., Borbinha, J., Calado, P. and Martins, B. (2017) *A Maturity Model for Information Governance – FinalVersion* (E-ARK Deliverable No. D7.5), Instituto Superior Técnico – Universidade de Lisboa,
www.eark-project.com/resources/project-deliverables/95-d75-1/file

Quebec (2015) Governance. *Thésaurus de l'activité gouvernementale*,
www.thesaurus.gouv.qc.ca/tag/terme.do?id=6152

Raj, P. and Periasamy, M. (2011) The Convergence of Enterprise Architecture (EA)

and Cloud Computing. In Mahmood, Z. and Hill, R. (eds), *Cloud Computing for Enterprise Architectures*, London, Springer London, 61–87, https://doi.org/10.1007/978-1-4471-2236-4_4

Riempp, G. and Gieffers-Ankel, S. (2007) Application Portfolio Management: a decision-oriented view of enterprise architecture, *Information Systems and E-Business Management*, **5** (4), 359–78, https://doi.org/10.1007/s10257-007-0052-2

Rogers, C. and Tennis, J. (2016) *General Study 15: Application Profile for Authenticity Metadata*, Final Report, InterPARES, http://interpares.org/ip3/display_file.cfm?doc=ip3_canada_gs15_final_report.pdf

Saffady, W. (2015) Records Management or Information Governance?, *Information Management*, **49** (4), 38–56.

Scott, A. (2013) How to Create a Good Information Security Policy, https://www.computerweekly.com/feature/How-to-create-a-good-information-security-policy [accessed 12 July 2018].

Shepherd, E. and Yeo, G. (2003) *Managing Records: a handbook of principles and practice*. London, UK, Facet Publishing.

Smallwood, R. F. (2014) *Information Governance: concepts, strategies, and best practices*. Hoboken, New Jersey: Wiley.

Surrey Health Borough Council (2015) Information Governance [Text]. https://www.surreyheath.gov.uk/council/information-governance [accessed 12 July 2018].

Wildhaber, B., Burgwinkel, D., Hagmann, J., Holländer, S., Neuenschwander, P. K., Schmutz, D. and Spichty, D. (2015) *Leitfaden Information Governance*, Zürich, Kompetenzzentrum Records Management, https://informationgovernance.ch/services/leitfaden-information-governance/

Willis, A. (2005) Corporate Governance and Management of Information and Records, *Records Management Journal*, **15** (2), 86–97, https://doi.org/10.1108/09565690510614238

6

Retention and disposition

Editor: Patricia C. Franks
Contributors: Alicia Barnard,
Eduardo Bonilla, Patricia C. Franks,
Claudia Carvalho Masset Lacombe Rocha,
Silvia Schenkolewski-Kroll and Assaf Tractinsky

Introduction

Attitudinal shifts fostered by technological advancements pose the greatest challenges to the disposition of records and information today. Some believe, and advocate, that we should keep everything because storage is cheap and we never know when we might need it. Google encourages us with statements like this: 'Never delete anything, always use data – it's what Google does' (Kershaw, quoted in Hardy, 2015). However, others believe that 'even in this world of "never delete anything", secure, compliant information disposition has its place!' (Franks, 2017).

If you are a supporter of this second premise, you understand that records cannot be disposed of unless the reasons for creating them in the first place are understood. *Disposition* can be defined as 'The destruction or transfer of records as specified by a retention schedule' (Pearce-Moses, 2018, s.v. disposition).

Retention is the responsibility of the organization to maintain 'records for a period of time until their authorized disposition by destruction or transfer' (Pearce-Moses, 2018, s.v. retention). The *retention schedule* provides a comprehensive list of each group of related records treated as a unit for retention purposes (*records series*) and the length of time each is to be maintained – regardless of their format (e.g. electronic and physical) and location (e.g. on premises and in the cloud). This holds true, as well, whether the records and information are in the physical custody of the organization or a third party.

In this chapter, we call upon the findings of four studies that explore the principles of records retention and disposition in a cloud environment and identify ten best practices based on those principles.

The first study, *Policies for Government Records Produced by a Community Cloud* (Barnard, 2018), addressed transparency, access to information and responsibility for records management in the cloud, including the topics of appraisal, retention schedules and disposition. The second study, *Preserving Records and Managing their Life-cycle in a Multi-provenance Digital Government Environment – a case study on a government electronic system: SIGEPE* (Lacombe Rocha et al., 2017), considered retention and disposition in the context of controlling records in the physical custody of a cloud service provider. The third study, *Retention and Disposition in a Cloud Environment* (Franks, 2016), introduced a checklist for retention and disposition functional requirements and applied it to 20 cloud services to identify gaps that exist between the functional requirements needed and those offered and the resulting risks presented to the organization. The final study, comprised of three phases, focused on the retention and disposition process concerning Israel's Ministry of Foreign Affairs website. The first phase, *Research on Retention and Disposition Processes in an Internet Website of the Government of Israel: The Ministry of Foreign Affairs Case Study* (Schenkolewski-Kroll and Tractinsky, 2015), considered solutions to retaining the website; the second, *Research on Users of the English Website of the Israel Ministry of Foreign Affairs as a Criterion for Appraising Records* (Schenkolewski-Kroll and Tractinsky, 2016), recognised the behaviour of visitors as a factor in appraisal of website records; and the third, *Archival Appraisal, Retention Schedules and Metadata in Web Sites – the case study of the Ministry of Foreign Affairs, Israel* (Schenkolewski-Kroll and Tractinsky, 2017), focused on website metadata for records management, especially appraisal and preservation.

A running theme throughout the studies is the importance of being able to trust that records and information are managed in a way that mitigates risk to the organization. Additional themes that emerged from the studies include ways in which collaboration between records managers, IT departments and vendors and recognition of the human factor are essential to the effective management of digital records, particularly those stored in the cloud.

Trust and digital records

Trustworthiness of records is directly linked to users' trust in governments and enterprises responsible for the records. In general, trustworthiness refers to the accuracy, reliability and authenticity of a record (Pearce-Moses, 2018, s.v. trustworthiness). However, 'in the context of electronic records, trustworthiness often implies that the system is dependable and produces consistent results based on well-established procedures' (Society of American Archivists, 2018). Traditional records environments have established best practices and procedures for retention and disposition of analogue records. By contrast, the fragility and vulnerability of digital materials endangers their trustworthiness, which in large part depends on reliable retention and disposition.

Systems that adhere to national or international standards, such as records management applications certified as compliant with *DoD 5015.2 – Electronic Records Management Software Applications Design Criteria Standard*, tend to engender trust in users of the system and their constituents. While this standard was developed in the pre-cloud era, cloud vendors can also achieve certification; for example, Collabware CLM for SharePoint claims that their system is certified to control all aspects of the content lifecycle, including security, retention, review and disposition (Gravity Union, 2018).

While cloud services have the potential to contribute to the trustworthiness of digital records, evidence suggests that there is some resistance to their use. For example, records and information management (RIM) professionals have been sceptical of these services and their impact on records, as well as their own ability to mitigate risks associated with records management. Governments charged with the responsibility of operating in a transparent manner fear that poor governance of information and records will be exposed, causing citizens to lose confidence in their government. Collaboration among records managers, IT departments and third-party vendors may be the key to establishing trust in digital records and cloud services.

Value of collaboration

Records and information managers involved in preparing retention and disposition schedules for records held on premises can contribute their expertise to decisions made when employing cloud technologies. Our research, however, shows that records and information management professionals revealed that not all were involved in such decisions and many were not aware of the types of cloud services employed across their organizations. Instead, decisions regarding the lifecycle of electronic records in the cloud often fall solely to IT departments and/or are entrusted to the third-party vendor (Franks, Poloney and Weck, 2015).

In a study of records managers, fewer than 25% of survey respondents indicated retention and disposition considerations were included when selecting cloud services. Even fewer (14%) believed their organization performed disposition of content stored in the cloud – some noting that retention periods had not yet been met for cloud content. A number of respondents failed to answer technical questions about disposal actions, indicating 'don't know'. The one question that elicited the largest number of 'yes' responses was 'Can records be deleted according to the retention/disposition schedule?'. However, fewer responded 'yes' to a similar question about copies of records on back-up servers. And fewer still answered 'yes' when asked if destruction could be automated (Franks, Poloney and Weck, 2015).

Cloud systems must provide agencies with conditions that enable them to manage records in the same way they manage traditional records stored within each agency's environment. However, service providers are often unaware that creators need to exercise this control. This lack of control may have led to the initial scepticism of records managers around promises made for cloud computing and the inability of others within the organization to understand the impact the use of cloud services will have on the records management programmes. Another factor that may have led to this scepticism and lack of understanding by many RIM professionals is that vendors often do not address retention and disposition functionality when describing their products. Anecdotal evidence suggests this is changing, with a greater awareness among RIM professionals and an increased effort by cloud service providers to include retention and disposition functionality in their products.

Records appraisal in diverse systems

Appraisal has more than one definition. Archival *appraisal* is defined as 'the process of assessing the value of records for the purpose of determining the length and conditions of their preservation' (Pearce-Moses, 2018, s.v. appraisal). In the records management field, *appraisal* is the 'process of evaluating business activities to determine which records need to be created and captured and how long the records need to be kept' (International Organization for Standardization (ISO), 2016). The ARMA International Glossary, 2016, takes a different approach by describing both appraisal and functional appraisal. *Functional appraisal* is considered the 'process of assessing the enduring value of records by determining the functions of the organization to be documented, identifying which offices or individuals created records in carrying out those functions, and selecting the records that provide the most complete and concise documentation of those functions' (ARMA International, 2016).

Appraisal according to functionality

Retention and disposition considerations must be addressed when evaluating diverse systems that meet diverse functional requirements. The studies referred to in this chapter explore retention and disposition capabilities in both government and enterprise settings, including community clouds, private clouds and websites.

A *community cloud* is a cloud infrastructure deployment model in which a specified group of organizations with common privacy, security or legal concerns collaborate to share resources that may be managed by the organizations or a third party, on or off premises. One study examined records management in the federal government in Mexico's portals: INFOMEX for access to information petitions and POT for transparency obligations (Barnard, 2018).

A *private cloud* is defined in the InterPARES Trust (hereinafter ITrust) Glossary as 'a deployment model in which a provider manages and supports infrastructure, platform, or software as a service for the exclusive use of a consumer' (Pearce-Moses, 2018, s.v. private cloud). An example of a system in a private cloud is SIGEPE, which controls all personnel management activities for federal government agencies in Brazil. The agencies have access to the system on the internet and the records are kept in a centralised database and repository under the responsibility of a consortium of IT government enterprises (SERPRO-DATAPREV). In this case, the exclusive consumer of the private cloud is comprised of all institutions under the Federal Public Administration of Brazil (Lacombe Rocha et al., 2017).

A *website* is a collection of web pages related by content or domain. An extensive study conducted in three phases examined records management in Israel's Ministry of Foreign Affairs website. The study describes websites as innovative tools of mass communication that can serve as platforms for the representation of organizations and individuals. The ability to continuously update records that appear on the website is a special characteristic that provides current information as often as several times a day during critical periods and every few weeks (or longer) when dealing with permanent administrative materials (Schenkolewski-Kroll and Tractinsky, 2015, 2016, 2017).

Rather than reviewing a specific system, Franks and her research team investigated a wide array of cloud vendors and their applicability to different records management needs according to a checklist developed by the study, the 'Checklist for Retention and Disposition Functional Requirements' (Franks, 2016). The checklist, which can be applied to any type of cloud service, identified 25 functional requirements segmented into seven categories: Privacy and Security Considerations; Establishing Disposition Authorities; Applying Disposition Authorities; Executing Disposition Authorities; Documenting Disposal Actions; Reviewing Disposition; and Integration. The cloud services investigated were divided into the following eight categories: File Sharing and Cloud Storage; Records Management Extender; Infrastructure/Platform/Managed Services; Litigation Support and

Discovery; Archiving Solution; Enterprise Content Management; Long-term Digital Preservation; and Backup and Data Protection. Because not all cloud services are designed to perform the same functions, features were different among categories and then among providers within those categories.

A summary of the findings indicates capabilities present or absent in a majority of the cloud offerings, but the evaluation of the specific cloud service employed or under consideration is of much more value to the organization. An analysis of responses to each of the items on the checklist for the cloud services studied revealed retention and disposition features present and absent based upon the purpose of the cloud service. For example, Smarsh, a prominent archiving solution for a range of digital information platforms including social media, websites, e-mail and instant and mobile messaging, provides government records management services, such as the application of retention periods and support for freedom of information requests; however, the ability to execute disposition authorities was lacking at the time of the review (Franks, 2016).

Units of appraisal

Just as capabilities differ by system and purpose, units of appraisal also differ. In the case of websites, website sections may be the best unit of appraisal for web content, due to specific content characteristics in the various sections and the heightened chance for technical difficulties encountered in harvesting websites at lower levels (such as at the page level). However, Mexico's community clouds – INFOMEX for disclosure of public requests and responses and POT for accomplishing transparency obligations – provide both proactive disclosure and disclosure in response to a public request. Questions asked during this study included how records for both transparency obligations and access to information are managed by the federal government in Mexico's community cloud. The units of appraisal in this case were records and record groups. Brazil's private cloud system, SIGEPE, offers similar units of appraisal. However, there was a need to further classify information by authoritative records versus copies of records due to their separate nature.

Defining purpose and provenance

Retention schedules: authoritative records versus copies

The difference between authoritative records and copies of records presents risks associated with records management in the cloud. This is because the authoritative records were meant to be created to accomplish a specific activity and not produced for transparency purposes. For example, records reproduced to fulfil the transparency function in a transparency portal might differ in format or in content from the original ones.

Transparency is an obligation of governments to become more accountable to their citizens. Citizens of democratic countries have the fundamental right to ask the government for public information and to receive the answers to which they are entitled. Government transparency is the outcome of the actions taken to meet the obligation for disclosure of specific government data or the release of information in response to an individual request by a member of the public. In relation to transparency obligations, the record shared with the public is a copy of the original made for the express purpose of sharing information rather than fulfilling the record's original purpose. By contrast, a request for information and a response to that request produces two or more files (either digital or analogue) created for different reasons. A failure to address the retention periods and appraisal criteria for each case places records at risk. Important questions associated with this risk include:

- Because functions differ depending on the reasons for generating records, should authoritative and derivative files have different names, classification codes and retention periods?
- Should there be one file with access privileges specifying different retention periods and disposal criteria – or, is it necessary to create different files with different names, retention periods and disposal criteria according to the purposes for which they are generated?
- Would it be reasonable to employ micro-appraisal in cases when responses to access to information requests answered by different areas of the agency are not present in other records and might have historical values?
- Should the cloud co-ordinator also maintain an authentic copy of the authoritative record?

Maintaining a chain of custody

A new challenge for the management and preservation of digital records in the cloud is found in the extra steps that must be taken to ensure that the chain of custody is not broken and trust is established when records are entrusted to cloud computing services. Mitigating risk arising from a broken chain of custody is especially important for open government systems that utilise cloud services committed to transparency and access to information requests. Government transparency requires good governance of information and records entrusted to officials and public servants. For example, if the records' provenance is not clearly defined at the moment of transfer to the historical archives, the authenticity of each record and the context of a group of records are at risk. Although some vendors offer services to help maintain the chain of custody, records managers are responsible for ensuring that the chain of custody from creation through to final disposition remains intact.

Considering human factors

The human factor is easy to overlook amidst concerns over the implementation and functional requirements of digital systems. For example, human involvement is necessary to interpret results when studying electronic records users. To appraise the value of the website of Israel's Ministry of Foreign Affairs, researchers created a formula for measuring the usefulness of a website section in order to calculate an appraisal metric that correlates geographical location of returning visitors to their interest in specific sections. (For more information about the Web Analytics used to measure citizen engagement in the study, please see Chapter 4, Citizen Engagement). It was found that industrial countries consistently received high results, but developing countries sometimes received low results in sections that should have received high results. To explain this discrepancy, a records manager must consider the nature of the relations between a specific country and Israel.

User behaviours should also be taken into account when appraising records to determine retention periods. For example, Israel's Ministry of Foreign Affairs website is predominantly a public relations site, which means its social value is of the utmost importance in the appraisal of its records. In particular, returning visitors (users who visit the site at least twice) are important in identifying records that have value because those users have found information on the site and returned knowing that information is likely to be found there again. Therefore, counting returning visitors and the time they spend on the site is significant when determining the importance of sections that should remain available for use.

Ultimately, records and information managers must be aware of what is happening with data, records and information across the entire organization, because there are some decisions that must be made when managing records that should be entrusted to humans rather than machines. For example, records managers must recognise the difference in types of records before appraising them according to appropriate standards for each type of record. They must also recognise the difference in types/uses of records before applying metadata, which differs by use. For example, records must contain or be linked to sufficient metadata to describe the record structure, business context, relationships to other records, retention and disposal rules and to produce an audit trail. Records creators maintain the responsibility for the retention and disposition of digital records, regardless of services offered by cloud vendors.

Ensuring accountability

Records creators are responsible for establishing policies regarding requirements (e.g. appraisal criteria, retention periods and specific characteristics of records and information generated in or posted to the cloud) that should be included in their official classification schema and disposal schedule. Traditionally, creators fulfil these responsibilities in order to ensure that records are maintained as long as required in a manner that assures the characteristics of authoritative records – authenticity, that is, identity and integrity, reliability, and usability – are unaltered. This also ensures that disposition is performed with acuity based on criteria established according to records management best practices.

For records in the cloud, however, another question arises: Who is (or should be) responsible for controlling the records' life cycle – the creator or the service provider? Case studies carried out throughout the ITrust project have shown that organizations maintain the responsibility for controlling records in the cloud in theory; however, many cloud environments do not provide the creator with the ability to control the records life cycle. When this is the case, researchers have identified two ways to overcome the problem. The first is to develop the capability of the system to export records so they can be captured by each agency's Electronic Records Management Systems (ERMS). Thus, creators could manage their records in the same environment in which they control traditional records. The second is to develop specific features in the cloud platform to support each agency in controlling its records within the cloud throughout the records life cycle. Even in cases where creators may not be directly responsible for the performance of a specific function, such as digital preservation, the creator must at least monitor the process and performance of the system.

Though records creators and managers are ultimately responsible for records, it is appropriate in some cases for a vendor or party other than records managers and creators to manage records in the cloud. For example, the responsibility of storing records in a cloud environment involves attention, protection and guarantee of access in the long term. In some cases, the service provider takes on this responsibility because the service provider has physical custody of the records. Thus, the service provider is able to control the records' digital components and monitor issues related to technological obsolescence and media fragility in order to carry out its storage responsibility.

When a service provider assumes responsibility for preservation, it must demonstrate its capacity to do so and must make explicit how this is accomplished by means of a formal and publicised preservation policy. This preservation policy must demonstrate that the service provider has in place procedures for maintaining the authenticity and accuracy of the records, technology monitoring strategies, file formats policy, access control policy, guarantee of service continuity and hardware and software infrastructure. Metadata standards are used to depict the business context in which the records were created, dependencies and relationships among records and records systems, relations to legal and social contexts and relationships to agents who create, manage and use the records. Initial metadata is derived or attributed at the time the record is created – the point of capture for records. Metadata will continue to accumulate over time and will be used, among other things, to document a record's changes. Depending upon the nature of the cloud service, such as cloud digital preservation, solutions can be selected that permit ingest not only of the digital objects but also the metadata appended by the creator/agent. In other instances, such as social media archiving solutions, records will be created in the cloud environment and captured by the service providers using their own metadata schema. A discussion between the client and the provider regarding the metadata standards in use and supported must take place before the records are entrusted to the provider.

Metadata for retention and disposition

A major requirement for records management systems is the capability to employ metadata for the retention and disposition of digital records. Metadata, for example, is a possible solution for issues that might arise from government recordkeeping systems, such as determining retention schedules, understanding context and documenting disposal actions. -

Metadata guidelines that exist in the field of records management are addressed in the ICA's *Principles and Functional Requirements for Records in Electronic Office Environments, Module 2: Guidelines and Functional Requirements for Electronic Records Management* (International Council on Archives (ICA), 2016), the most general of records management standards; the DoD's *Electronic Records Management Software Applications Design Criteria Standard* (Department of Defense (DoD), 2007), which is at the intermediate level; and the *MoReq 2010* specification (MoReq, n.d.), which is a standard for applications in systems and the most detailed among them. All the above records management standards include processes for determining disposition authority and executing the function of disposition in accordance with appraisal and retention schedules, destruction, additional examination and transfer.

Unfortunately, there is almost no reference in common international standards and procedures, such as ISO 15489-1 (International Organization for Standardization (ISO), 2016) and ISO 23081, parts 1, 2 and 3 (ISO/TC 46/SC 11, n.d.), to the metadata of websites or their appraisal. However, researchers Rogers and Tennis provide a model, IPAM (InterPARES Authenticity Metadata) schema, which expands and presents metadata fields required to reinforce authenticity of records according to the InterPARES model (Rogers and Tennis, 2016).

In the case of websites, it is important to consider metadata on the site's section and subsection levels and according to three metadata parameters that assist in website records appraisal and preservation: the period of time pages remain in a section or sub-section; the reason for changing the pages; and whether the frequency of change results from pre-ordained circumstances or ad hoc decisions that change in accordance with circumstances. In some cases, it may be possible to pre-determine how long pages remain in a section or subsection (days, weeks, or months). For example, the Foreign Policy section of Israel's Ministry of Foreign Affairs site has a known high frequency of change (i.e. one to three documents a month). Reasons for changing pages include special or one-time events. Examples of pre-ordained changes are permanent sections which publish programmes at set times. As an example of ad hoc changes, Israel's Ministry of Foreign Affairs site's 'About Israel' section changes according to events occurring within Israel.

The basic metadata fields of a website and the sections it contains should include those that are required for appraisal and disposition. Of the four values that drive appraisal and appear in the management of electronic records (legal, administrative, research and social), the latter two – research and social values – stand out based on the characteristics of websites. Additionally, three parameters (frequency of change, reason for change and reason for frequency of change) assist in the management of website records for appraisal and disposition. Also relevant to the creation of metadata for websites is the fact that, although it may be possible to reuse some metadata when a site section or subsection changes (e.g. content management system), other metadata must be created uniquely with each change (e.g. [date] modified). Furthermore, special cases may require the creation of metadata ex nihilo.

Shenkolewsky-Kroll and Tractinsky (2017) have created a table of metadata elements for websites and website sections for the Israeli Ministry of Foreign Affairs website. The authors developed the table by combining existing metadata elements from various standards with three new elements: web platform date, web content structure change and link to file outside the system.

Regardless of the system employed, metadata is pertinent to risk mitigation, since it is used to accomplish essential tasks, including providing security and protecting privacy; establishing, applying and executing disposition authorities; reviewing and documenting disposal actions; and enabling integration with other systems (Franks, 2016).

Evaluating systems to mitigate risks

There are benefits and risks to any initiative. While all risks cannot be avoided, they can be identified and either accepted or mitigated. One way to identify risks presented by employing the services of a cloud provider is to determine the gap between the retention and disposition functionality needed and that offered. The Checklist for Retention and Disposition (Franks, 2016, Appendix 2) can be used to assist in identifying risk, whether evaluating existing cloud services or investigating new services. Two examples of the application of the checklist to different types of cloud providers illustrate some of the features that should be evaluated.

Of the 20 cloud services investigated in the development of the checklist, one provides unified compliance and eDiscovery workflows across an entire range of digital communications including social media, websites, instant messaging and mobile messaging. While the solution allowed the application of retention periods and deletion according to the retention schedule, other desirable features such as control over deletion of back-ups and ability to track multiple retention requirements were lacking.

A second vendor provides long-term digital preservation services and allows users to apply retention periods to content, automate disposal and automatically record and report disposal actions to the administrator. It also, however, does not allow deletion of back-ups according to the same retention schedule. While this situation may not be unusual due to the nature and purpose of back-up copies, the organization should be aware of the vendor's policy for the destruction of back-ups.

Technology is not the only challenge when it comes to records retention and disposition in the cloud. When records and information are stored on physical media (e.g. paper and microfilm), records managers are closely involved in appraisal, retention and disposition decisions. However, the move to the digital environment separated records managers from those who have physical custody of the records and information: information technology departments and third-party providers. In spite of the attitude of some that all information should be retained indefinitely, there are valid reasons for disposing of information that affords no value to the organization. Retention and disposition issues must be addressed whether storing records and information on premises or in the cloud and within systems owned and controlled by the enterprise or by a third-party provider.

It is important to consider the traditional parameters of legal, administrative, research and social values for appraisal of digital records. For example, ensuring the maintenance of the archival bond, reliability, authenticity and documentation of provenance are essential features of archival processing that may be overlooked when records managers do not maintain control over the records lifecycle. In particular, the control over the records lifecycle and the ability of each creator to send its own records to the archives is an important step in making explicit the provenance of the records. According to Adrian Cunningham:

> (…) the thing that separates archives from other forms of information is that they derive their meaning and value from their provenance. If you do not know the provenance of a document, then the document can be no more than a source of information out of context – an information object that is largely devoid of wider meaning.
>
> (Cunningham, 2016, 49)

In some cases, records managers can mitigate risks for digital records by following a parent organization's policies in the retention, destruction or transfer of traditional materials, such as *Israel Archive Law* or Australia's *Administrative Functions Disposal Authority* (Schenkolewski-Kroll and Tractinsky, 2015, 2017). However, traditional guidelines do not always apply to digital materials in the cloud and in the custody of a third party rather than on premises under the physical control of the organization. In these cases, it is up to records professionals to establish new guidelines and checklists for the evaluation of digital records and services to foster the creation of and adherence to standards and regulations for the retention and disposition of reliable, authentic and accurate digital records. Establishing these guidelines and checklists is necessary to provide a means for records managers to reveal gaps between cloud service offerings and pertinent retention and disposition functional requirements.

Conclusion

Records and information management professionals are in a position to aid their organizations in establishing in-house systems or acquiring the services of cloud providers that allow them to meet governing records retention and disposition requirements. Records managers can exert influence over retention and disposition decisions when collaborating with other stakeholders through a better understanding of ways that trust, risk mitigation, collaboration, system requirements and the human factor relate to records management in the cloud.

The following best practices derived from the studies covered in this chapter will assist RIM professionals and other stakeholders involved in evaluating cloud-based services in their work:

- Solutions to retention and disposition challenges presented by the use of cloud-based technologies rest upon the collaborative efforts of all stakeholders, including records and information management and archival professionals, information technology experts, business units and third-party providers.
- Retention and disposition decisions based on an approved appraisal process must be applied to records retained on systems as diverse as government portals, human resource systems, websites and third-party cloud services, including file sharing, social media archiving and long-term digital preservation.
- Units for appraisal will differ based on systems used; for example, sections may be the best unit for appraisal for website content.
- Retention schedules recognise the difference between authoritative records and copies; however, those distinctions are more difficult to make when records are stored in digital systems. Records management policies should clearly address these issues.
- Because records authenticity depends upon provenance and a documented chain of custody, this information must be maintained for all records created, managed, stored and preserved in a cloud environment.
- Human factors as indicated by interactions on websites should be considered as part of the appraisal process; for example, time spent on certain website sections may indicate a rationale for continued use even after the record has met its approved retention date.
- Ultimate responsibility for retention and disposition falls with the creator of the record (such as the department).
- Third-party providers with physical control over records may be required to delete records and back-up copies from systems on behalf of records owners, or must provide the tools to allow the creators to delete their own records from those systems and provide information as to when and how back-up copies will be destroyed. Responsibilities should be explicitly stated in a contract or service level agreement between the organization and the service provider.

- Metadata can/should be employed to assist in carrying out retention and disposition actions, as well as management and preservation of content.
- Cloud services must be evaluated to identify potential risks related to their retention and disposition capabilities and steps must be taken to mitigate those risks.

The studies reviewed in this chapter illustrate that there is no single solution to ensuring retention and disposition in a cloud environment – each situation is predicated on the legal, political and cultural environment in which the organization operates, as well as the gaps between the functionality required and that provided by the cloud services employed. Although ITrust offers valuable insights, new lines of research related to retention and disposition in a cloud environment continue to arise, such as how the use of blockchain technology to create an immutable record of transactions that establishes an unbroken chain of custody will impact retention and disposition of those records.

References

ARMA International (2016) *Glossary of Records Management and Information Governance Terms.* 5th edn, ARMA TR 22-2016, Overland Park, KS, ARMA International.

Barnard, A. (2018) *Policies for Government Records Produced by a Community Cloud.* LA02, Final Report, InterPARES Trust, https://interparestrust.org/assets/public/dissemination/abaITRUSTLA02CaseStudyreport.pdf

Cunningham, A. (2016) Describing Archives in Context: Peter J. Scott and the Australian 'Series' System. In Lemieux, V. (ed.), *Building Trust in Information,* Springer Proceedings in Business and Economics. Springer International Publishing.

Department of Defense (DoD) (2007) DoD Electronic Records Management Application (RMA) Design Criteria Standard, Version 2, www.esd.whs.mil/Portals/54/Documents/DD/issuances/dodm/501502std.pdf

Franks, P. (2016) *Retention and Disposition in a Cloud Environment.* NA06, Final Report, InterPARES Trust, https://interparestrust.org/assets/public/dissemination/NA06_20160902_RetentionDispositionInCloud_FinalReport_Final.pdf

Franks, P. (2017) Even in a 'Never Delete Anything World' Compliant Information Disposition Has Its Place, *Information Management,* **51** (6), 45.

Franks, P., Poloney, K. and Weck, A. (2015) *Executive Summary of Survey Distributed to Members of ARMA International,* InterPARES Trust, https://interparestrust.org/assets/public/dissemination/NA06_20150331_

RetentionDispositionClouds_ExecutiveSummary_Report_Final.pdf

Gravity Union (2018) Collabware CLM. *Gravity Union,*
www.gravityunion.com/collabware-clm/

Hardy, Q. (2015) Google Offers Cheap Storage for Certain Kinds of Data. *Bits Blog.*
11 March 2015, https://bits.blogs.nytimes.com/2015/03/11/google-offers-cheap-
storage-for-certain-kinds-of-data/

International Council on Archives (ICA) (2016) Principles and Functional
Requirements for Records in Electronic Office Environments, Module 2:
guidelines and functional requirements for electronic records management,
https://www.ica.org/en/ica-tools.

International Organization for Standardization (ISO) (2016) *ISO 15489-1 Information
and Documentation-Records Management, Part 1 Concepts and Principles,* Geneva,
ISO.

InterPARES (2018) InterPARES 2 Terminology Database,
www.interpares.org/ip2/display_file.cfm?doc=ip2_glossary.pdf&CFID=
16119752&CFTOKEN=94344076

ISO/TC 46/SC 11 (n.d.) *ISO 23081 Metadata for Records,*
https://committee.iso.org/sites/tc46sc11/home/projects/published/
iso-23081-metadata-for-records.html [accessed 6 July 2018].

Lacombe Rocha, C., Diogo Claudino, F., Gonçalves, D. and da Costa, F. (2017)
*Preserving Records and Managing Their Lifecycle in a Multi-Provenance Digital
Government Environment – a Case Study on a Government Electronic System: SIGEPE.*
LA01, Final Report, InterPARES Trust, https://interparestrust.org/assets/public/
dissemination/IPT_LA01_Report_eng_2017.pdf

MoReq (n.d.) MoReq2010, Module Requirements for Recordkeeping Systems,
www.moreq.info/ [accessed 6 July 2018].

Pearce-Moses, R. (ed.) (2018) *InterPARES Trust Terminology,* InterPARES Trust,
www.interparestrust.org/terminology.

Rogers, C. and Tennis, J. (2016) *General Study 15: Application Profile for Authenticity
Metadata,* Final Report, InterPARES,
http://interpares.org/ip3/display_file.cfm?doc=ip3_canada_gs15_final_report.pdf

Schenkolewski-Kroll, S. and Tractinsky, A. (2015) *Research on Retention and
Disposition Processes in an Internet Website of the Government of Israel: the Ministry of
Foreign Affairs case study,* EU01, Final Report, InterPARES Trust,
https://interparestrust.org/assets/public/dissemination/EU01_20150909_
RetentionDispositionProcessesIsraeliForeignAffairs_FinalReport_Final.pdf

Schenkolewski-Kroll, S. and Tractinsky, A. (2016) *Research on Users of the English
Website of the Israel Ministry of Foreign Affairs as a Criterion for Appraising Records.*
EU25, Final Report, InterPARES Trust,
https://interparestrust.org/assets/public/dissemination/EU25_20161001_
WebAnalyticsAndAppraisalMinistryForeignAffairsIsrael_FinalReport_Final.pdf

Schenkolewski-Kroll, S. and Tractinsky, A. (2017) *Archival Appraisal, Retention Schedules and Metadata in Web Sites – The Case Study of the Ministry of Foreign Affairs, Israel.* EU36, Final Report, InterPARES Trust, https://interparestrust.org/assets/public/dissemination/EU036_20171120_AppraisalWebsites_FinalReport.pdf

Society of American Archivists (2018) Glossary of Archival and Records Terminology, https://www2.archivists.org/glossary/terms/a/appraisal

7

Authentication

Editor: Hrvoje Stančić
Contributors: Hrvoje Stančić,
Mpho Ngoepe and
Jonathan Mukwevho

Introduction

This chapter discusses the certification of digital records and their long-term preservation as authentic records. Two scenarios in which the records' trustworthiness might be questioned are examined. The first scenario addresses digital records and their potential inadmissibility as evidence to external audits. The examples from the African context, and particularly from South Africa, are discussed, followed by an analysis of the framework to certify the trustworthiness of digital records that support the audit process.

The second scenario examines challenges of long-term preservation of digitally signed or sealed records relying on certificates which normally have a short life span. It focuses on long-term preservation of the validity information of digital signatures or seals. A blockchain-based model, showing that periodical re-signing or re-timestamping of records is not necessary, is presented. Even though the two scenarios are focused on the auditing process and the digitally signed or sealed records, both the framework and the model can be applied broadly, wherever records need to be relied on as accurate and authentic. In order to better understand the two scenarios, a discussion of the concept of authenticity is offered.

Authentic digital records

The widespread use of technology to conduct government activities has resulted in an increased creation of digital records. This development brings with it issues about the reliability and authenticity of digital records (Park, 2001, 270).

Duranti and Thibodeau (2006) identify three types of digital records: (1)

computer stored records; (2) computer generated records; and (3) computer stored and generated records. Computer stored records contain human statements. They are created in the course of business and can be in the form of, for example, e-mail messages or word-processing documents. They may be used as *substantive evidence*, i.e. evidence of their content. In comparison, computer generated records do not contain human statements. They are the output of a computer program designed to process input following a defined algorithm, for example server log-in records from internet service providers, ATM records, etc. They may be used as *demonstrative evidence*, i.e. evidence of the action from which they result. Finally, computer stored and generated records are a combination of the two previously mentioned types. An example of such a record may be a spreadsheet record that has received human input followed by computer processing, i.e. the mathematical operations of the spreadsheet program. These records may be used as substantive and/or demonstrative evidence.

A digital record can be considered authentic if it retains all the significant properties that determine its identity and integrity. The international records management standard, ISO 15489, considers an authentic record as one that can be proven to be what it purports to be, has been created or sent by the person purported to have created or sent it and has been created or sent at the time purported (International Organization for Standardization (ISO), 2016).

There are two senses in which the term authentication is used in archival practice. In the more colloquial sense of the word, it is a process of establishing that a record is what it is purported to be. In the second, legal and diplomatic sense, authentication is a declaration of authenticity made by a competent officer and consists of a statement or an element, such as a seal, a stamp or a symbol, added to the record after its completion. In this context, authentication only guarantees that a record is authentic at one specific time, when the declaration is made or the authenticating element or entity is affixed (Duranti, 2009; Duranti and Franks, 2015).

While authenticity means that a record is what it claims to be, reliability means that the record is capable of standing for the facts to which it attests (Lee, 2005). The authenticity and reliability of digital records generated and preserved as evidence of how public representatives executed their mandate is of utmost importance. Reliable and authentic digital records enable organizations to defend their actions, improve decision-making, prove ownership of physical and intellectual assets and support all business processes; they support overseeing service delivery, compliance with the legislative framework and standards and a seamless and effortless audit process (Mukwevho and Jacobs, 2012; International Council on Archives (ICA), 2008).

At the core of records and archives management is the idea that every record is linked to all the records belonging in the same aggregation by a network of relationships, which finds its expression in the archival bond. The archival bond is *originary*, because it comes into existence when a record is created, *necessary*, because it exists for every record (a document can be considered a record only if and when it acquires an archival bond) and *determined*, because it is qualified by the function of the record in the documentary aggregation in which it belongs (Duranti, 1997). The importance of metadata and their role in ensuring the reliability, authenticity, traceability and legal value of digital records where a network of relationships and more than one original order are possible is further discussed in Chapter 8 on intellectual control.

Taking into account all the above, the challenges of the creation and preservation of digital records that may be used as evidence will be discussed in the context of business processes and auditing first, and in the context of the long-term preservation of digitally signed or sealed records second. Both studies will illustrate the challenges that many institutions and businesses are facing today. Further discussion on the issues of digital preservation in the cloud can be found in Chapter 9.

Accepting digital records as evidence in the auditing process

Most professions, such as auditing, health, finance, human resources and law, rely on the strength of records management to perform their duties. For example, records management is increasingly becoming the tool that enables organizations to fulfil the requirements of auditors. Auditing is an independent assessment whereby auditors check on the transactions of an organization using records as supporting documentation (Dandago, 2009). To be in a position to express a positive audit conclusion, it is necessary for the auditor to obtain sufficient appropriate evidence. Lack of supporting documentation during the audit process is an indication of poor governance and lack of accountability, which can lead to disclaimer opinions and increased audit costs (Ngoepe, 2012). Therefore, if auditing is to be undertaken, relevant reliable and authentic records will be required as evidence.

During the audit process digital records of any of the three types identified earlier may be presented as evidence by auditees. However, there is always a challenge, as in many countries government entities have implemented electronic content management (ECM) while others have enterprise resource planning (ERP) systems and still others generate digital records without the benefit of any controlled system (Ngoepe, 2017). As a result, the following scenarios or combination of scenarios are likely to exist in organizations: ERP, ECM and informal systems (Katuu, 2012).

Enterprise Resource Planning (ERP) business system

Automated business systems create or manage data about an organization's activities. They include applications whose primary purpose is to facilitate transactions between an organizational unit and its customers, for example, an e-commerce system, client-relationship management system, purpose-built or customised database, and finance or human resources systems. Business systems typically contain dynamic data that is commonly subject to constant updates (timely) and can be transformed (manipulable) and hold only current data (non-redundant). For the purposes of this chapter, business systems exclude Electronic Records Management Systems (ERMS). Electronic records management systems contain data that is not dynamically linked to a business activity (fixed), cannot be altered (inviolable), and may be non-current (redundant). They are specifically designed to manage the maintenance and disposition of records. They maintain the content, context, structure and links between records to enable their accessibility and support their value as evidence. Electronic records management systems are distinguished from business systems for the purpose of this chapter because their primary function is the management of records while the systems discussed here tend to contain 'data' rather than 'documents', although they can also be used to store documents. If business systems have a dedicated module or component which has specific ERMS functionality, this module is deemed to be a records management system, as indicated in the next section below.

Electronic Content Management (ECM) system

For purposes of this chapter, an Enterprise Content Management (ECM) system, Electronic Document and Records Management System (EDRMS) or Electronic Records Management System (ERMS) are used interchangeably as long as they include specific records management functionality. Any system that is designed to store 'office-type documents' in such a way that they are managed according to records management criteria and can be shown to be unaltered, meets the requirements for an ERMS.

Informal system

Any system that does not meet either of the definitions above can be considered 'informal'. These may consist of:

- Local hard drives that store electronic documents outside of records management control

- Shared drives that store documents
- Collaboration environments, such as Microsoft SharePoint, which have not been specifically configured to include records management functionality and controls
- Portable media, unless these are classified and managed according to a file plan and strict records controls
- Electronic document management systems (EDMS) without formal classification, the ability to edit and amend.

Taking an example from Africa, many records management professionals lament the fact that auditors do not always accept digital records as evidence to support audit queries, due to lack of guidelines (Ngoepe and Ngulube, 2014). The problem is compounded by the general poor management of records, which results in organizations presenting inaccurate and unreliable records as evidence to support the auditing process. The situation is worse in the digital environment as it is difficult for organizations to prove the authenticity of digital records to support the audit process or to present records as evidence in the court of law. For example, media reports indicate that the South African government struggled to authenticate the Gupta leaked e-mails (a series of explosive e-mails showed the extent of the Gupta family's control over cabinet ministers and state-owned companies and their CEOs and boards. The authenticity of the e-mails has been questioned.) Another situation where the authenticity of cell phone records was questioned is the murder case of Olympic runner Oscar Pistorius versus the State of South Africa. Due to these situations and others like them, public-sector external auditors may not accept digital records as evidence during the audit cycle. This is the case in many countries, such as Ghana (Akotia, 1996), Botswana (Mosweu, 2011), sub-Saharan Africa (Nengomash, 2013), Kenya (Katuu, 2015) and Zimbabwe (Chaterera, 2016) to mention a few.

According to Ngoepe (2014), the Auditor-General of South Africa regards the reliability and authenticity of records as key components of any entity risk management process. For instance, at the moment of transitioning between systems, digital records are at the greatest risk of losing their authenticity. Major risks occur during capturing of metadata as digital records are liable to be altered, to lose their original identity or to be separated from metadata required to establish their authenticity (Bearman, 2006). The Australian National Audit Office (2016) identifies particularly complex business requirements and the large number of electronic business systems in use as the main challenges for governmental bodies in achieving robust records management in today's digital environment. As a result, the use of such systems creates the risk that inaccurate or incomplete information could be generated, accessed and used when making decisions and during the auditing process and service delivery. Possible consequences arising from these risks may include adverse publicity, inefficient business activity and a weakened capacity to prosecute or defend allegations, as well as the inability to prove ownership of physical and intellectual property (International Council on Archives (ICA), 2008).

A framework to authenticate digital records for the auditing process

In order to help organizations to authenticate digital records, a framework has been developed. The framework can be applied in different contexts such as a court of law or financial, academic and health institutions. It is limited to digital records generated in the various systems deployed by an organization to enable and execute its business processes in order to fulfil its regulatory obligations. These could be either business systems or record management systems.

The main methods for creating and retrieving digital records as authentic include profiling records and retrieving records in context.

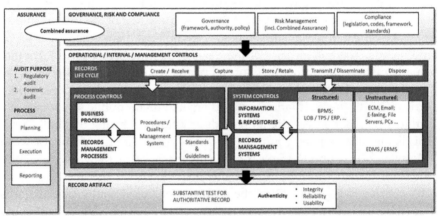

Figure 7.1 *A framework to authenticate digital records for the auditing process* (Ngoepe and Mukwevho, 2018, 26)

The framework shown in Figure 7.1 identifies the various elements that need to be considered during the audit process. Each of these elements has a potential impact on the authenticity of electronic records that may be used as evidence during the audit. While the focus is on a regularity audit, the same principles should be adopted in any form of audit.

Though the emphasis is on the auditees' electronic records and systems, the auditors should take care that the authenticity of their own records generated during the audit process is evaluated using the same principles.

Any record received, captured, stored and used during the audit process should be similarly evaluated.

An audit process includes preliminary engagement activities, an overall audit strategy, detailed planning and execution, concluding, reporting and quality control. During the audit process auditors meet the heads of business units or sections or senior managers within the public institution wherein records are requested or made available. Asset-related records, such as asset registers, predetermined information such as strategic plans, supporting documents of achievements, human resource records such as leave files, minutes of meetings of selection committees, and supply chain management records such as payment batches, as well as tender documents, are made available.

The workflow for assessing the reliability and authenticity of digital records in each records phase (i.e. creation/approval/capturing and records storage and preservation/archiving) during the audit process is reflected in Figure 7.2. A checklist to help with this process (Ngoepe and Mukwevho, 2018) consists of focus areas, such as business process, records management, IT general controls, application controls and a substantive test of record artefacts. Each area is further subdivided into requirements, accompanied by assessment details or key questions. The assessment can be done against the existing information and system-generating records, which can be used as evidence during audit process. Such systems include ECM, ERP or any informal systems and are presented in Table 7.1 on the next page.

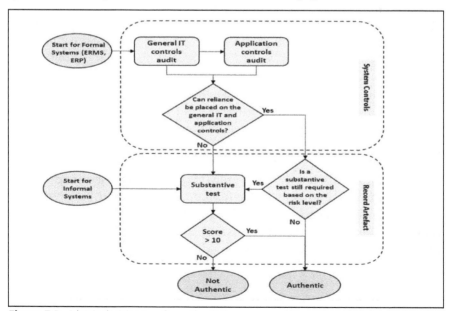

Figure 7.2 *A basic decision tree for authenticity assessment* (Ngoepe and Mukwevho, 2018, 40)

Table 7.1 *System categories*

System category	Explanations
ECM and ERP	Reliance can be placed on the general IT/system controls in that a presumption of authenticity can be made. The assurance provider might not need to conduct substantive tests or more substantive tests of transactions or business activities.
Informal systems	Reliance cannot be placed on the general IT/system controls in that a presumption of authenticity cannot be made. The assurance provider might need to conduct substantive tests or more substantive tests of transactions or business activities. In relation to digital records authenticity in the context of a business process, this involves assessing the authenticity of the record based on its characteristics (including metadata), context, content and structure of the electronic record itself. In such a situation, all tests for record authenticity should check whether the record meets the criteria of an authoritative record as per ISO 15489-1: 2016 – Information and documentation – Records management – Part 1: Concepts and principles.

When an auditee/public institution using ECM or ERP scores enough on IT general controls and application/process controls, the auditor may presume that the evidence derived from that system is reliable and authentic and allows for a judgment to reach a sound conclusion.

When auditee/public institutions using informal systems do not score enough points on IT general controls and application/process controls but score them on the substantive test of the record instead, the auditor may presume that the evidence derived from that system is authentic and reliable and allows for a judgment to reach a sound conclusion.

The framework's checklist still needs to be piloted with auditees. Also, much could be gained from training public auditors on records management processes and on how to assess the authenticity of digital records as well. In addition, records management officials could benefit from being part of the audit team during the audit cycle in order to learn about the auditing process.

This could prove to be even more important now that businesses are increasingly starting to use digital signatures and seals, at least in the European Union, and archivists are facing challenges with the long-term preservation of authentic records providing evidence. This aspect will be discussed next.

Supporting long-term preservation of digitally signed or sealed records with blockchain

The result of e-business and digital communication is the creation of an ever-increasing number of digital records with digital signatures or digital seals attached to them. Therefore, it is necessary to analyse the challenges of long-term preservation of such digital records.

An electronic seal is technically the same as an electronic signature (Cryptomathic, n.d.). The terms *electronic signature* and *digital signature* are often used interchangeably to mean the same thing. In this chapter, the term *electronic signature* is used when referring to the signatures in which the identity of the signatory cannot be verified, while the term *digital signature* is used when referring to signatures where the Certificate Authority (CA) confirms the identity of the signatory. The European eIDAS Regulation makes the following distinction: a digital signature can be associated only with a natural person and the signing key must be under the sole control of the signatory with the aim to sign, while a digital seal can be associated only with a legal person and the signing key must be under the sole control of the process assigning a seal with the aim to ensure integrity and origin (European Parliament, 2014; Kirova, 2016).

In order to be preserved for the long-term, digitally signed records must present the characteristics of authenticity (i.e. identity and integrity) and usability and this requires a more complex approach to preservation compared to digital records which are not digitally signed or stamped. Just as there is a difference between the short-term and long-term preservation of digital records, there is a difference between the preservation of digital records that are digitally signed or sealed and those that are not. Digitally signed or sealed records contain one more level of complexity, which makes their preservation more complicated.

Even though digitally signed records can be preserved for the long term, they may lose their legal validity if they cannot be validated or if they lose the property of non-repudiation. If an error occurs in the process of digital signature validation, the trustworthiness of the digital record may be questioned. This issue arises because re-validation of historical digital signatures is not usually supported by common software and requires reliable long-term preservation of digital certificates, certificate revocation lists (CRL) and, for the longer term, other elements of historical public key infrastructure (PKI). If any of the elements of this system malfunction, digital signature validation will fail. This is especially important when preserving records that contain advanced digital signatures, which will be discussed later (Herceg, Brzica and Stančić, 2015).

A digital signature is a code, created according to cryptographic principles using the Public Key Infrastructure connected to a digital object, which serves as proof that the object has not been tampered with, and in some cases can be used to authenticate the sender's identity (Mihaljević, Mihalhević and Stančić, 2015). A digital signature represents the basic technology used to check a digital document's authenticity and a method of protection of a document or electronic communication content, whereas the digital certificate which it relies on makes it possible to confirm the identity of a natural or legal/juridical person. Thus, the basic requirement for a digital signature is the validation or confirmation of the signatory and of the authenticity of the content of the signed communication (Katulić, 2011).

Although a digital signature has the same purpose as a traditional wet ink signature, there is an important difference between the two. While, with some exceptions, the wet ink signature of the same person on many different paper documents is generally expected to be the same on all of them, the signature of the same person on many different digital documents will be a different binary string, though it will still be associated with both the document and the signatory. In other words, a person signs each digital document with a different digital signature because a digital signature is sent attached to a message in the form of a binary string. If the same string were used for multiple documents, anyone who received a digitally signed document could simply copy the string and attach it to another document, thus forging someone else's signature.

Apart from the basic electronic signatures, which the European Telecom-munications Standards Institute (ETSI) defines as essentially the equivalent of a handwritten signature with data in electronic form being attached to other electronic subject data as a means of authentication, there are also *advanced electronic signatures*. According to the eIDAS Regulation, whose definition is based on the Directive 1999/93/EC (which has since been superseded), the *advanced electronic signature* must meet the following requirements:

> a) it is uniquely linked to the signatory; b) it is capable of identifying the signatory; c) it is created using electronic signature creation data that the signatory can, with a high level of confidence, use under his sole control; and d) it is linked to the data signed therewith in such a way that any subsequent change in the data is detectable.
>
> (European Parliament, 2014)

The PKI system provides the components necessary for managing (issuing, verifying and revoking) public keys and certificates (as well as their storage and preservation). It also provides secure authentication of participants in the communication, exchange of documents with the possibility of encryption, digital signing and co-signing and a unique registry of public keys in the form of a digital certificate.

The basic element of this system is the *digital certificate*. It is used for more demanding public key encryption implementations. A digital certificate confirms the connection between a secret key owned by a particular person and the associated public key. It is a system in which the identity of the person is stored together with the corresponding public key and the entire structure is digitally signed by a trusted third party (certification service). A digital certificate is issued for a limited period (usually two to five years). The certificate may be terminated or revoked if the user or the certificate has been compromised. There are two ways of knowing whether a digital certificate is revoked. The first is to check whether the certificate revocation information has been published on the CRL. The second is to check the OCSP (Online Certificate Status Protocol) – an internet protocol which is used for obtaining the revocation status of a certificate. This means that there must be direct trust or a trust chain to the certification authority certifying the digital certificate.

According to Blanchette (2006), from an archival perspective there are three possible options for dealing with digital signatures in the context of long-term preservation:

1 *Preserve the digital signatures:* This solution involves the deployment of considerable resources to preserve the necessary mechanisms for validating the signatures and does not address the need to simultaneously preserve the intelligibility of documents.
2 *Eliminate the signatures:* This option requires the fewest resources but impoverishes the authority of the document, as it eliminates the signature as one technical element used to verify its authenticity. (It is widely considered bad practice to discard signature elements altogether. Elimination is more often understood now as a refusal of an archival institution to do re-validation.)
3 *Record the trace of the signatures as metadata:* This solution requires few technical means and records both the existence of the signature and the result of its verification. However, digital signatures lose their special status as the primary form of evidence from which to infer the authenticity of the document. Of course, this approach requires the recognition of the archival institution as the trusted third party who preserves and authenticates the metadata.

Another possible approach is to use official state registers of created records in combination with early archival intervention. Dumortier and Van den Eynde's position is that archival institutions should establish a Trusted Archival Service

(TAS) and use it to preserve digitally signed records with the digital signatures (Dumortier and Van den Eynde, n.d.). They claim that by using TAS, the archives could at any point later in time validate the digital signatures. This approach to the preservation of valid, digitally signed records has been recognised in archival practice but has yet to see a widespread implementation.

Earlier InterPARES projects have recommended recording the trace of the signatures as metadata (Roeder et al., 2008, 50–1). According to this approach, archival institutions should check the validity of the signatures, i.e. of the certificates, at the point of ingest. This could be achieved by technical re-validation of signatures or by obtaining assurances from the relevant authority. The next step in the process of ingest would be recording the information on the validity in the metadata and eliminate the signatures. The records and the accompanying metadata would then be preserved in the digital archives. This procedure implies that users trust the digital archives and the metadata associated with the records. This approach is based on the traditional digital preservation model and precedes the development of disruptive technologies such as blockchain and distributed ledger technologies (DLT) (Nakamoto, 2008). However, the new technologies which favour disintermediation, i.e. do not require trusted third parties, may improve the process of long-term preservation of digitally signed records.

These technologies offer a fourth option based on the principles at the core of blockchain and distributed ledger technologies, i.e. registering the validity of the digital signature in a blockchain.

Blockchain

One of the possible solutions to the long-term preservation of digitally signed records is blockchain technology. Blockchain is best known as the technology that supports digital currencies (cryptocurrencies), but is already being applied in various other areas for a variety of purposes. This technology is by its very nature an authenticating technology because everything that is being recorded using it cannot be changed or deleted.

The digitally signed records are not themselves stored on the blockchain – only their hash values are. This is an important aspect to understand because the blockchain, in its essence, is a distributed (peer-to-peer) database and for some records it is important that they not leave the system in which they reside (e.g. security classified records). The distributed database of transactions, i.e. hashes that may or may not be accompanied by metadata, is built using the network of interconnected nodes, thereby creating a distributed ledger. Each instance of the distributed ledger holds an exact copy of the ledger and its blockchained records.

The term 'blockchain' is coined from the terms 'block' and 'chain'. A block contains one or more transactions, i.e. hash values representing records to be registered on the blockchain. The 'chain' term is used to denote that the blocks are chained, i.e. interconnected, or, more precisely, that each block relies on the previous one. This chain grows linearly in an append-only manner, creating an immutable chain of transactions. Blockchain solutions rely on the underlying technologies and concepts – hash algorithms, Merkle trees and distributed consensus (Stančić, 2018).

A cryptographic hash is a *one-way* function that 'does not provide any way to trace its input values by its outputs, … [i.e.] it is impossible to recover the original input data based on the hash value' (Drescher, 2017). Another characteristic of the hash algorithm is that it is *pseudo-random*. This means that it is unpredictable, but also that even if, intentionally or unintentionally, only one digit is changed in the binary stream, the resulting hash will be significantly different from the original one. This also implies that the hash function is *deterministic*, i.e. that it will always result in the same hash out of the same input data (Drescher, 2017).

Hash values may be hashed together. The resulting values can in turn be grouped and hashed together until a final 'top/root hash' has been calculated. This approach was first introduced in 1980 by Ralph C. Merkle (1980). Since the structure resembles an upside-down tree structure it was named the Merkle tree. In this approach, if any of the branch hashes changes (e.g. a record is tampered with), the check of all the upper level hashes calculated on it would fail.

Distributed consensus is a type of consensus in which every participant (server/node) checks every event in the ledger ('main book'/database). Consensus is used to determine authenticity. The event, for example the registration of several records on the blockchain, will be formally confirmed and a block containing the hash values of the records to be registered will be sealed only if 50% of nodes plus 1, the so-called 'qualified majority', confirms it.

The blocks typically contain hash values of the records, possibly some metadata, and a previous block's hash (except for the first or so-called genesis block). The system then asks all the participating nodes to confirm the creation of the new top hash (i.e. block). As per the distributed consensus principle, a new block is confirmed when the qualified majority agrees upon it. New blocks, when confirmed, are timestamped and recorded by every participating node, thereby creating the distributed ledger. The resulting hash is than referenced by the next block, as shown in Figure 7.3 on the next page.

There are at least four positive aspects of the blockchain that need to be outlined. First, although it is possible to store records on the blockchain, this is usually not done. The data, information, documents or records that are

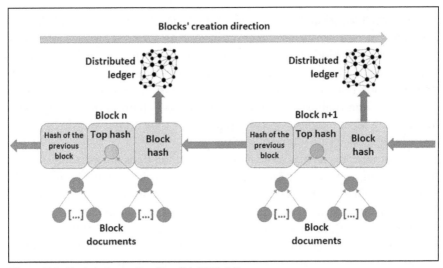

Figure 7.3 *Blockchain creation* (Stančić, 2018, 13)

registered on the blockchain never leave the system in which they reside and remain under institutional control. Second, adding new blocks makes the whole chain stronger, because the chain is made longer and more hashed blocks reinforce the previous ones. Third, any attempt to modify a block would invalidate all subsequent blocks and would be easily detected. Therefore, no changes to the already created blocks are possible. Fourth, the blockchain contains proof that a hash, and in that sense that data, a document or record, was part of the original set of hashes the chain was built upon, as well as the proof of the time it was registered in the blockchain.

What is lacking from the archival perspective is the archival bond. Lemieux and Sporny realise that 'even though the time-ordered nature of the transactional records is preserved, the link to their procedural context, and relationship to other transactional records relating to the same procedure, is not' (Lemieux and Sporny, 2017, 1439). They suggest that 'through use of ontologies to represent the procedural context of ledger entries, it is possible to instantiate the archival bond between ledger entries as records of a variety of transactions' (Lemieux and Sporny, 2017, 1442). Taking into account all the characteristics of the blockchain and its underlying technologies and concepts, it may be concluded that the blockchain can be used to:

- Confirm the integrity of a record
- Confirm that a record was in existence or created at a certain point in time (i.e. not after it was timestamped and registered in the blockchain)
- Confirm the sequence of entries in the blockchain

- Support/enhance the non-repudiation of a record
- Ensure that the digital processes cannot be manipulated
- Improve the validation possibilities of digitally signed or sealed records during their long-term preservation.

The last point will be argued in the context of the description of the TrustChain model.

TrustChain model

The model was developed as part of the InterPARES Trust research study Model for Preservation of Trustworthiness of the Digitally Signed, Time-stamped and/or Sealed Digital Records (TRUSTER). It will be referred to as the TRUSTER VIP (Validity Information Preservation) solution, or simply TrustChain. It represents the fourth possible approach to the long-term preservation of digital records that have digital signatures or seals attached to them. The TrustChain model allows archives and other institutions preserving digitally signed or sealed records to avoid having to re-sign (or timestamp) records periodically before their digital certificates expire in order to keep their validity verifiable.

The TrustChain, as a blockchain solution, is envisioned as being maintained by an international alliance of archival institutions. The system could also be implemented by a single institution, although the degree of security of the validation would then be significantly reduced.

The TrustChain achieves its goal by checking a document's signature validity and, if the result is positive, writing the signature's hash (and possibly some document metadata) in the blockchain. Signature validity is checked by all participating institutions or, if their number is high, by some of them. If the signature is deemed valid, the information is permanently stored in the TrustChain blockchain (see Figure 7.4 on the next page) (Bralić, Kuleš and Stančić, 2017). Having signature validity information written into an immutable blockchain provides evidence that the signature was valid at the point of its TrustChain entry creation and that neither the record (as assured by the signature) nor the blockchain entry has been tampered with since then.

While it is true that, like other methods, for example addition of archival timestamp(s) as defined by ETSI EN 319 102-1 (ETSI 2016), TrustChain relies heavily on the PKI concept and thus on the asymmetric cryptographic algorithms, there is no need to periodically re-sign the data because of the way the data is stored. TrustChain's blockchain data structure is what enables it to avoid the pitfalls of compromised private keys or outdated cryptographic algorithms. Once an algorithm becomes outdated, TrustChain voting nodes

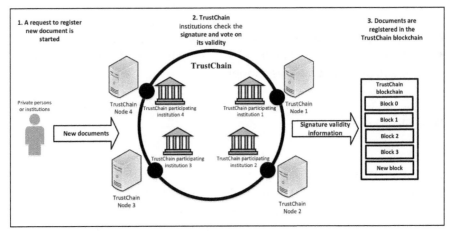

Figure 7.4 *TrustChain concept* (Stančić, 2018, 30)

merely need to change the algorithm they use to sign their votes. Blocks signed with a compromised or outdated key do not need to be re-signed. If an attacker wanted to re-sign them with altered data, they would need to change and re-sign all the subsequent blocks as well and eventually they would run into a block signed by an uncompromised key (and a safe algorithm). In short, we could say that (as in other linked data models) adding a new block to the TrustChain re-signs (or re-confirms) all the existing entries, or that the entire (block) chain is as strong as its strongest link or, in this case, as the strongest block, which will always be the most recent one.

The confirmation process of the (expired) digital signatures begins with finding the hash of the relevant records in the TrustChain blockchain. For this, the TrustChain relies on the blockchain entries' metadata – those can be, as Bralić, Kuleš and Stančić propose, ISAD(G)'s essential set of elements as well as information pertaining to the archival bond (Lemieux & Sporny, 2017). Once the hash with the related entry metadata is identified, all that needs to be done is to recalculate the hash from the original record and compare it to the one written in the TrustChain. If these hashes match, one can reliably claim that the record and its signature have remained unchanged since the date indicated by the blockchain record timestamp (Bralić, Kuleš & Stančić, 2017). Therefore, although the digital signature or seal, i.e. their certificates, may have expired since the time of registration to the blockchain, one could effectively operate with them as if they are still valid.

Conclusion

This chapter began by addressing the challenges of creation, maintenance and long-term preservation of authentic records that can be used as evidence during the auditing processes. A framework to authenticate digital records for the auditing process, incorporating methods of profiling records and retrieving records in context, was explained. Next, building the case for preserving records as evidence, a blockchain-based solution to the specific challenge of preservation of digitally signed or sealed records with short validity period of signing certificates was presented. The reason for the development of the TrustChain was to preserve certificate information, or at least to preserve information about its validity at a certain point in time. To the knowledge of the TRUSTER Team researchers, none of the existing timestamping services meet this requirement. Of course, successful implementation of the TrustChain system requires significant infrastructure and a number of participating institutions, as well as further development. While timestamping services are standardised and commercially available right now, it is the view of the researchers that the TrustChain is a better solution. The TRUSTER VIP Solution 'TrustChain' demonstrates that such a system is possible and that periodical re-signing (re-timestamping) of records is not necessary. Both studies argue for more standardised procedures in order for digital records to remain authentic throughout their preservation period and to be accepted as evidence.

References

Akotia, P. (1996) *The Management of Public Sector Financial Records: the implications for good government*, Legon, University of Ghana.
www.msu.ac.zw/elearning/material/1174370018Pino%20Akotia%201996%20on%20governance.pdf

Australian National Audit Office (2016) *Recordkeeping Including the Management of Electronic Records*, 26 January 2016, https://www.anao.gov.au/work/performance-audit/recordkeeping-including-management-electronic-records

Bearman, David (2006) Moments of Risk: identifying threats to electronic records, *Archivaria*, **62**, 15–46.

Blanchette, J.-F. (2006) The Digital Signature Dilemma, *Annales Des Télécommunications*, Mai/Juin, 908–23.

Bralić, V., Kuleš, M. and Stančić, H. (2017) A Model for Long-Term Preservation of Digital Signature Validity: TrustChain, *ResearchGate*, 89–113, University of Zagreb: Department of Information and Communication Sciences, Faculty of Humanities and Social Sciences,
https://www.researchgate.net/publication/321171227_A_Model_for_Long-term_Preservation_of_Digital_Signature_Validity_TrustChain.

Chaterera, F. (2016) Managing Public Records in Zimbabwe: the road to governance, accountability, transparency and effective service delivery, *Journal of the South African Society of Archivists*, **49**, 116–36.

Cryptomathic (n.d.) *What Is an Electronic Seal?*.
https://www.cryptomathic.com/products/authentication-signing/
digital-signatures-faqs/what-is-an-electronic-seal [accessed 8 July 2018].

Dandago, K. (ed.) (2009) *Advanced Accounting Theory and Practice*, London, Adonis & Abbey.

Drescher, D. (2017) *Blockchain Basics – A Non-Technical Introduction in 25 Steps*, Apress.

Dumortier, J. and Van den Eynde, S. (n.d.) *Electronic Signatures and Trusted Archival Services*,
www.expertisecentrumdavid.be/davidproject/teksten/DAVIDbijdragen/Tas.pdf

Duranti, L. (1997) The Archival Bond, *Archives and Museum Informatics*, **11** (3–4), 213–18.

Duranti, L. (2009) From Digital Diplomatics to Digital Records Forensics, *Archivaria*, **68** (Fall), 39–66.

Duranti, L. and Thibodeau, K. (2006) The Concept of Record in Interactive, Experiential and Dynamic Environments: the view of InterPARES, *Archival Science*, **6** (1), 13–68.

ETSI (2016) *ETSI EN 319 102-1: Electronic Signatures and Infrastructures (ESI); Procedures for Creation and Validation of AdES Digital Signatures; Part 1: Creation and Validation*, www.etsi.org/deliver/etsi_en/319100_319199/31910201/01.01.00_30/
en_31910201v010100v.pdf

European Parliament (2014) eIDAS-Ecosystem, https://www.eid.as

Herceg, B., Brzica, H. and Stančić, H. (2015) Digitally Signed Records – Friend or Foe?. In Anderson, K. et al. (eds), *INFuture2015: e-Institutions – Openness, Accessibility, and Preservation – Proceedings*, 147–50, University of Zagreb, Department of Information and Communication Sciences, Faculty of Humanities and Social Sciences, https://doi.org/10.17234/INFUTURE.2015.18

International Council on Archives (ICA) (2008) *Principles and Functional Requirements for Records in Electronic Office Environments – Module 3: Guidelines and Functional Requirements for Records in Business Systems*, www.naa.gov.au/Images/
Module%203%20-%20ICA-Guidelines-Principles%20and%20Functional%
20Requirements_tcm16-95420.pdf

International Organization for Standardization (ISO) (2016) *ISO 15489-1 Information and Documentation-Records Management, Part 1 Concepts and Principles*, Geneva, ISO, https://www.iso.org/standard/62542.html

Katulić, T. (2011) Razvoj Pravne Regulacije Elektroničkog Potpisa, Elektroničkog Certifikata I Elektroničke Isprave U Hrvatskom I Poredbenom Pravu, *Zbornik Pravnog Fakulteta U Zagrebu*, **6** (14), 1343–4.

Katuu, S. (2012) Enterprise Content Management (ECM) Implementation in South Africa, *Records Management Journal*, **22** (1), 37–56, https://doi.org/10.1108/09565691211222081

Katuu, S. (2015) Managing Records in a South African Health Care Institution – A Critical Analysis. PhD Thesis, Pretoria, South Africa: University of South Africa.

Kirova, M. (2016) *eIDAS Regulation (Regulation (EU) N°910/2014) – FUTURIUM – European Commission*, https://ec.europa.eu/futurium/en/content/eidas-regulation-regulation-eu-ndeg9102014

Lee, B. (2005) *Authenticity, Accuracy and Reliability: reconciling arts-related and archival literature*, Discussion paper, Vancouver, BC, InterPARES Trust, www.interpares.org/display_file.cfm?doc=ip2_aar_arts_lee.pdf

Lemieux, V. and Sporny, M. (2017) Preserving the Archival Bond in Distributed Ledgers: a data model and syntax, *Proceedings of the 26th International Conference on World Wide Web Companion*, 1437–43.

Merkle, R. (1980) Protocols for Public Key Cryptosystems, *IEEE Symposium on Security and Privacy*, 122–34.

Mihaljević, M., Mihalhević, M. and Stančić, H. (2015) *Archival Science Dictionary: English-Croation, Croatian-English*. FF Press.

Mosweu, O. (2011) Auditing, Records Inadequacy and the Lamentations of the Auditor General in Conducting Performance Audits in the Botswana Public Service. Paper presented at the *Archival Conference on Guarding Against Collective Amnesia: is there a role for records and archives?* Pretoria, South Africa.

Mukwevho, J. and Jacobs, L. (2012) The Importance of the Quality of Electronic Records Management in Enhancing Accountability in the South African Public Service: a case study of a national department, *Mousaion*, **30** (2), 33–51.

Nakamoto, S. (2008) *Bitcoin: A Peer-to-Peer Electronic Cash System*, https://bitcoin.org/bitcoin.pdf

Nengomash, C. (2013) The Past, Present and Future of Records and Archives Management in Sub-Saharan Africa, *Journal of the South African Society of Archivists*, **56**, 2–11.

Ngoepe, M. (2012) *Fostering a Framework to Embed Records Management in the Auditing Process in the Public Sector in South Africa*, PhD Thesis, Pretoria, South Africa, University of South Africa.

Ngoepe, M. (2014) The Role of Records Management as a Tool to Identify Risks in the Public Sector in South Africa, *South African Journal of Information Management*, **16** (1).

Ngoepe, M. (2017) Archival Orthodoxy of Post-Custodial Realities for Digital Records in South Africa, *Archives and Manuscripts*, **1** (45), 31–44.

Ngoepe, M. and Mukwevho, J. (2018) *Ensuring Authenticity and Reliability of Digital Records to Support the Audit Process*, AF06, Final Report, InterPARES Trust.

Ngoepe, M. and Ngulube, P. (2014) The Need for Records Management in the

Auditing Process in the Public Sector in South Africa, *African Journal of Library, Archives and Science*, **24** (2), 135–50.

Park, E. (2001) Understanding 'Authenticity' in Records and Information Management: analyzing practitioner constructs, *American Archivist*, **64** (2), 270–91.

Roeder, J., Eppard, P., Underwood, W. and Lauriault, T. P. (2008) Authenticity, Reliability and Accuracy of Digital Records in the Artistic, Scientific and Governmental Sectors: Domain 2 Task Force Report. In Duranti, L. and Preston, R. (eds), *International Research on Permanent Authentic Records in Electronic Systems (InterPARES) 2: Experiential, Interactive and Dynamic Records*, Padova, Associazione Nazionale Archivistica Italiana, www.interpares.org/ip2/display_file.cfm?doc=ip2_book_ part_3_ domain2_task_force.pdf

Stančić, H. (2018) *Model for Preservation of Trustworthiness of the Digitally Signed, Timestamped And/Or Sealed Digital Records (TRUSTER Preservation Model)*, EU31, Final Report, InterPARES Trust, https://interparestrust.org/assets/public/ dissemination/TRUSTERPreservationModel(EU31)-Finalreportv_1_3.pdf

Suvak, W. (2015) Authentication. In Duranti L. and Franks, P. (eds) *Encyclopedia of Archival Science*, Rowman & Littlefield Publishers, 116–19.

8

Intellectual control

Editor: Giovanni Michetti
Contributors: Özgür Külcü, Giovanni Michetti,
Richard Pearce-Moses, Chris Prom,
Corinne Rogers, Joe Tennis, Kat Timms
and Sevgi Koyuncu Tunç

Introduction

This chapter explores intellectual control over records, focusing on metadata, records management and arrangement and description as strategies to exercise such control.

Archivists have been exploring the implications of digital technology on traditional archival practice for some time. The cloud and networked storage present distinct challenges for arrangement and description. Archivists should question assumptions underlying traditional approaches and they should look for opportunities to use technology to enhance existing practice. A thoughtful consideration of the traditional principles and concepts underscores their value and why archivists should maintain them. At the same time, further exploration of what original order is in the digital era demonstrates enormous new possibilities that complement – rather than replace – traditional approaches.

Section 1 of this chapter identifies and explores some of the assumptions and opportunities in order to help archivists understand that decisions to use the cloud and networked storage are often made without fully addressing recordkeeping and preservation implications, especially with regard to archival description.

Section 2 presents some considerations on metadata and authenticity based on the InterPARES 2 Benchmark and Baseline Requirements, moving through the Chain of Preservation Model assertions about documentable actions during the records lifecycle, and then focusing on the InterPARES Trust work on the IPAM (InterPARES Authenticity Metadata) Vocabulary. These models help archivists and records managers cope with the empirical questions that surface when dealing with metadata and records: how much is too much and how much is enough to support the presumption of authenticity of digital records?

Section 3 focuses on usability and human–computer interaction in electronic records management systems (ERMS). Such systems help capture, create, store, classify and access – in a word, manage – records based on authority. The features that an ERMS should support are determined by specific laws and regulations, but we should never forget that these systems are managed and used by humans. The interaction between human and computer can be analysed and evaluated – the qualitative and quantitative outputs of such interaction can tell us whether a system is usable or not. This section deals with Heuristic Evaluation of an ERMS' usability.

Role and meaning of arrangement and description in the digital environment

Giovanni Michetti, Chris Prom, Richard Pearce-Moses and Kat Timms

Archivists have been exploring the implications of digital technology on traditional archival practice and questioning assumptions underlying traditional approaches for some time. In particular, it is not uncommon to hear that respect for original order is no longer relevant when working with digital records (See Trevor Owens, *The Theory and Craft of Digital Preservation* (preprint, June 2017) https://osf.io/preprints/lissa/5cpjt). Such an attitude discounts the important role original order (defined as the last order the records had when they were in active use) plays in the very nature of archives as trustworthy records. A thoughtful consideration of the traditional principle underscores its value and why archivists must maintain it. At the same time, further exploration of original order in the digital era demonstrates new ways of complementing – rather than replacing – traditional approaches.

This section provides a checklist that identifies and explores some of these assumptions and opportunities. It is not intended to be comprehensive or prescriptive, but to prompt further reflection and discussion. As technology evolves, so do the possibilities for innovation. At the same time, many archives have established practices that are effective and efficient and adopting some of the ideas suggested here may not be practical or desirable.

The following considerations might help archivists and records managers assess whether a decision to use the cloud and networked storage was made without fully addressing the recordkeeping and preservation implications, especially with respect to archival description. The checklist may help records professionals identify risks and possible approaches in existing systems.

Arrangement

The systems and methods a record creator uses to store and organize records are significant because they place records in context. That context supports increased understanding of the records as an organic whole that extends beyond any individual record. In short, the sum is greater than its parts. As important, preserving the relationships among records is essential to maintaining their authenticity.

Following the principle of respect for original order, archivists should attempt to identify and preserve the creator's system of arrangement. This principle is an ideal, largely based on archives of governments and structured organizations. It presumes that the records creator has adopted some sort of systematic approach to organize the records and that such a system is reasonably easy to identify.

Personal, community, and even some government and organizational archives, in the absence of a robust records management programme, may have no apparent internal order or the order may have been lost at some point. When confronted with records in disarray, archivists may joke that they are under no obligation to preserve 'original chaos'. In other cases, the original order may have been disturbed and an archivist's attempts to reconstruct the creator's order may reflect the archivist's best efforts more than the creator's intent. With born-digital materials, the original order might be dependent on system configuration or external metadata that are not available to the archivist.

Archival arrangement is frequently hierarchical. Record creators commonly use hierarchies to organize records into a simple, effective taxonomy paralleling the way the creator organized its business units and functions. Similarly, individuals use simple hierarchies to group related activities to simplify filing and retrieving their records. To a large extent, digital storage continues to promote hierarchical organization through the use of folders and subfolders in the file system, although some systems may rely on additional metadata to support their management in alternate views or in ways that complement a hierarchical file system.

In the age of tangible records, the creator's physical arrangement imposed a single order. That order typically resulted from an organic process that established a relation among records, creating a documentary context that a person, organization, or software agent can use to authenticate the records (*Authenticity* refers to the trustworthiness of a record as a record (i.e. the quality of a record that is what it purports to be and that is free from tampering or corruption). *Authentication* is the act of verifying a record's authenticity.) Archivists privilege the creator's arrangement as it captures the archival bond, that is, the network of original relationships among records arising from the circumstances of creation that provide context and support their authentication.

In the digital era, many orders are possible and there may be no single original order. Creators can arrange records in a variety of ways to facilitate access. For example, lists of e-mail messages may be sorted by recipient, sender or date, or they may be filtered by search terms. A record stored in a cloud-based file management console such as Google Drive or Dropbox may be associated with or created by multiple users and each user may have that document associated with different folders. These relationships, tracked using the storage system metadata, will often be lost when files are downloaded or may be available only through specialised application programming interfaces (APIs).

Users, including the creator and researchers, often see other relationships among the records beyond the creator's original order. In the age of tangible records, users were obliged to navigate the creator's order, making notes to reveal those relationships. In the digital era, when arrangement is virtual rather than physical, using metadata and software to discover those relationships is significantly easier. Discussion of these other relationships is covered under description and access below.

Provenance and respect for original order remain important concepts to protect the records' trustworthiness (i.e. accuracy, reliability, and authenticity)

Such protection serves to:

- Ensure the source of the records is properly documented.
- Ensure that the chain of custody is properly documented.
- Capture metadata about files that is appropriate to the particular provenance, creator or context one is seeking to document, while also respecting the ability to document alternate provenances or facilitate the discovery of other relationships.
- Respect original order by considering how the creator organized and used the records to identify aggregates (e.g. collections, fonds, record groups, series, subseries, dossiers and any other grouping of records that reflects some unifying characteristic) and their relationships.
- Document the creator's system of arrangement to offer a human-readable description of the original order and context under which records were arranged, rather than leaving users to make their own assumptions based on implicit knowledge hidden in finding aids.
- Provide processing notes that document the archivist's activities and decisions regarding how the arrangement is presented to the user.

- Recognise that because an archive is 'a living organism which grows, takes shape, and undergoes changes' (Muller, Feith and Fruin, 2003, 19), the creator may have changed the organization of the materials through their life. Also, the original order, that order in which the creator last used them, may be different from the first order and any subsequent received order, and may convey information about how the archive took its shape over time.
- Recognise that because it is relatively easy to integrate accretions of records into existing archives in a digital environment, it is important to make clear to users that the virtual and chronological orders are not the same, and that different parts of the archives were accessioned at different times.

An arrangement based on a hierarchy of aggregates established by the creator remains a practical technique to manage large quantities of records

It is important to remember:

- That while document management and cloud storage systems may flatten the physical storage structure, the records are often organized into a logical hierarchy because record creators are familiar with that organization. Do not confuse orders that are an aspect of the storage system with logical orders record creators rely on to keep and access records.
- That depending on the system used and specific management techniques employed in organizations or collaborating groups, the records may have a common arrangement for all users, or each user may have his or her own arrangement and hierarchy.
- That preserving a hierarchy of aggregates (for example, series, subseries, files) makes it easier for archivists to manage and for users to understand large bodies of records as units, rather than having to manage each record individually.
- To carefully consider which hierarchies should be preserved and base such decisions on the specific context, activity or function one wishes to document. The decisions made should be documented and made available to users.
- That if records are rearranged to facilitate other access pathways, archivists should document the original order and discuss the activities that led to the new order. This documentation will serve as the basis for users to understand the records' context.

Technology offers novel techniques to enhance and expand traditional approaches

Archivists need to recognise that:

- Digital records may have been stored in systems that organized the records in a variety of ways according to the creator's needs. The aggregations and order may be based on different metadata elements or a search that created an ephemeral subset of records. For example, a user may access e-mail by sorting the messages by sender, date, subject or keyword search, depending on the sought information.
- Records creators may have used multiple arrangements – resulting in different contexts – to access the records. Archivists may want to bring users' attention to the fact that there were multiple original orders and they may want to document or provide the ability to recreate those different arrangements. As examples, individual records within a series may have been dynamically searched and sorted using a variety of techniques; or a listing of e-mail or documents may have been sorted by filename, date, format or size, depending on how they were being searched for a particular purpose.
- Many organizations have adopted technologies that are user based, not role based. As a result, policy-driven records management often devolves to personal information management practices, resulting in a loss of systematic approaches to control of the records.
- Storage systems may have important metadata that is not readily visible and can be easily lost. Google Drive, Dropbox and similar technologies offer APIs and other means to access that metadata.
- Archivists should be directly involved in the design, selection and implementation of systems for storing active records to ensure that the systems meet essential records management requirements.
- Archivists should be directly involved in data modelling and functional requirement specification building for preservation repositories that will store records emerging from multiple contexts, such as desktop workstations, mobile devices, cloud services and corporate networks, to make it easier to document the relationships among records, creator and functions.

Description and access

Archival description serves several overlapping purposes. Documenting the archives facilitates archival management by the archivist. Description also provides a simple, efficient and secure means for users' access; reading an overview of the archives can help them determine which specific items they want to request for closer inspection. Finally, documentation of the creator's arrangement helps to maintain the records' authenticity.

In many countries, archival description historically focused on describing individual records. Because of the increased number of records and resulting backlogs, description evolved to focus on the records' context of creation and arrangement as aggregates. In some instances, finding aids also included lists of the folders or items within the aggregates. This approach assumed that a user would be able to determine which records to inspect by navigating the creator's arrangement. Archivists might provide additional avenues of access by indexing the finding aids by entity names and topics or by creating topical guides to archives. Archivists would also use reference interviews to help determine users' interests and point them to relevant archives based on their own, personal knowledge of the holdings.

In the digital era, technology provides archivists with many tools to enhance and expand description and access. For example, manually describing items has long been considered impractical, but technology can automate the process and create detailed lists of digital objects quickly and inexpensively. At a minimum, a simple listing of directory and file names is trivial, although the value may be limited if the names are not meaningful For example, the Unix tree command can generate a graphic display of the directory structure, and may also include the files within each directory and subdirectory with size and time stamps. Even if of limited use for access, it can be an important archival management tool to quickly document all the files received. Integrating item-level metadata from the recordkeeping system or extracting them from the document may make the listing more useful. Keyword and topical analysis tools can also supplement descriptions. Full-text searches of born-digital records (and, as OCR improves, of scanned records) provides a level of access long considered impossible.

These tools are imperfect but will, no doubt, improve and become more useful over time. Until then, archivists should consider their use, weighing their potential, if limited, benefits against their negligible costs.

Existing archival description standards and automated tools (e.g. Access to Memory, ArchivesSpace) reflect traditional practice and, to a large extent, emphasise hierarchical relationships among the records. These standards and tools may be supplemented using a linked data paradigm. With linked data, particular descriptive nodes can be identified and connected to each other, including by reference to language-agnostic URIs.

Using such a strategy might lead to the creation of large networks of data that, taken as a whole, represent an alternate mode of archival description. Yet even within this large network, semantic enrichment – that is, the process of adding layers of metadata to content – allows computers to process data and make sense of it so that people can find, filter and connect information. In this way archival data can be identified by language-agnostic URIs and connected through properties that can be referenced through URIs as well. This leads to the creation of large networks of data that altogether make up archival descriptions. On the one hand, such fragmentation of information creates new and numerous points of direct access to resources, since in theory linked data are an unlimited source of access points. On the other hand, linked data takes users beyond search – users may discover archival materials by moving around in the digital network. For this reason, linked data supports discovery thanks to its intrinsic nature: the underlying graph is not only a data architecture, but also a network of nodes that can be used as a path to explore freely the vast quantity of online resources.

Respect for provenance remains a core principle for access
Recommendations:

- Archival description should include a description of the entities that are associated with context of creation:
  - Records produced by an entity are a primary source of information about that entity and topics associated with that entity.
  - Ideally, general administrative histories or biographical notes would be maintained separate from, but linked to, the descriptions of associated records, rather than being embedded in the descriptions of the records.
  - Administrative or biographical notes appropriate only to a particular set of records may be recorded in a biographical or historical note contained in the description of the records.
  - Archivists must establish good practices that meet local needs and system capabilities to balance the best place to store such information.
- Archival description should also include general administrative histories or biographical notes describing entities that are subjects of the material, but such links should make clear that the records are linked in a 'subject of' role, not a 'creator of' role:
  - Such a note may either be included in a separate file, embedded in the descriptive record, or split among the two, according to the needs of the archives.
- In addition to providing access points based on creators' names, archivists should provide access based on the creators' characteristics.

For example, a topical heading 'Governors – Arizona' can be used to link creators who were or are part of that office.

High-level descriptions, even if incomplete, are essential for archival management and can provide users at least limited access to records
Recommendations:

- All accessions should be described at a minimum level to ensure that all records can be identified and located. Accession records should be created as soon as possible after receipt of the records.
- All holdings should have, at a minimum, a brief description at the highest level, that is, they should be described at least as a whole.
- More detailed descriptions and descriptions of lower levels (series, subseries, item levels) must balance potential benefits for archival management and access against resources necessary to generate detailed descriptions and other demands, such as backlogs.
- All holdings should be discoverable by users, even if they are not immediately available for reference, within limits of legal and donor restrictions. Minimal descriptions at the accession or archives level can support discovery based on the records' most essential characteristics.

Description of aggregates below the archives (archival fonds) level based on original order remains a practical means to support archival management and access
Recommendations:

- To the extent to which a creator arranged records to facilitate its own access and use, that order may remain useful to support initial, minimal level access by archivists and users. Consider the benefits of establishing a new, different arrangement over an existing arrangement against the costs of the effort and potential damage to the records' context.
- Emphasise the records' context in aggregate-level descriptions, in particular the inter-relationship among aggregates, so that users can better interpret and understand them.
- Abstract the content of the records in aggregate-level descriptions to help users determine whether they should invest time examining the records in that series more closely.
- Prioritise description in terms of time and resources needed to create or capture metadata, as well as use and relevance to the archival institution

mission. Consider which metadata elements, especially those stored separately from the records, must be preserved to support authentication and evidential value, as well as enabling discovery and use.

Archival descriptions should include subject analysis

Recommendations:

- Archivists should facilitate access to records based on the information they contain, including people, organizations, topics, places, timeframes and other dimensions appropriate to the archives' mission.
- Archival description systems should be able to create browsable lists of access points to help users locate relevant records. The ability to search data assumes that the search terms are explicit in the data, and adding topical headings using a controlled vocabulary can help find records when commonly used search terms are not present in the records. In some instances, users may spot relevant records by browsing. For example, a search for 'trains' may miss a collection that uses the term railroads, but someone browsing a listing would likely make the connection.
  - Subject analysis may be done at the aggregate level or item level, depending on the nature of the records and available resources.
  - Access points can also support secondary filter and faceting functions that enhance the ability to narrow search results.

Descriptions are a primary interface between users and the records

Recommendations:

- Archivists should follow appropriate descriptive standards, such as ISAD, ISAAR, EAD, EAC, RAD and DACS:
  - Archivists that implement descriptive systems using other standards should create a map between the system and standards.
- Metadata values should be normalised to the extent possible. For example, archivists should use data value standards such as Virtual International Authority File (VIAF), Library of Congress Name Authority Files (LCNA) and Library of Congress Subject Headings (LCSH).
- Archival descriptions should be designed to maximise analysis and reuse.
- Archivists should embrace the linked data paradigm, since it is inherently shareable, extensible and reusable.
- Descriptive systems (print and online) should follow principles of good usability.

Description at the item level using automated techniques is a practical and useful means to support access for a variety of purposes and to discover relationships beyond the creator's original order

Recommendations:

- Consider using tools to extract metadata from and synthesise descriptions of born-digital and OCRed records to provide more atomic descriptions that may help users find relevant documents while also reducing the number of documents they must consult. Item-level descriptions and extracted metadata elements make use of a wide range of properties whose values may be searched and analysed in order to establish connections and discover different perspectives/arrangements of the archives.
- Remember that while item-level descriptions may add complexity to the picture, they may also hinder recognition of the aggregates making up archives.
- Promote innovative uses of visualisation tools and techniques to allow greater freedom when representing archives. Traditional description is dominated by written word, narrative and hierarchies; visualisation tools can leverage on the graph information model to enhance archival description.

Archival descriptions must include sufficient information for preservation

Recommendations:

- Archivists must capture sufficient information to ensure that the records, especially digital records, will remain accessible into the future and that users will have trust in the records' authenticity.
- Archivists should provide a human readable overview of material or technical aspects of the collection, such as requisite software, the inclusion of specialised formats or other technical aspects of the collection that may impact users' ability to access or work with the materials. If needed, such information may be provided at the item level too, in order to document any further technical details that may be relevant to access and use specific materials. To this aim, it is recommended to adopt an existing standard such as PREMIS.

Role of metadata in relation to authenticity

Joe Tennis and Corinne Rogers

Records' authenticity is guaranteed not only by showing the identity of records and demonstrating their integrity, but also by demonstrating the integrity of the systems in which they are created and stored. As investigated in the previous InterPARES research projects, authenticity is assessed and demonstrated by evaluating records' identity and integrity metadata. However, when the systems in which records are created and stored are cloud systems, one needs to ask whether the established models of metadata and the design requirements for preserving authentic digital records change. Records and archives professionals need to understand the new records environments and what can be expected from them with regard to metadata and system integrity. Further, they need to understand to what degree the human- and machine-readable assertions about records in the cloud contribute to assessing the authenticity of those records.

Literature discussing metadata of records in cloud applications, including metadata added by cloud service providers (CSPs), covers different metadata concerns. Askhoj et al. (2011) have elaborated a model specifically designed for the cloud computing environment that provides a simple, OAIS-compatible approach to representing how digital objects and necessary metadata can be transferred from content creation systems to archives systems. Daconta, Metadata Program Manager at the Department of Homeland Security, (2013), has introduced the notion of a formal taxonomy in the context of the Federal Enterprise Architecture's Data Reference Model: in order to guarantee enhanced search and access in government departments he recommends seven metadata description types. The National Archives of Australia (2011) has produced a checklist most concerned with maintaining links between records in the cloud and those in internal systems. Tonkin and Allinson (2006) mention authenticity explicitly and suggest using digitally signed metadata to protect custodial information and increase trust in the records. Many authors explore the need for interoperable, automated metadata generation. Smit et al. (2012) present a cross-cloud adaptive resource management solution that offers a provider-agnostic, extensible method capable of collecting comparable metadata for different content service providers through an automated inter-cloud broker.

In the context of creating metadata derived from the Chain of Preservation model (Duranti and Preston, 2008), InterPARES has created the InterPARES Authenticity Metadata (IPAM) set (Rogers and Tennis, 2016). Assuming that metadata is the set of machine- and human-readable assertions made about a record or body of records, the IPAM set is a comprehensive listing of assertions that can be made about records and aggregations of records from creation, across the threshold of preservation, documenting disposition as well. There are 428 unique and repeatable terms in the IPAM set. This large vocabulary is the ideal and maximum set of metadata to preserve the identity and integrity of records over the lifecycle. Because it is ideal and because there are such a large number of metadata assertions in the set, the question surfaces: do we need all of these metadata assertions? In the cloud environment we do not have clear controls and if authenticity is based on identity and integrity, then metadata must figure in at some point. So what are the ideal (i.e. consistent with the theory) and realised (i.e. consistent with the practice put in place by archivists and records managers in the contemporary networked environment) requirements for authenticity in systems with suspect or unclear controls? Also, what new metadata requirements surface from this new systems context? It is possible that the models and the metadata derived from the theoretical models will not match the requirements for maintaining identity and integrity of records over the lifecycle. If that is the case, what new metadata requirements surface in the cloud context?

The InterPARES Authenticity Metadata (IPAM) set identifies all the metadata that:

> … should be necessary and sufficient to support the presumption of authenticity of records, interoperate between systems and across time, be adequate for archival description, and be useful for both retrieval and meaningful display of records.
>
> (Rogers and Tennis, 2016)

Given the great many metadata assertions that are necessary for supporting authenticity, it is worth investigating whether it is possible to re-package, re-organize or represent the IPAM metadata in a more condensed way, highlighting similarities, common themes/activities, or the like, in order to elaborate a useful conceptual or instructional tool that might make the IPAM set more approachable in implementation scenarios, particularly in a distributed computing environment. To this aim, a matrix has been created analysing the IPAM assertions in order to identify the types of things (entities) or activities/processes they represent. In effect, the matrix's representation of the assertions privileges a function/activity point of view, while the IPAM document had enumerated them in alignment with the underlying COP model, which followed an implied linear progression. Grouping the assertions by common function/activity was envisioned to enable identification of commonalities. Therefore, a matrix of processes and entities/types has been designed as follows:

Columns (i.e. processes):

1. Records' Creation (Capture, Identify, Declare, Execute)
2. Preparing Transfer of Records

3. Transferring or Placing Records into a System for Keeping
4. Processing the Transfer of Records upon Receipt
5. Managing Kept Records
6. Describing Kept Records
7. Providing Access to Kept Records
8. Destroying Kept Records

Rows (i.e. entities/types):

1. Identifiers
2. Agent + Role
3. Contextual Bond
4. Dates
5. Relationships (e.g. Attachments)
6. Form
7. Technical (e.g. Format)
8. Location
9. External Documentation/Links to System Metadata
10. Rights and Access
11. Authentication
12. Subject

Following the objective to consolidate the IPAM assertions, each of the groupings below represent an attempt to 'genericise' the processes:

- Column #2 (Preparing Transfer of Records): This includes both preparing completed (active) records for transfer to a recordkeeping system and preparing records for transfer to a designated preserver.
- Column #3 (Transferring or Placing Records into a System for Keeping): This includes transferring completed records to a recordkeeping system; placing kept records in storage; transferring kept records to a designated preserver; and placing preserved records in storage.
- Column #4 (Processing the Transfer of Records upon Receipt): This includes processing records transfers and accessioning records.
- Column #5 (Managing Kept Records): This includes managing active records in a recordkeeping storage system and preservation activities following accessioning into a preservation system.
- Column #7 (Providing Access to Kept Records): This includes managing requests for kept records and managing requests for preserved records.

The categorisation of the IPAM assertions in this matrix has been informed by the categorisation scheme contained in the IPAM document:

- Attachments (AT)
- Authentication (AU)
- Archival Bond (B)
- Date(s) (D)
- External Documentation (DO)
- Form (F)
- Handling (H)
- Location (L)
- Persons (P)
- Rights and Access (R)
- Subject (S)
- Technology (T)

It is worth highlighting some interpretations of the IPAM model which have provided the ground for the categorisations:

- Row #2 (Agent + Role): Category 'P' for persons was interpreted more broadly than defined in the IPAM model. As 'Agents', they are not limited to individuals or legally defined entities involved with the original creation or receipt of the record but also include individuals who manage the records and request the records later on.
- Row #5 (Relationships (e.g. Attachments)): This category may have been under-used. While metadata regarding attachments is easy to segregate (AT), 'Relationships' could be broadly interpreted. Likely more of the 'Contextual Bond' metadata (and possibly others) could have been slotted in this row; or, this row could have been limited to just attachments.
- Row #9 (External Documentation/Links to System Metadata): the IPAM model describes the 'DO' category as 'external documentation and system metadata (policy, context, appraisal, transfer, audits of system activity, requests on the records – but also rights information – deed of gift[)]'. This metadata is further defined as 'links to information that governs preservation, transfer, and access to the record(s) over time'.
  — Metadata assertions classified as type 'DO' include:
    - authorisations/rationales (e.g. for transfer, for modification to records, for rejection of records), that is, the 'why';
    - indication of records and other documentation received (e.g. upon transfer), that is, describing 'what' was transferred and received, including information about quantity and characteristics;

- rules under which transfers were made (e.g. terms and conditions);
- indication of measures used to verify records, confirm their authenticity, confirm preservation feasibility for them, etc.;
- rights information; and
- most details about access requests to the record (e.g. who requested which record, when, what access rights they held, notification of records sent, verifying that requested records are reconstituted in authentic form, redaction of records requested, rejection of requests, etc.).
— All of these assertions belong together in the 'DO' category because they originate from sources external to the records themselves, including from the system, while the other categories of metadata represent intrinsic or atomic elements. The 'DO' assertions effectively function as pointers to external documents or sources, many of which would possess their own family of intrinsic or atomic metadata assertions.

True to the underlying Chain of Preservation model, which followed a record through a linear lifecycle process, the IPAM metadata assertions are record-centric. That is, metadata assertions are predominantly associated with individual records. There is some reference to aggregate-level metadata, pertaining to groupings or sets of records (e.g. transfer package metadata), but this is not highlighted as such and it is the exception rather than the norm. Other models for records-related metadata often include aggregates, hierarchies and notions of relations between entities. In the case of IPAM, different records-related entities can be perceived by an analytical reader (e.g. records, agents, activities, etc.), but they are not presented in IPAM as a relational model.

In some cases, either as building an enhancement to IPAM or when devising implementations of it in its current form, it may be useful to further consider metadata requirements for aggregates of records that undergo a process as a unit (e.g. description, access, preservation). There may be additional metadata that is relevant to record relative to the management of these aggregates as units, over and above the metadata required at the level of the individual record.

Another potentially valuable enhancement of the IPAM application profile would be to clarify which metadata need to be retained indefinitely throughout the life of a record (or a record aggregation) and which may be discarded at various points along the way. Hypothetically there may also be cases in which granular metadata (e.g. twenty assertions) could be eventually discarded at a particular point in the process because they have in effect been summarised by a new metadata assertion that is applied at that point (e.g. an indication that Y happened, which can replace the previous grouping of twenty assertions that had represented Y in detail). That said, this hypothesis is yet untested and it is uncertain that description (i.e. such a singular metadata assertion) would necessarily permit the elimination of all metadata previously accumulated (for Y). It might also depend on how description was scoped (using what standard, for what purpose – i.e. just for discovery or also for archival management) and how it specifically accommodated authenticity concerns.

Electronic records management systems and usability
Özgür Külcü and Sevgi Koyuncu Tunç

Organizations need to have a sound records and information management system. In particular, it is necessary to take adequate measures to guarantee that records can be created, sorted, filed, transferred, used, stored and accessed to support business activities. Most organizations use Electronic Records Management Systems (ERMSs) intensively for this purpose. Such applications can be evaluated not only in terms of performance, security and functionality. ERMSs are expected to enable efficient records management from creation to either preservation or destruction, so they are also required to be robust in terms of usability, because non-usable systems reduce efficiency by slowing down operations.

Bayram, Özdemirci and Güvercin (2015) have analysed the functionality of the ERMSs developed by Turksat in 2012 in three different organizations and have determined that one of the most important features of an ERMS is an architecture that is easy to adapt and flexible to meet the needs of different operational rules, management models, organizational structure and information infrastructure. Many national and international standards have been developed in order to foster interoperability and ease coping with different models and structure. However, such standards hardly touch on usability and its role to improve efficiency.

Some scholars have identified the major problems that are likely to be encountered when introducing and establishing an ERMS in an organization (Önaçan, Medeni and Özkanli, 2012):

- Resistance of personnel
- Low computer literacy and fear of technology
- Absence of full support from the top management
- Business processes supported by unspecified and/or non-standardised records management
- Role conflicts

- Issues with the application software
- Increased workload
- Inexperience.

In particular, some studies have highlighted that users perceive the systems as being non user-friendly (Önaçan, Medeni and Özkanli, 2012). Therefore, it is very important to investigate usability as a key factor for consolidating records management systems and programs within an organization.

The usability of an ERMS can be assessed using the heuristic method. Heuristic evaluation (HE) is described as a fast, low cost and effective method for performing usability tests on software in many different areas. HE is classified as 'evaluation by expert analysis' and is distinct from 'evaluation by user participation' because it is not implemented by real users. Throughout the process, several expert evaluators apply their predefined, representative tasks under the guidance of specific usability guidelines (Blandford et al., 2004; Gray and Salzman, 1998; Nielsen, 1994; Preece, 1993). It is recommended that field experts and usability and human-computer interaction experts be included in a balanced evaluating team. The outcome of an HE is a list of usability problems affecting the system, identified according to the heuristic methods used or any other criteria defined by the evaluators (Dix et al., 2004).

Usability guidelines help the evaluators identify interface problems while helping designers choose between design alternatives. One of the most popular guidelines for user interface design was proposed by Nielsen (1994). According to his so-called usability criteria, there are ten aspects that need special care when designing and evaluating user interfaces. The following points were defined focusing on websites and user experience while visiting websites, but they can easily be extended to any generic interface:

1   System status visibility: The system should keep users informed of what is happening in relation to the current situation, on a continuous basis and in the context of appropriate feedback. One of the most important elements for the users is that they know the answer to the questions 'Where am I?' and 'What's next?'.
2   System and real world match: The system should be able to speak with the users and understand the terms, words and concepts used by the users. Can the website reflect the user's language, tasks and goals? Since publicly available websites pertain to different demographics (age, education, interests, etc.), the system needs to be addressed to all users.
3   User control and freedom: In order for users not to feel lost in the websites if they follow a wrong path on the site, they must be able to return easily to the point where they were before.

4   Consistency and standards: Users should not have to think whether different words, situations and actions have the same meaning. The application should be self-consistent.

5   Preventing errors: Rather than getting an error message, careful design should help avoiding the occurrence of an error.

6   Recognition rather than remembering (or minimising the memory burden): Objects, activities and options should be made visible in order to minimise the memory burden.

7   Flexibility aimed at efficient use: Accelerators not visible to novice users should be used. Generally, experienced and inexperienced users of the system show different usage behaviours. It is important to address both groups.

8   Aesthetic and simple design.

9   Error Messages: Users should be able to identify and resolve the problems they encounter. Any error message should provide a solution or establish a connection to a solution.

10   Help and documentation: Although it is more preferable to use the system without documentation, it may be necessary to provide documentation and assistance to the user.

Similarly, Shneiderman (1980, 1987) has provided eight simple rules on usability:

1   Design must be consistent.

2   Design must include shortcuts and tips.

3   System should provide information messages about the transactions.

4   Process sequence for each process group must be specific and sequential.

5   Users should be able to make mistakes, and there should be descriptions in case of error.

6   System should allow to undo transactions.

7   System should give the impression that the operations that are happening are under user's control.

8   Resources should be used efficiently, memory space should not be occupied too much.

Donald Norman (1988) devised four simple, user-centered design rules:

1   It should be obvious what the user can do at any time.

2   The general structure of the user system should be shown so that the user can navigate himself.

3   The user needs to be informed about the current status of the system.

4   The user should not be confused with designs that are out of general
    use.

Wickens et al. (2003) categorised the design principles and dealt with them
in detail under separate headings:

Perceptual Principles
1   The items on the screen should be legible.
2   The user should not be asked open questions.
3   Designs contrary to users' expectations should be avoided.
4   Compatibility between forms allows the user to learn faster.
5   Confusion should be eliminated by providing distinctive signals for
    different situations.

Logical Model Principles
1   The images and icons used should be similar to the objects they
    represent.
2   The movement of moving items must conform to the logic model of the
    user.
3   Principle of attention.
4   The cost of accessing information should be minimised.
5   It is possible to detect the information more quickly by giving the user
    more than one channel.
6   The user should not have to remember some information. The
    information to the user should be presented in options.
7   The user should be provided with some predictive information to help
    him make plans for the future.

The usability guidelines mentioned above have been used to define a checklist
specifically designed for investigating ERMS:

Heuristic Evaluation Criterion List
1   System state visibility
2   Matching the system with the real world
3   User control and freedom
4   Consistency
5   Preventing errors
6   Remember instead of recognition
7   Flexibility and utilisation efficiency
8   Aesthetic and simple design
9   Error messages

10   Help and documentation
11   Include shortcuts and tips
12   Do not allow undo transactions
13   Contrary to general usage design
14   Readability of items on the screen
15   Open question to user comment
16   Better fit between forms and faster user learning
17   Elimination of confusion by providing distinctive signals for different situations
18   The images and icons used are similar to the objects they represent
19   Minimising the cost of accessing information (e.g. number of clicks)
20   Giving information to the user from multiple channels (e.g. picture and text)
21   Do not provide more information to the user
22   Screen elements that are expected to be clicked are large enough and co-exist.

This checklist has been used to evaluate the usability of the ERMS at the Hacettepe University, Turkey. The system was analysed via the Heuristic Walkthrough by four different user types (faculty secretary, faculty dean, department chair and department secretary). All the pages were categorised according to their functionality. The user was changed according to the business rules, since each user role has different authorities and responsibilities (e.g. defining parameters, creating, signing, sharing and filing documents).

Thirty pages were analysed by the Heuristic Walkthrough and this study identified many weaknesses and areas to consider for improvement in the ERMS system: around 85 interface mistakes (in terms of usability) were found, 47 of which were categorised as serious (i.e. in need of urgent revision), 26 in the mid-range and 12 non-critical mistakes related to the look-and-feel of the interface. The results can be summarised in the form of a list of suggestions for improving the usability of an ERMS:

- Common elements should look similar so that users can remember their function
- Useless elements should be made invisible according to the user role
- Design of the active and inactive elements should be changed
- Inappropriate object titles should be made more understandable
- Warning and information messages should be added where needed
- Elements in a page should be arranged in order to guide the user
- Images on the icons should express the meaning of the buttons
- Custom error page should be used for unhandled exceptions.

Heuristic evaluation is cheap and intuitive and it does not require complex planning. Nonetheless, it allows the researcher to easily discover the factors that affect the usability of an ERMS and to propose suggestions to correct any issue in the interface design. However, there will still be problems experienced by users because the working environments, personal capabilities and different points of views cannot be simulated completely by usability experts.

Conclusion

Intellectual control is defined as '[t]he control established over archival material by documenting in finding aids its provenance, arrangement, composition, scope, informational content and internal and external relationships' (International Council on Archives (ICA) and InterPARES Trust, 2016). However, the deep meaning of intellectual control has to do with understanding records, their mutual relationships and their significance in relation to the business processes. Therefore, not only arrangement and description but also management of contextual information from the early stages of a record's life is key to exercise such control.

The investigation of the issues arising when arranging and describing records in the cloud has shown the fundamental role of the traditional principles and the need to maintain them, but at the same time has suggested the need to review them in order to explore the possibilities for innovation and to complement – rather than replace – the traditional approaches. Metadata play a significant role in this respect – research has demonstrated that a consolidated set of metadata such as the InterPARES Authenticity Metadata (IPAM) set can be re-packaged, re-organized and represented in a different, more condensed way in order to ease implementation in distributed computing environments. Investigation in this area has also highlighted areas for future research: which metadata need to be retained indefinitely throughout the life of a record?; and how to balance a granular, record-centric approach with the need to describe and manage records aggregations?

These issues are not limited to the archival domain – assuming a peculiar perspective on electronic records management systems (ERMSs), research has demonstrated that the usability of such systems is a key requisite, because non-usable systems reduce efficiency by slowing down operations. Heuristic evaluation can be used to perform usability tests on ERMSs and evaluate the quality of interaction between humans and computers – in other words, to assess the quality and degree of intellectual control over records.

References

Askhoj, J., Sugimoto, S. and Nagamori, M. (2011) Preserving Records in the Cloud, *Records Management Journal*, **21** (3), 175–87. https://doi.org/10.1108/09565691111186858

Bayram, Ö., Özdemirci, F. and Güvercin, T. (2015) Determining Institutional Discrepancies for ERM Software Applications, *International Journal of Integrated Information Management*, http://ejournals.teiath.gr/index.php/JIIM/article/download/3059/2810

Blandford, A., Keith, S., Connell, I. and Edwards, H. (2004) Analytical Usability Evaluation for Digital Libraries: a case study. In *Proceedings of the 4th ACM/IEEE-CS Joint Conference on Digital Libraries 2004*, 27–36. Tucson: ACM Press.

Daconta, M. (2013) Big Metadata: 7 ways to leverage your data in the cloud. *Reality Check* (blog), 13 December 2013, http://gcn.com/blogs/reality-check/2013/12/metadata.aspx

Dix, A. J., Finlay, J. E., Abowd, G. D. and Beale, R. (2004) *Human-Computer Interaction*, 3rd edn, Harlow Essex, Pearson Education Limited.

Duranti, L. and Preston, R. (2008) *Research on Permanent Authentic Records in Electronic Systems (InterPARES) 2: Experiential. Interactive and Dynamic Records*, Padova, Associazione Nazionale Archivistica Italiana.

Gray, W. D. and Salzman, M. C. (1998) Damaged Merchandise? A Review of Experiments That Compare Usability Evaluation Methods, *Human-Computer Interaction*, **13** (3), 203–61.

International Council on Archives (ICA) and InterPARES Trust (2016) Multilingual Archival Terminology Database, www.ciscra.org/mat/

Muller, S., Feith, J. A. and Fruin, R. (2003) *Manual for the Arrangement and Description of Archives*. Translated by A. Leavitt, Chicago, IL, Society of American Archivists.

National Archives of Australia (2011) A Checklist for Records Management and the Cloud, www.naa.gov.au/Images/Cloud_checklist_with_logo_and_cc_licence_tcm2-41355.pdf

Nielsen, J. (1994) Heuristic Evaluations. In Nielsen, J. and Mack, R. L. (eds), *Usability Inspection Methods*, New York, John Wiley & Sons.

Norman, D. (1988). *The Design of Everyday Things*, New York, Basic Books.

Önaçan, M. B. K., Medeni, T. D. and Özkanli, Ö. (2012) Benefits of Electronic Document Management System (EMS) and a Roadmap for EMS Configuration within the Organization, *Court of Accounts Journal*, **85** (April-June), 1–26.

Preece, J. (1993) *A Guide to Usability: human factors in computing*, The Open University, Addison-Wesley.

Rogers, C. and Tennis, J. (2016) *General Study 15: application profile for authenticity metadata*, Final Report, InterPARES, http://interpares.org/ip3/display_file.cfm?doc=ip3_canada_gs15_final_report.pdf

Shneiderman, B. (1980) *Software Psychology: human factors in computer and information systems*, Boston, MA: Little, Brown & Co.

Shneiderman, B. (1987) Designing the User Interface: strategies for effective human-computer interaction, *ACM SIGBIO Newsletter*, **9** (1), 6.

Smit, M., Pawluk, P., Simmons, B. and Litoiu, M. (2012) *A Web Service for Cloud Metadata*, White Paper, York University, http://cloudymetrics.com/servicescup.pdf

Tonkin, E. and Allinson, J. (2006) Signed Metadata: method and application, *International Conference on Dublin Core and Metadata Applications*, http://dcpapers.dublincore.org/pubs/article/view/861

Wickens, C. D., Lee, J., Liu, Y. D. and Gordon-Becker, S. (2003) *Introduction to Human Factors Engineering*, 2nd edn, Upper Saddle River, NJ, Pearson.

9

Exploring digital preservation in the cloud

Editor: Adrian Cunningham

Contributors: Adrian Cunningham,
Ken Thibodeau, Hrvoje Stančić
and Gillian Oliver

Introduction: an alternative to in-house digital preservation

Digital preservation initiatives and implementations have been in the past, and are still today, overwhelmingly in-house endeavours. In this paradigm, digital records that meet certain criteria are transferred from the creator to an archival repository, where professionals use in-house processes, facilities and software to ingest, process, transform (when deemed necessary), describe, store and secure archival information packages (AIPs) and disseminate renderings of digital records (DIPs) for use by researchers and other designated users. The software used is either developed and owned by the archives in question or is used under some kind of licencing arrangement (either commercial or open source). The preserved digital records are stored using (hopefully secure) in-house storage systems that may or may not have external network connections to the wider internet. In some cases, the AIPs may be stored entirely offline as 'dark archives', with suitably redacted and rendered DIPs accessible over the wider network via a search engine or discovery interface.

The in-house approach partly reflects the small, often 'cottage industry' scale of early digital preservation implementations, whereby archivists learn incrementally about digital preservation by doing it themselves on a small scale and gradually ramp up as expertise, resources, infrastructure and digital holdings expand over time. The approach also reflects a strong preference by professionals to have direct and total control of their archival holdings within the secure boundaries of their institutional repositories and infrastructure, reflecting the long tradition of archives as places of secure custody. There is a natural reluctance to trust this vital core business of archives, or part of it, to third parties.

The in-house approach, however, has some potential drawbacks. With digital preservation expertise still being somewhat scarce in the archival profession, in-house programmes sometimes struggle to develop and maintain a critical mass of the diverse archival and technical skillsets that are necessary to sustain a long-term digital preservation implementation. Very few such implementations have sought and received accreditation or benchmarking as 'trustworthy digital repositories'. Arguably, therefore, some of these are deficient in one or more ways, and may indeed be blissfully unaware of their shortcomings.

The field of information technology is fast-moving and highly innovative. A risk, therefore, with in-house implementations is that they may get left behind using outdated processes, software and hardware as the industry matures rapidly. Investments made in owning and deploying yesterday's solutions may hinder the uptake of new and better solutions, approaches and technologies.

Small-scale, in-house infrastructure is often, on a per-unit basis, expensive to maintain and operate – lacking as it does the ability to benefit from economies of scale and the flexibility to expand easily and cost-effectively when necessary.

The drawbacks of in-house owned and operated information technology are well understood in the IT industry. The industry has responded by adopting 'as-a-service' outsourcing models for software, platforms and infrastructure. Under the 'as-a-service' model, organizations do not own or maintain their own software and storage systems. Instead they engage third parties to provide them as a service to deliver designated business outcomes. The potential advantages of the 'as-a-service' approach include:

- Economies of scale
- Expansion of consumption of the volume of service required can be easily and flexibly accommodated
- Highly skilled experts may be reliably obtained from large service providers rather than needing to be recruited as in-house staff
- Software and hardware can be kept up to date by the service provider, thus removing the need for constant in-house updating/upgrading of technologies.

An increasingly popular form of IT as-a-service is the so-called 'cloud', where data may be stored anywhere in the world in massive network-accessible storage systems. Cloud services may be public or private, with private cloud services being available only to designated paying customers under agreed terms and conditions (McLeod and Gormly, 2017).

The major advantages of in-house preservation are that it offers the greatest degree of control and the maximum opportunity for aligning to local policies, objectives and circumstances. Contracting, especially with cloud service providers, can provide archives with access to the richest technical resources, but also entails the greatest risk of loss of control and knowledge of how preservation is carried out. Moreover, the technologies implemented by service providers may not be optimal and in some cases may not even be appropriate for the preservation of authentic records. Cloud services may also run afoul of legal requirements regarding data residency, data protection, privacy and intellectual property rights.

It has become common for governments all over the world to encourage, if not mandate, the use of IT as-a-service and/or cloud services in order to enable government agencies to avail themselves of the advantages described above. The economics of IT as-a-service are especially attractive to cash-strapped governments. In some cases, these advantages are reaped using 'whole-of-government' IT services such as a jurisdiction-specific government private cloud. In other cases, governments encourage their agencies to use third-party services sourced from the private sector. Either way, there is a noticeable trend away from small, in-house IT implementations – though in some cases in-house approaches are permitted if it can be demonstrated that they can deliver superior or more cost-effective outcomes. Archival programmes are increasingly coming under pressure from parent departments, government policy regimes and funding arrangements to adopt IT as-a-service for all aspects of their operation, including digital preservation. Even when archivists are not placed under this pressure, it would be remiss of them to ignore the potential advantages of IT as-a-service for addressing their digital preservation needs.

This is not to say that one approach, either in-house or as-a-service, is inherently better than another. As described above, each has its potential advantages and disadvantages. Nevertheless, archivists who are considering (or who are being forced to consider by government policy regimes) the adoption of digital preservation as-a-service must be able to make informed decisions before they commit to it. In reality, the choice is rarely a simple 'either/or' or 'all or nothing' decision. Increasingly, archival programmes may choose to adopt mixed models that combine some aspects of in-house and in-the-cloud approaches.

An initial objective of the InterPARES Trust Project (hereinafter ITrust) was to test the relevance and utility of the 'Chain of Preservation' (COP) model, which was developed in earlier iterations of InterPARES (Duranti and Preston, 2008), in the cloud. Research showed that, while the COP model is not completely transferable to the cloud, it can be adapted for application to cloud services. These findings are discussed in more detail below. In addition, and perhaps more significantly, ITrust also researched the pros and cons of adopting internet-enabled digital preservation services from third parties and the use of the cloud in such contexts, and developed sound advice for archivists who choose to go down that path. Given the potential advantages of IT as-a-service, the possibilities associated with digital preservation as-a-service cannot be ignored. Nor should digital preservation as-a-service be blindly adopted without fully understanding the risks associated with relying on third parties to perform what has previously always been regarded as an important part of the core functions of archival programmes.

Essentially, the decision to adopt digital preservation as-a-service comes down to questions of trust. Can the services on offer be trusted to deliver the outcomes required in a reliable way over the long term? Can the risks associated with such third-party services be managed adequately? This requires knowing, understanding, and being able to articulate and communicate the desired outcomes and to put in place mechanisms for monitoring and assuring their delivery – together with mechanisms for intervention, rectification and redress when services fail to deliver on those outcomes.

In New Zealand, for example, government mandates to use cloud services motivated the early adoption of cloud computing by the National Library's National Digital Heritage Archive (NDHA). The New Zealand government requires agencies to use cloud services rather than in-house IT services 'because they are more cost effective, agile, are generally more secure, and provide greater choice' (ICT.govt.nz, 2018). The National Archives, UK, has issued guidance for archives using the cloud for storage (Beagrie, Charlesworth and Miller, 2014), but the experience of the NDHA appears to be unique in terms of a national memory institution taking the significant step of outsourcing services for digital heritage. Consequently the NDHA provided an excellent case study to explore the consequences of outsourcing preservation services (Oliver and Knight, 2015).

Despite the emphasis on cost effectiveness as a key driver for shifting to the cloud (ICT.govt.nz, 2018), the NDHA experience highlighted negative cost implications, at least for the short term, due to accounting practices. In-house IT infrastructure is funded from capital expenditure, whereas the use of cloud services is supported by operating budgets. Therefore it may appear that costs are increasing rather than decreasing. If the key stakeholders involved (e.g. management, funding bodies) are not aware of this, there may be significant risks posed to maintaining services provision at existing levels. Conclusions from this research pointed to the need for archivists to articulate preservation issues strategically in order to cast short-term disadvantages in terms of long term benefits. Also highlighted was the need to clearly differentiate the requirements of cultural heritage institutions from those of everyday office environments (e.g. in terms of data quantity, longevity required and spikes in activity level) in order to negotiate appropriate service levels with vendors (Oliver and Knight, 2015).

Choosing a trusted cloud service for digital preservation

When switching from in-house to cloud services, or from one cloud service provider (CSP) to another, users rarely consider the issue of whether their data, documents or records will be preserved for the long term, remaining accurate and authentic. Usually, they are focused on the daily business and availability of the service. When choosing between different cloud service providers users will assess the essential characteristics of the cloud services, for example whether a service offers on-demand, elastic change of the amount of computing resources available to the user, or the usage of the resources can be precisely measured. They will also consider the type of a service being offered, Infrastructure-as-a-Service (IaaS), Platform-as-a-Service (PaaS), or Software-as-a-Service (SaaS), as well as the pricing model. However, those intending to use cloud services not only for storage but also for long-term preservation should evaluate the chosen CSP on a different level. From the archival, long-term preservation perspective, the service being offered should be thoroughly investigated against ten different categories: (1) general information about the service; (2) governance; (3) compliance; (4) trust; (5) architecture; (6) identity and access management; (7) software isolation; (8) data protection; (9) availability; and (10) incident response (Stančić, Bursic and Al-Hariri, 2015).

These categories are explained below using the example of the IaaS model.

1. General information about the service

General information relates to the basic questions about the CSP and to three specific areas: storage, service, and networks (Rackspace, 2017). Users should investigate what technologies are being used and how the implemented storage, servers, networks and technology affect the security and privacy of the system.

2. Governance

Governance is the key factor in assuring security over data produced by a company. In this category, users should examine how they can verify the integrity of the data stored by a CSP and how they can monitor the security of their data. Potential users should examine how the CSP ensures that the data from different users are kept separate in a multi-tenant system on the one hand, and on the other, that the client's data is not shared with unauthorised employees, i.e. those not responsible for a certain task. Finally, the usage of audit mechanisms and enforcement of policies should be assessed.

3. Compliance

For a company considering IaaS it is important to be aware of which jurisdiction the CSP is governed by, where, geographically, the data is stored, and whether any part of the service is subcontracted. Along with those critical issues, it is also important to verify whether the service being considered is compliant with relevant standards, such as ANSI/TIA-942 Quality standard for data centres (TIA-942.org, n.d.), ISO 27001:2013 Information security management systems (International Organization for Standardization (ISO), 2013), and ISO 9001:2015 – Quality Management (International Organization for Standardization (ISO), 2015).

4. Trust

This category addresses the fundamental grounds for judging the trust-worthiness of a CSP. It is important to find out whether the CSP implements risk management systems – the technical and physical measures of protection that secure service from unauthorised access, usage, discovery, interruption, alteration and destruction of data. For example, one should ask what kind of physical and logical security is set up for virtual servers and applications against attacks like DoS (Denial of Service) or DDoS (Distributed DoS).

Another important issue in the context of trust deals with the ownership of the data given to the custody of the CSP as well as that of the metadata generated by the CSP about preservation actions (e.g. who owns the technical metadata about the conversion or migration process that are needed for judging the authenticity of a record). Existence of the certificates of compliance with the trust-related standards such as ISO 14721:2012 Open archival information system (OAIS) (International Organization for Standardization (ISO), 2012), ISO 16363:2012 Audit and certification of trustworthy digital repositories (International Organization for Standardization (ISO), 2012), are also important.

5. Architecture

Since the hardware and software architecture used to deliver cloud services can vary significantly, the actual set-up can have repercussions for security. Therefore, it must be investigated what type of architectural solutions the CSP has implemented, e.g. measures of protection against attack on hypervisor, virtual machine monitor, images, proprietary code, client (on user's computer) and server. It is also important to learn whether the process of virtual machine images management is used or not. By knowing this, the users can understand whether the processes of creation, storage and use of virtual machines are governed, i.e. procedures exist and are documented.

6. Identity and access management

Data sensitivity and privacy of information have always been areas of concern for organizations. The identity proofing and authentication (see also Chapter 7: Authentication) aspects of identity management entail the use, maintenance and protection of personally identifiable information (PII) collected from users. The data collected by the provider of the purchased service include details about the accounts of consumers, customer-related activities, meter and charge for consumption of resources, logs and audit trails, and other metadata that are generated and accumulated within the cloud environment, data of an organization's initiatives (e.g. the activity level or projected growth of the company), as well as metadata generated by the CSP. In the wrong hands, the loss of these data can be damaging to the client's business. All of the above-mentioned data – ancillary data – should be protected and potential users given assurance of this protection.

7. Software isolation

In order to achieve the flexibility of on-demand services, cloud service providers have to use high degrees of multi-tenancy over a large number of platforms. The multi-tenancy in an IaaS cloud computing environment is typically done by multiplexing the execution of virtual machines from potentially different consumers on the same physical server. Multi-tenancy in virtual machine-based cloud infrastructure, together with the way physical resources are shared among the guest virtual machines, give rise to new sources of threat, for example the man-in-the-middle attack. Therefore, it is important to assess how the service prevents these kinds of threats.

8. Data protection

Data protection should be applied to data-at-rest, data-in-transit and data-in-use. The data-at-rest may be protected by an encryption mechanism, while the data-in-transit may be much harder to encrypt. A fully homomorphic encryption scheme allows data to be processed without being decrypted. Sharma (2013) explains that the aim of homomorphic cryptography is to ensure privacy of data in communication, storage or use by processes that use mechanisms similar to conventional cryptography, but with added capabilities of computing over encrypted data, searching encrypted data, etc. Thus, homomorphism makes secure delegation of computation to a third party possible. It can help preserve customer privacy while outsourcing various kinds of computation to the cloud, not just storage (Sharma 2013). Making sure that the data stays computationally accurate is as important as the preservation of its integrity. The issue of data remanence – the residual representation of data that has been at some point nominally erased or removed – should also be addressed by checking if the CSP applies any media sanitisation techniques.

Generally, encryption of data-at-rest is not recommended for data that is being managed in a long-term archival preservation system, due to the risks associated with key management over the long term. If keys are lost or if the ability or technology to manage the keys is not actively maintained over the long term, then all access to the data will be forever lost. This risk has to be assessed against countervailing security risks associated with storing unencrypted data in network-accessible storage, even when the storage has state of the art perimeter security and firewalls, as determined and professional hackers may be able to breach the perimeter security. One compromise might be to encrypt 'at rest' only the most highly sensitive data, while keeping an entirely offline unencrypted copy of that data in secure vault storage in the archival repository (i.e. not in the cloud) to guard against the risk of total loss of data in the event of some future malfunctioning of the encryption key management regime. The downside of this approach, however, is then the need to manage and synchronise duplicate digital preservation regimes for the preservation treatments of the two different sets of instances of the data, one encrypted and one decrypted.

It should also be kept in mind that the CSP can be located in one country and its data centre(s) in another. Therefore, the possible implications this situation has on the data being stored and backed up for disaster recovery purposes has to be clearly understood. The information on the geographic location(s) where the data are stored and backed up can result in an increase or decrease of trust regarding the security of an organization's records. Furthermore, the laws and regulations of the country where the records are being stored need to be understood in case of a legal action or loss and recovery of data.

9. Availability

Users should investigate whether the CSP guarantees service availability in case a court orders a seizure of equipment, because, in multi-tenant systems, the data, documents and records from more than one customer will be stored in the same physical equipment. Also, the provider can encounter facility damage or loss due to natural disasters or human-influenced incidents, or it can go out of business or bankrupt, or have other kinds of financial difficulties. Continuity of customer access to data in such circumstances is vital and must be legally guaranteed.

Regardless, every organization considering a cloud service should have a contingency plan. If the organization relies on IaaS for data storage and processing, such a plan should have a business continuity solution for prolonged or permanent service disruptions, especially with mission critical operations, until restoration of the service.

10. Incident response

Incident response involves an organized method for dealing with the consequences of an attack against the security of a computer system, equipment failure or other kinds of service provision disruption. The CSP's role is vital in performing incident response activities, including incident verification, determination of the scope of the incident and assets affected, attack or failure analysis, containment, data collection and preservation, problem remediation, and service restoration. Each layer in a cloud application stack generates event logs. These data are accessible and under the control of the CSP. One should investigate the existence of an incident response plan as well as whether the CSP keeps a forensic copy of incident data for legal proceedings or in case it is needed by the client. Aiming for business transparency, the incident response plan should also include the reporting phase in the course of which the customers will be informed about the incident and the way the CSP resolved it.

The issues indicated in the above ten categories sometimes overlap across categories, for example the issues addressing multi-tenancy or compliancy-related issues, legal aspects or security. The reason is the multi-layered nature of the risks and the overarching impact of a negative event.

The checklist developed by ITrust, available in English and Spanish (Stančić, Bursic and Al-Hariri, 2016a, 2016b), could be used to provide sufficient information on a CSP IaaS service. It allows one to assess the service and determine whether it operates in a responsible, reliable, accurate, secure, transparent and trustworthy way, as well as whether it considers privacy issues, duty to remember (i.e. digital preservation) and the right to be forgotten (i.e. safe deletion). The developed checklist could also be used by the CSPs to prepare themselves to be assessed on its basis and to make sure that they cover all aspects that are relevant to the long-term preservation of records in the cloud.

Preservation as a Service for Trust (PaaST)

The objective of preserving digital information over considerable time runs against the high probability that the means of keeping the information intact and accessible will become ineffective or even unavailable in relatively short order. Digital preservation also confronts an obverse tension in that the longer the technologies used for preservation remain viable, the greater the likelihood that they will pose barriers to more recent tools which people would prefer to use to access and exploit the information. These tensions are compounded when digital preservation is accomplished by contracting with cloud service providers because, generally, those who commit to contracts with CSPs will not control and often not know what technologies they use. In this context, digital preservation is a 'black box' process, in that the responsible parties cannot directly observe what goes on. This phenomenon is, however, not limited to the cloud or to contracted services. The dimensions of the black box are hardware, software and time. Even when digital preservation is performed in-house, the responsible parties cannot predict what technologies will be available or effective for preservation in the future. The only certainty is that technology will continue to change.

In the physical sciences, the difficulties posed by black box processes are surmounted by varying the inputs and observing the consequent changes in outputs. In software development, the black box model is used in requirements testing, where the specifics of how software programs work are irrelevant. For any requirement, what matters is that the process produces the desired outcome from the specified input. This model can be applied to digital preservation, where the input is the object we wish to preserve and, given that it is not a persistent physical object but a configuration of bits, the output is a reproduction of the input. What matters are not the internal components of the process used in preservation, but whether the output faithfully reproduces the input. This is a core concept underlying the ITrust Preservation as a Service for Trust (PaaST) project (Thibodeau, 2018).

A second, closely related core concept is that digital preservation must be verifiable. As explained below, this requires specifying what it is about the information being preserved that must remain invariant over time and in the face of changes in technology.

The PaaST project focused on articulating requirements for digital preservation that would not only be appropriate for preservation in the cloud, but also be applicable to other scenarios, including in-house preservation, a combination of in-house and contracted capabilities and even multiple contracts with various providers offering different services. Parallel development of a domain model of preservation using the Unified Modeling Language (UML) (Object Management Group, 2017) fostered greater precision and consistency in articulating the requirements (hereinafter, terms that correspond to classes or other elements of the domain model are in italics.) Consistent with the black box approach, the requirements and the domain model are neutral with respect to the technologies used for implementation. Technical neutrality is essential. Requirements for digital preservation must be immutable, regardless of changes in the available means of implementing them. Otherwise, one could only assert that information had been carried across time, not that it had been preserved.

In order to accommodate both flexibility in assigning responsibilities and inevitable changes in technology over time, PaaST introduces the concept of a *preservation environment*, rather than using the expression archival information system. A *preservation environment* is an implementation of PaaST requirements, including the set of objects that are preserved under those rules, and a comprehensive body of preservation management information describing the objects as well as the actions taken with respect to them, together with the technological infrastructures and tools used. A *preservation environment* may consist of several, independent systems or applications, used either simultaneously or successively, where each one constitutes a *local preservation environment*. For example, an archives might enter into a contract for digital preservation where the contractor stores the records to be preserved and performs all preservation and access functions, but the archives itself maintains an online database covering all of its holdings, both analogue and digital, so that researchers have a single place where they can go to discover any and all records of interest. The database and the contractor's system would have to be interoperable so that data about digital records in the database are complete and accurate. In this case, the preservation environment would include both the in-house database and the contractor's system.

Classifying digital objects for preservation

Potential candidates for preservation are digitally encoded *intellectual entities*, where an *intellectual entity* is defined as an object that is capable of conveying information. There are no *a priori* restrictions on the kinds of *intellectual entities* that could be preserved under the PaaST requirements. An *intellectual entity* could be a text, photograph, map, music or anything else that is meaningful to persons. *Intellectual entities* also include things that are meant to be processed on computers, such as software programs, databases, geographic information systems, data from environmental sensors, etc. Accordingly, the domain model classifies *intellectual entities* in two main categories, depending on whether they are intended to be read by humans or machines. Preservation of human- and machine-readable objects differs in what is involved in their reproduction or instantiation. Reproducing a *machine-readable intellectual entity* entails loading it in a *runtime version* on an appropriate computing platform. A *human-readable intellectual entity* must also be loaded as a *runtime version;* then it must be output in a *rendering* suitable for human use.

Intellectual entity is a broad, general concept. To be instantiated, *intellectual entity* must be enhanced with additional specifications. The PaaST domain model includes two distinct facets for adding such specifications. The first provides additional details on what the *intellectual entity* is in itself through more specific subtypes of *machine-readable* and *human-readable intellectual entities*, such as software, database, text, photograph, etc. The requirements enable these subtypes to be further refined at lower levels to provide whatever types and specificity are needed in a particular *preservation environment*. The second path for specifying an *intellectual entity* is describing how it is represented in bits. A digital representation of an *intellectual entity* is called a *binary encoding*. A *binary encoding* has two types of parts. One, its *digital components*, specifies how it is stored in strings of bits. The other, *manifestation*, indicates how it is reproduced in *runtime versions* and *renderings*. An *intellectual entity* can have more than one *binary encoding;* for example, a textual document could be created as a word-processing file but be output in HTML for publishing on the web or exported in PDF for distribution. Each of these versions constitutes a different *binary encoding* of the same document.

Digital preservation is achieved only by reproduction. Even if the bits are stored perfectly, unless it is possible to load the files correctly on a computer and, in the case of human-readable objects, to output the *intellectual object* in an appropriate form, the object cannot be said to be preserved. Thus, every *binary encoding* must include at least two types of *digital components*: the first type is *content component*, which holds the specific content of the *intellectual entity*, and the second is *software component*, which is software suitable for producing the appropriate *runtime versions* and *renderings*. A *binary encoding* could include a third type of *digital component*, an *instantiation component* that contains data that the software applies in manifesting the *intellectual entity*, such as a font library, style sheet, data model or schema. A single *digital component* could be an element in many *intellectual entities*. For example, an XML schema could apply to hundreds or even thousands of textual documents, and the same piece of software could be used to reproduce unlimited numbers of objects. Moreover, a bit string could be a different type of *digital component* in *binary encodings* of different *intellectual entities*. For example, an XML schema is an *instantiation component* of the documents that implement it, but it could be managed as a distinct *intellectual entity* in its own right. In such a case, the schema would be the *content component*. The particular role of a given bit string in a *binary encoding* is clarified by means of a *component description*.

For example, in many sectors of industry, commerce, government and science there are data standards issued in the form of XML schemas. Whenever records that implement such standards are preserved, the relevant schema would be needed as an *implementation component* for each of the records. Moreover, such standards often undergo successive versions and it might be determined that the version used be preserved in order to enable understanding of changes in what data was considered important or useful in a given sector over time. In such cases, the standard would be the *intellectual object* being preserved and the XML schema would be the *content component* of that object (for examples, see XML Standards Library at http://schemas.liquid-technologies.com/).

An *intellectual entity* may also have multiple *manifestations*. Each specification of a different form or report that can be output from a database, for example, defines a different type of *manifestation* of the database and, when there are user selected options, such as the time period or geographical coverage of a report, each selection results in a different *manifestation*. A *manifestation description* identifies which *digital components* are used in a particular *manifestation* and describes how they are processed to generate the appropriate *runtime version* or *rendering*.

The PaaST requirements are applicable both to *intellectual entities* that are single *items* and to *collections* of *items*, such as *records series, multivolume publications* and *periodicals*. *Collections* may be nested, such as articles in an issue of a journal, issues in a volume of the journal and successive volumes.

An *intellectual entity* that is selected for preservation is called a *preservation target*. Any *intellectual entity* may be designated as a *preservation target*. A *preservation target* is distinguished from an *intellectual entity* not selected for preservation in that some of the *features* – attributes or operations – of a *preservation target* must be qualified explicitly as *permanent features*. A *permanent feature* is one that should remain invariant regardless of changes in *binary encodings* of the preservation target, in technologies used to accomplish preservation, or in responsibilities for control or execution of preservation. In principle, any feature of an *intellectual object* could be designated as permanent. The designation of *permanent features* can vary according to the purpose of preservation or the policies or standards applied. For example, preservation of scientific data for continuing research use, including potential repurposing, could entail identification of different *permanent features* than in the case where the data were preserved as records of an individual scientist or research institute.

For example, a significant amount of observational data in the earth sciences is initially organized based on the instrument or observatory where the data was collected; however, rather than maintain successive datasets from a particular source as a separate time series, scientific data centres frequently merge sets of similar data from multiple sources to provide broader geographic, even global, coverage which is better suited to scientific research. The resultant databases are usually organized by data type rather than source. If, however, the data were to be preserved as part of the records of an observatory or other creator, then its provenance should be respected by keeping it separate from data from other creators and in the structure originally imposed on it.

Decisions about what features of a *preservation target* should be permanent should make it possible to generate a *manifestation* of the *preservation target* that is capable of conveying the same information as the initial *preservation target*. Three criteria for identifying *permanent features* support this objective:

- **Uniqueness**: *permanent features* should differentiate a *preservation target* from any other. For example, if several editions of a book originally published in hard copy were scanned and preserved, each edition would constitute a distinct preservation target and the binary encodings of each edition should include all those elements of content and appearance which distinguish it from other editions.
- **Instantiation**: the *permanent features* should support realisation of the characteristics that a *preservation target* should have when manifested. For example, it is possible to depict the visible properties of a physical object precisely and completely using either traditional engineering drawings or a 3D computer model; however, if display of the computer model included the ability to rotate it through a 360° solid angle, the information it is capable of conveying could be substantially diminished if it were converted to a set of 2D drawings. The ability to rotate the model then would be a permanent feature of the model.
- **Integrity**: *permanent features* should specify the elements that make up and are necessary to reproduce a *preservation target*, as well as their interrelationships. For example, a natural language document might contain heterogeneous types of content, such as photographs, figures or

tables. Each of these elements must be preserved. The correct placement of each element in the document and its relationship to specific elements of the text, such as captions and footnotes, are also integrity features.

These are not exclusive categories. The same feature may satisfy more than one criterion.

Specification of *permanent features* provides a way around the black box in digital preservation. By stipulating an equivalency relationship between the *permanent features* of the *preservation target* ingested into a *preservation environment* and any subsequent representation or *manifestation* of that target, it establishes an empirical basis for verifying if a *preservation target* is preserved successfully.

Verifying that *permanent features* remain unchanged requires defining where and how they are expressed. *Permanent features* may be expressed in *digital components, manifestations,* or both. A *permanent feature expression* that details how the feature is embodied and how it can be tested is part of either the *component description* or the *manifestation description,* depending on where the feature is expressed.

In many, especially complex cases, determining what is specifically required to verify preservation of a *permanent feature* will involve an element of judgement. In the example of a 3D model given above, information that establishes that the *software components* in a *binary encoding support rotation of the display* might be deemed sufficient verification that this feature is preserved. This is not the case for a geographic information system, where the ability of users to select arbitrarily different data elements from different layers and to vary the way they are displayed might require user interaction for verification.

Judging the success of preservation obviously requires that *permanent feature expressions* be verifiable. *Permanent feature expression,* then, should indicate the means of verification. The way a feature is verified also will depend on its location. The expression of *permanent features* in *digital components* or *runtime versions* may be verifiable using automated tools, but expression in a *rendering* may require human observation. If the expression can be verified by an automated tool, the tool should be identified in the description of the expression of the feature. If verification is by human inspection, the *permanent feature expression* should indicate whether passive observation of a *rendering* is sufficient or specify any required interaction.

A *permanent feature* that is an attribute of the *preservation target* has three facets that should be considered in describing the expression of the *feature*: its existence, its value and the manner in which it is expressed. In the case of e-mail, for example, every message should include as *permanent features* the attributes of sender and addressee but might not include any copy because CCs and BCCs may not exist. Their designation as *permanent features* is contingent on whether they exist in individual messages. The values of some permanent attributes of e-mail can be specified *a priori* and those values should be preserved in every instance. In an individual's e-mail account, every outgoing message should identify that individual as the sender and the same individual should be either the addressee or a recipient of a copy of every incoming message. The identifiers of any other addressees or copy recipients should be preserved even though they cannot be specified in advance.

The way an attribute is expressed can be crucial in the information conveyed by an object. Changing the colour space of a digital image, for example, could entail loss of information. Deciding whether and what characteristics of *renderings* should be identified as *permanent features* is another judgement call.

When a *permanent feature* is an operation of the *preservation target*, the function the operation performs and any required return value or post-condition should be considered in describing the expression of the *feature*. Essential return values for a 3D model, for example, include appropriately rendered shape factors, such as curvature and compactness, and the appropriate transformation of such features as the model is rotated. A post-condition is a predicate that must be true after an operation is performed. A post-condition for the rendering of a textual document, for example, would be that the rendering display appropriately content that was distinguished from other text by features such as colour, type size or italics.

The *permanent features* of a *preservation target* should be specified no later than when the target is initially ingested into a *preservation environment*. These specifications, called *benchmark values*, should be ascertained either from information about the *preservation target* or examination of the initial *binary encoding(s)* that represent it, or both. When *benchmark values* are specified in both sources, they should be compared to ensure consistency. The success of preserving a *preservation target* is evaluated by comparing the *benchmark values* of *permanent features* with the expression of those *features* in *digital components* and *manifestations* thereafter. The *permanent features* in all subsequent reproductions of the *preservation target* and in any new *binary encoding* properly should conform to their *benchmark values*.

An *intellectual entity* can have another role in a *preservation environment*. It can help persons to understand or make valid use of *preservation targets*. In this role, an *intellectual entity* is called *heuristic information*. *Heuristic information* is a subtype of 'representation information', as defined in the OAIS standard (ISO, 2012). *Heuristic information* is distinguished from other *intellectual entities* not by content or form, but by its relationship to *preservation targets*. *Heuristic information* is especially important in preservation because the context in which a *preservation target* is retrieved and used differs – increasingly with the passage of time – from that in which it was created and used originally. While the ability to repeat the results of experiments is crucial in science, the conduct of historical research in archives practically never involves repeating the actions in which preserved records were created. In digital preservation, differences stemming from the context of use are exacerbated by changes in the technology needed to retrieve, use and even to encode *preservation targets*. The evolution of natural language and changes in other means of communication can also impact the interpretation of a *preservation target*. The PaaST requirements and domain model support specifying how an instance of *heuristic information* clarifies a *preservation target*; that is, whether it applies at the level of the *intellectual entity* or to one or more of its elements; moreover, this specification is customisable in different environments.

Because *heuristic information* is qualified as such not by its intrinsic characteristics but by its relationship to one or more *preservation targets*, an *intellectual entity* could be both a *preservation target* in its own right and *heuristic information* regarding another *preservation target*. For example, the data model is essential for instantiating a database (instantiation component), but it is also important to enable people to understand the content and structure of the database (*heuristic information*). Items of *heuristic information* that were produced in the same context by the same creator often should be designated as *preservation targets* even when the motivation for preserving them derives entirely from their contribution to understanding related *preservation targets*.

The preceding paragraphs have described the 'what' of digital preservation: information objects and their digital encodings and the way they are classified and described for preservation in a *preservation environment*. The next section describes 'how' preservation is accomplished via the PaaST requirements.

Preservation actions

Digital preservation is accomplished in a series of steps or workflow. The particular steps, their sequence and timing vary according to policies and procedures in effect and the division of responsibilities in different *preservation environments*. Some institutions require that *preservation targets* in various formats be converted to a canonical or standard format as part of the ingest process. Others may perform format migrations only when the received formats become obsolete. Others may use emulators rather than changing received formats. To accommodate these and other variations in what is done for preservation and under what conditions preservation actions are performed, the PaaST requirements are organized in groups of related activities, called services, that can be invoked as needed in accordance with policy; moreover, not all requirements within a service need be implemented – individual requirements can be invoked as appropriate in each situation.

In the experience of the National Archives of the United States, for example, as much as 30% of accessions of digital records contained significant discrepancies between the records creators' descriptions of the records transferred and the digital files actually received. The occurrence of such problems, however, diminished substantially, even to zero, in the case of records creators who regularly and frequently transferred records from the same systems or series (Henry and Southerly, 1999). When processing accessions in such cases, an archives would not need to use as many of the capabilities for inspecting transfers provided by PaaST requirements as it would in reviewing initial transfers from records creators.

PaaST requirements also enable policymakers to define additional requirements to add greater specificity appropriate not only to relevant policies but also to the types of intellectual entities being preserved. Finally, in support of customisation, PaaST includes a service for defining and implementing preservation rules that specify under what circumstances preservation actions are performed, what are acceptable outcomes and how problems should be addressed.

The requirements are organized in three main groups: preservation action capabilities, information management capabilities and preservation management capabilities. Preservation action capabilities encompass those actions which accomplish the preservation of *preservation targets*. Information management capabilities enable creation, updating, maintenance, quality control and use of the data and information needed to carry out, manage and evaluate preservation. Preservation management capabilities enable assessment of whether preservation actions have been carried out properly, whether the objects used in digital preservation are what they should be and, crucially, whether *preservation targets* have been preserved successfully and whether policy objectives have been met.

Preservation action capabilities execute the functions that accomplish digital preservation. These include: bringing *preservation targets* into and under the control of a *preservation environment*; ensuring *digital components* are stored in a way that guarantees their integrity and accessibility; implementing changes in *preservation targets* or in the technology needed to operate on and provide access to them; and providing to authorised parties access to information about *preservation targets*, copies of the *digital components* of *preservation targets* and access to *manifestations*. Preservation action capabilities rely on both information and preservation management capabilities.

Information management capabilities support creating and managing *preservation management information* about objects, actions and actors. These capabilities include organizing, managing and reporting information and data. There are five main classes of *preservation management information*: (1) *preservation target data* that describe *preservation targets* or any of their specialisations, elements or their subclasses; (2) *digital type registry* describing generic properties of types of *digital components*, such as the formats of data files, the types of data that a software program operates on, the way elements of an *instantiation component*, such as a schema or style sheet, are expressed in *content components*, et al.; (3) *preservation action data* that describe *preservation actions* performed, the parties and *preservation targets* involved and the results or outcomes of the action, including any problems encountered and their resolution; (4) *preservation rules* which are business rules that govern execution of one or more *preservation actions* and impacts one or more *preservation targets*; and (5) *actor* identifying an individual who is authorised to or does participate in carrying out a *preservation action*.

Information management capabilities support organizing information into classes and sets. A class is a group of objects all of which have at least one feature in common. A class may have subclasses. Every subclass inherits all the features of the superclass. For example, all subclasses of textual document, such as report and letter, inherit the property that content is primarily printable natural language. A set is a group of objects demarcated by the association among the members. Members of a set can belong to multiple classes and thus may not have any common feature. A set may have subsets, but the subsets do not necessarily inherit any feature of the superset other than the attribute or attributes that determine membership in the set. For example, a website may comprise a set of heterogeneous objects, such as text, photographs and audio, where the only common property is that they are all parts of the site. Capabilities for managing a class or set of objects encompass defining the group and implementing it in the data management system. They do not address individual members of an aggregate. Class and set management facilitate implementing different preservation policies and fine tuning a *preservation environment* to the types of *intellectual entities* being preserved and their technical characteristics. For example, a preservation policy that stipulates standard-isation of file formats would need to be implemented by defining a class, and probably a hierarchical set of classes, encompassing all formats that should be converted to the same canonical format. In contrast, implementing a policy that addressed format obsolescence by using operating system emulation would entail defining the set of software programs that execute properly under a particular operating system version.

Preservation management capabilities include defining and enforcing *preservation rules* and capturing data about their implementation, assessing the status of preservation efforts and verifying the success of the preservation. A preservation assessment involves inspecting *preservation management information* or *digital components,* comparing related *preservation management data,* or comparing *preservation management data* with the *digital components* or realisations of the *manifestations* they describe. Inspection of a *preservation target* would include examining management data about the target itself and also its *permanent features, binary encodings, component descriptions, manifestation descriptions, permanent feature expressions* and *manifestations.* The inspection should aim at determining if all the objects needed to preserve the *preservation target are present and adequately and appropriately specified; if associations among objects are defined and appropriate; and if related features in different objects are consistent.*

For example, if the *preservation target* were a relational database, every table in the database should be embodied in a *content component* in storage and described in a *component description* that corresponds to the data in storage; the data elements in each table should be defined in a data model, which is a type of *instantiation component;* this component should also exist in storage; the data model should also specify parent/child relationships between tables and the specified primary and foreign keys should be data elements in the related tables; each parent/child relationship would be a *permanent feature* of the database and should be specified in a *permanent feature expression;* every *binary encoding* of the database should include as a *software component* the database management system necessary to load and operate on the database. A preservation assessment of the database would need to verify each of these conditions, as well as many others that are necessary to the preservation of a relational database.

Verification determines whether *preservation targets* have been preserved successfully and also whether *heuristic information* does clarify the *preservation target* or *targets* with which it is associated. Verifying preservation entails verifying that *preservation targets* can be instantiated. If a *preservation target* cannot be instantiated, its preservation is, to say the least, incomplete. Verification requirements also address the preservation of *preservation collections.* Preservation of the *collection* entails preserving the *items* that are its members and the relationships among them. Verifying preservation of a series of records, for example, would include determining whether the files described in the *preservation target* for the series were present in the *preservation environment* and whether the files could be arranged in accordance with the order described as a permanent feature of the series, with similar tests being performed for the records in each file.

Requirements for verifying *heuristic information* include determining that the *preservation target(s)* with which it is associated exist and that the association is appropriate. This verification could be done by automated or human methods. The generic requirements for verifying that a human-readable *preservation target* can be instantiated also apply to *heuristic information*.

Archival preservation

PaaST requirements are articulated to enable preservation of practically any type of digital information for as wide a variety of objectives and purposes as possible, but the requirements encompass a special case, archival preservation; that is, the preservation of records. Archival preservation extends the generic data model with specialisations. It does not require other additional classes. For example, a *record* is a type of *item* and a *record aggregate* is a type of *collection*. *Records* and *record aggregates* that are preserved are specialisations of *preservation target*. Similarly, the specific features that are essential to preserving preservation targets as records are *archival permanent features*; that is, specialisations of *permanent feature*. As in the general case, PaaST requirements allow the particulars of archival preservation to be fine-tuned to different situations. For example, the *record aggregate* class can be used to specify a traditional hierarchical system of records organizations, but the same structure can also be used for more complex situations, such as the Australian series system. Furthermore, PaaST requirements support preservation of the provenancial context of records by supporting not only the preservation of *records* and *record aggregates*, but also *heuristic information* that elucidates the relationships of the *records* to their creators, the activities in which the creators used them and also the interrelationships among *records*. As in general, *heuristic information* that clarifies the archival characteristics of records and which was generated by the records creator should be included in the aggregate of the records of that creator.

Heuristic information that contributes to understanding *intellectual entities* as *records* often comes from sources other than the records creators; for example, from works of history or descriptions created by the archives that preserves the records. While such documents cannot be considered to be parts of a *record aggregate*, even at the highest level, PaaST provides a persistent basis for associating third-party heuristic information with a collection in the class, *preservation network*. A *preservation network* is a set of objects related to a *preservation target*, including its *binary encodings, heuristic information* that supports its comprehension and use, other *preservation management information* about it and any other *preservation targets* associated with the *preservation target* that is the focus of the network, for example related *records* that are parts of different archival fonds. A *preservation network* might be articulated, for example, to define a corpus of materials, both records and heuristics information, from multiple sources, related to a significant historical event, development or person. *Preservation networks* can also be defined for *preservation targets* that are not preserved as *records*. For example, a dataset preserved for use in scientific research could be associated with publications that used the data in a *preservation network*.

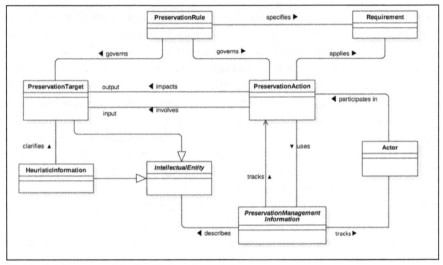

Figure 9.1 *Overview of the PaaST domain model*

PaaST in a nutshell

Figure 9.1 presents an overview of the main classes of objects in the PaaST domain model and their relationships in the form of a UML class diagram. The two central classes in terms of their importance for digital preservation are *preservation target*, what is preserved, and *preservation action*, what is done to preserve *preservation targets*. A *preservation target*, a subclass of *intellectual entity*, is involved as input in every preservation action and every *preservation action* impacts at least one *preservation target* as output. A *preservation action* applies one or more *requirements*. Which *requirements* are applied in a given action is specified in a *preservation rule* that also governs the conditions under which the actions are taken and the *preservation targets* that are involved as input or output. Although not shown in Figure 9.1, *preservation rules* also specify the *actors* who are allowed or required to participate in *preservation actions* as well as the mode of their participation. *Preservation actions* use *preservation management information*, for example, to identify the *binary encodings* associated with a *preservation target*. *Preservation actions* also generate *preservation management information* that tracks the actions performed and their impacts on *preservation targets*. Another subclass of *intellectual entity*, *heuristic information,* clarifies preservation targets for people interested in them.

PaaST defines a comprehensive set of functional requirements and a parallel domain model that support preservation of digital information regardless of the technologies used or who uses them. The requirements are intended to enable authentic digital preservation in the cloud, but the requirements are valid in other scenarios as well, including in-house preservation and situations where digital preservation includes both in-house and contracted services. Moreover, the PaaST approach is applicable to cases that include:

- Heterogeneity in the types of information objects being preserved
- Variety in applicable directives, such as laws, regulations, standards, policies, business rules, and contractual agreements, including varying conditions of ownership, access, use, and exploitation
- Variations in institutional arrangements and relationships between or among the parties involved
- As wide a spectrum of circumstances as possible from best practices to worst cases.

The PaaST requirements and domain model enable adaptation by allowing for flexibility in the assignment of responsibilities, selective implementation of requirements, articulation of additional requirements, extension and adaptation of the domain model, variation in the specification of what is required to identify as an information object in accordance with different purposes of preservation and different characteristics of the objects being preserved.

Other considerations: cloud-enabled digital preservation and access for records not transferred to archives and 'dark' repositories as-a-service

The ITrust project also considered some other issues associated with the shift towards the use of internet-based third parties for digital preservation. One issue that is common with government records is that only a small proportion of public records that require long-term preservation ever get formally transferred to the control of a government archival institution. Commonly, a much larger volume of digital records, those deemed to require long-term temporary retention (e.g. longer than ten years) but not requiring permanent retention, will remain in the control and custody of the creating agency or its successor. Because these records will very likely outlive the native software application in which they were created and initially managed, they will require digital preservation intervention and management. As such skills are unlikely to be possessed by the creating or controlling agency, accessing purchasing arrangements (which may be brokered by the archival institution on behalf of its parent government) to enable the agencies in question to pay for digital preservation services from a trusted third party may be an attractive option.

Legal responsibility for preserving records in this scenario usually rests with the records creating or controlling agency, rather than an archival authority, regardless of whether or not the agency recognises value/utility in the records for its ongoing business operations. Often, the preservation obligation may be viewed as nothing more than an onerous and unwelcome compliance requirement. The challenge here, therefore, is that value-added, third-party preservation services are likely to be noticeably more expensive than standard cloud data storage services, where no long-term data preservation treatments are provided. Will the custodial agencies in question be prepared to pay the necessary premiums to ensure the longevity of the digital records that they have responsibility for? What factors might either predispose or encourage creating agencies to make adequate investments in the longevity of their valuable, long-term digital records?

Another variable from jurisdiction to jurisdiction is the extent to which archival authorities are permitted, mandated, resourced and/or inclined to take a leadership role in enabling the preservation of digital records that they will never take custody of. The issue is both significant in terms of the legal and evidential implications associated with the potential loss of vital records and huge in terms of the volume of records that require long-term preservation. Whole-of-jurisdiction leadership is needed to put in place suitable and sustainable solutions, but will archival authorities wish to exercise that leadership and, if so, will the custodial agencies take advantage of the solutions made available to them?

Related to the above is the issue of whether government archives have a leadership role to play in ensuring that the access systems that are put in place for the holdings in their institutional repositories can be extended to encompass distributed holdings of digital public records in the custody of government agencies. Two key research questions were as follows:

- How can government make digital public records that are kept in the creating agency's custody available in a trustworthy and user-friendly manner?
- How can government deal with the privacy and ethical concerns that come with making public records available online?

There were two main factors considered in this study:

- The technical dimension: the practical elements. The actual technology for enabling access and discovery. What kind of system one will use to make records available and how one is going to do it.
- Cultural elements. There are cultural barriers. It can be difficult to want to give up control of information because one has the best intentions and wants to keep it safe and secure. How does one get custodians to open up? How does one get governments to take open government seriously?

So, while government archives may have obligations and responsibilities to provide access to digital public records outside of their custody, one has to consider the ethics of doing so:

- Openness is essential to good government and in an environment where information is withheld, there will be inevitable tensions and mistrust. The people have a right to know how their taxes are being collected and spent. Thus, the presumption ought to be that government should make its records available to the public unless they can show good cause for why they should be withheld (for example, matters of national security).
- If government is to be open and searchable, it is ethical to conduct programmes to educate the public on how to use the resources available to them. New technologies for accessing public records constitute new opportunities to rethink traditional trade-offs between conflicting values such as privacy and transparency (Spelay, 2016).

Further research needs to consider the enormous amount of heterogeneous data and metadata that needs to be controlled and how to implement a system that is stable, scalable and sustainable enough to preserve record integrity and privacy while also providing user-friendly access to millions of people.

The need for archives to explore new business models raised questions about archival authorities providing a new type of service – 'dark' repositories (i.e. entirely offline, secure storage infrastructure for digital preservation masters) for trusted storage for external customers, including other archival institutions. As a first step towards exploring the feasibility of this, preliminary research to assess archival institutions' attitudes towards outsourcing and awareness of cybersecurity was undertaken. This study consisted of an online survey of archival institutions worldwide, asking about current and future digital preservation policies and awareness/understanding of 'dark archives' (Oliver, 2018).

The survey was e-mailed to 237 public and private archival institutions located in the United States of America, Europe, Australasia and Canada. The institutions ranged from local government, national and cultural to corporate (banking and company) archives. The response rate was low (21%), with most responses coming from the public sector, so generalisations are not possible, but findings certainly reflect our anecdotal knowledge of this sector. Sixty-five per cent of respondents judged their digital preservation policies to be average to poor. Interest in outsourcing digital preservation requirements was expressed, but perceived barriers to doing so were cost and security considerations. Further research, preferably involving interviews or focus groups, is necessary to fully investigate the feasibility of this new service model, but these early indications certainly suggest a very real willingness to entertain the notion of outsourcing storage responsibilities for digital archives. Developing a practical scenario specifying costs and service levels would be advantageous as a starting point for discussion (McLeod and Gormly, 2018).

A related question, that requires further research, is whether archival programmes might in the future be willing and able to source 'dark archival' services from private sector service providers. Questions arise though on how might such a service operate and, given the more labour intensive nature of offline storage and the additional manual handling involved, whether such a service would be affordable and demonstrably more secure than the online alternative.

Conclusion

The digital preservation research findings reported in this chapter are wide-ranging, exploring several new initiatives and approaches. The paradigm shift involved in outsourcing services and deployment of cloud computing necessitated the development of practical advice and tools to guide selection of service providers and the detailed articulation of a comprehensive new standard, PaaST. The concept of a preservation environment, core to PaaST, provides the flexibility necessary to achieve digital preservation objectives in today's challenging and complex technological environment. Nevertheless, questions remain, and this is why this chapter ends by highlighting areas for further research. There are several options emerging for archival institutions with regard to digital preservation and it is hoped that the research reported here will motivate more investigation and, ultimately, innovative practice.

References

Beagrie, C., Charlesworth, A. and Miller, P. (2014) *The National Archives Guidance on Cloud Storage and Digital Preservation.* 1st edn. The National Archives.

Duranti, L. and Preston, R. (2008) *Research on Permanent Authentic Records in*

Electronic Systems (InterPARES) 2: Experiential Interactive and Dynamic Records. Padova: Associazione Nazionale Archivistica Italiana.

Henry, L. J. and Southerly, T. (1999) Archivists and Statistical Literacy, *Of Significance: A Topical Journal of the Association of Public Data Users: Statistical Literacy,* **1** (1), 31–4.

ICT.govt.nz (2018) *Why Agencies Must Use Cloud Services.* https://www.ict.govt.nz/guidance-and-resources/using-cloud-services/ why-agencies-must-use-cloud-services/

International Organization for Standardization (ISO) (2012) *ISO 14721:2012 – Space Data and Information Transfer Systems – Open Archival Information System (OAIS) Reference Model.* https://www.iso.org/standard/57284.html

International Organization for Standardization (ISO) (2013) *ISO/IEC 27001:2013 – Information Technology – Security Techniques – Information Security Management Systems — Requirements.* https://www.iso.org/standard/54534.html

International Organization for Standardization (ISO) (2015) *ISO 9001 Quality Management.* https://www.iso.org/iso-9001-quality-management.html

McLeod, J. and Gormly, B. (2017) Using the Cloud for Records Storage: issues of trust, *Archival Science,* **17** (4), 349–70. https://doi.org/10.1007/s10502-017-9280-5

McLeod, J. and Gormly, B. (2018) Records Storage in the Cloud: are we modelling the cost?, *Archives and Manuscripts,* March, 1–19. https://doi.org/10.1080/01576895.2017.1409125

Object Management Group (2017) *About the Unified Modeling Language Specification Version 2.5.1.* https://www.omg.org/spec/UML/About-UML/

Oliver, G. (2018) *Dark Archives as a Service.* AA03, Final Report. InterPARES Trust. https://interparestrust.org/assets/public/dissemination/AA03FinalReport.pdf

Oliver, G. and Knight, S. (2015) Storage is a Strategic Issue: digital preservation in the cloud, *D-Lib Magazine,* **21** (3/4). https://doi.org/10.1045/march2015-oliver

Rackspace (2017) *Understanding the Cloud Computing Stack: SaaS, PaaS, IaaS.* https://support.rackspace.com/how-to/understanding-the-cloud-computing-stack-saas-paas-iaas/

Sharma, I. (2013) *Fully Homomorphic Encryption Scheme with Symmetric Keys.* Master's Thesis. Kota: Rajasthan Technical University. http://arxiv.org/ftp/arxiv/papers/1310/1310.2452.pdf

Spelay, M. (2016) *Trusted Online Access to Distributed Holdings of Public Records: a literature review.* AA05. InterPARES Trust. https://interparestrust.org/assets/public/dissemination/AA05_FinalReport.pdf

Stančić, H., Bursic, E. and Al-Hariri, A. (2015) *Ensuring Trust in Storage in Infrastructure-as-a-Service.* EU08, Final Report. InterPARES Trust. https://interparestrust.org/assets/public/dissemination/EU08_20160727_ EnsuringTrustStorageIaaS_FinalReport_Final.pdf

Stančić, H., Bursic, E. and Al-Hariri, A. (2016a) *Checklist for Ensuring Trust in Storage*

in Infrastructure-as-a-Service. EU08. InterPARES Trust.
https://interparestrust.org/assets/public/dissemination/EU08_IaaS_
Checklistv1.2_.pdf

Stančić, H., Bursic, E. and Al-Hariri, A. (2016b) *Checklist for Ensuring Trust in Storage in Infrastructure-as-a-Service*. EU08. Translated by A. Barnard. InterPARES Trust.
https://interparestrust.org/assets/public/dissemination/EU08_20161110_
IaaSChecklist_v1-2_Spanish.pdf

Thibodeau, K. (2018) *Preservation as a Service for Trust (PaaST)*. NA12. Final Report.
InterPARES Trust. https://interparestrust.org/assets/public/dissemination/
PreservationasaServiceforTrust1_0-FINAL.pdf

TIA-942.org (n.d.) TIA-942: Certified Data Centers, Consultants, Auditors,
www.tia-942.org/ [accessed 8 July 2018]

10

Cultural heritage – Indigenous perspectives

Editor: Gillian Oliver
Contributors: Gillian Oliver, Mark Crookston,
Lisa Nathan, Elizabeth Shaffer and
Richard Arias-Hernandez

Introduction

This chapter summarises findings from two InterPARES Trust (hereinafter ITrust) research projects that are particularly relevant to the work of libraries, archives and museums, the institutions that constitute the cultural heritage sector. In Canada, researchers explored the extent to which pluralised perspectives were reflected in the early policies of a cultural heritage institution – a court mandated centre tasked with acknowledging a history of violence, while firmly rooted in that history. New Zealand researchers considered issues relating to trust from the perspective of Indigenous views of digitised language resources. These studies reflect the differing priorities and concerns of the regions in which they were based, nevertheless both have findings that are relevant to other countries and jurisdictions.

Multiple and diverse perspectives

Archives and archivists play critical roles in ensuring that national memories do not solely represent dominant or majority perspectives. As conjectured by Anne Gilliland and colleagues:

> … recordkeepers and archivists play a central role in shaping cultural identity and memory, forming national historical legacies, and ensuring societal and institutional accountability through their role in capturing, managing, and preserving records and making them accessible to users.
>
> (Gilliland et al., 2008, 88)

The extent to which this happens in everyday practice will undoubtedly influence trust in the institutions enabling access to cultural heritage. The digital environment provides considerable opportunities to work with a broader range of communities and perspectives than many archives and archivists have in the past. Research in Canada and New Zealand provides further insight into the issues and challenges involved in this complex area.

Canada: policy and plurality

Researchers in Canada undertook a case study of the National Centre for Truth and Reconciliation (NCTR), Winnipeg, Manitoba, investigating how making information digitally accessible influenced initial steps to address issues of plurality and trust related to records made available by the NCTR. The following background provides a historical account of the context leading to the establishment of the NCTR as it is critical to acknowledge and understand the resilience of the Indigenous peoples in that nation-state, the multitude of harms, abuse and denial that the NCTR exists to address and the ongoing influence of practices and institutions with colonial foundations.

Background

Canada's Indian Residential School Settlement Agreement (IRSSA), signed in 2006, was the culmination of over a decade of civil litigation. The agreement included Schedule N, an extra-judicial component of the settlement, which mandated that Canada engage a truth and reconciliation commission and fund a national research centre to preserve the commission's findings. With Schedule N, the coalition of residential school survivors – First Nations, Inuit and Métis peoples represented by the Assembly of First Nations – defined the residential school program as a policy of systematic human rights violations, requiring more than jail time or financial penalties for historical redress. The settlement was a result of decades of work by Indigenous peoples (and allies) to force Canadians to acknowledge over one hundred years of developing policies and institutions to assimilate or eradicate Indigenous peoples.

In 1842, the Bagot Commission produced one of the earliest policy documents to recommend education as a means of 'aggressive civilization of the Indian' (Miller, 1996). The proposal recommended the creation of technical and agricultural training schools located far away from the influence of Indigenous families and communities. The recommendations of the Bagot Commission were followed by laws and reports that promoted a similar strategy: the Gradual Civilization Act of 1857, the Act for Gradual Enfranchisement of the Indian in 1869 and The Davin Report in 1879. The Davin Report recommended the creation of a nationwide system of schools in which Indigenous children would be intentionally separated from their parents to reduce the influence of their own cultural traditions (Stanton, 2010).

In 1892, the Government of Canada passed an order-in-council that mandated the operation of residential schools run by the Catholic, Anglican and Presbyterian churches of Canada. In 1920, Duncan Campbell Scott, Deputy Superintendent of Indian Affairs, made residential school attendance compulsory for children between the ages of 7 and 15 (Miller, 1996) and by the 1930s, over 70 schools were in operation throughout the country (Troniak, 2011). Federal agents were responsible for monitoring Indigenous communities to ensure attendance and parents who resisted were jailed or forbidden to leave their reserves.

There were schools in each territory and province except for Newfoundland, Prince Edward Island and New Brunswick. It is estimated that over the course of the Indian Residential School program's history around 150,000 children were forcibly removed from their First Nation, Inuit and Métis communities and placed in the care of church-administered schools, which were typically financed by the federal government (Milloy, 1999).

Duncan Campbell Scott's expressed goal in mandating compulsory attendance for Indigenous children was to 'kill the Indian in the child' (Miller, 1996). Students were discouraged from speaking their native languages and practicing cultural traditions. If they were caught, they experienced severe punishment. Throughout the years, students lived in substandard conditions, endured physical and emotional abuse and rarely had opportunities to participate in family life. Most were in school ten months out of the year, while some were forced to stay year-round. All correspondence from the children was written in English, which many parents could not read. Brothers and sisters at the same school rarely saw each other because all school activities, meals and dormitories were segregated by gender (Miller, 2003).

Culpability

When the Assembly of First Nations Chiefs called unsuccessfully for a federal investigation into the administration of residential schools in 1989, they sought to challenge the prevailing narrative of the Indian Residential School program, which up to that time had characterised residential schools as a misguided but benevolent attempt to help Indigenous peoples adapt to an increasingly modernising society.

Indigenous communities pieced together a more comprehensive history by challenging the state narrative that portrayed the harms resulting from residential schools as 'crimes of benevolence'. Included in this history is Duncan Campbell Scott's suppression of Dr Peter Bryce's Report on the

Indian Schools of Manitoba and the Northwest Territories, which documented the high death rates among children in the residential school system (Milloy, 1999).

While there were undoubtedly caring teachers and administrators within the residential school system, the effect of the schools on many students was to prevent the transmission of traditional skills and cultures. Those who escaped physical or sexual abuse suffered the trauma of separation from family, the confusion of being taught that their culture was inferior and the loss of their language and spirituality. Eventually, the government concluded that the schools were not successful tools of assimilation. In 1969, the government withdrew from its partnership with the churches and administration of the schools began to be transferred to Indian bands (Miller, 1996).

Community organizing

Most Survivors of the residential school system express experiencing a sense of isolation and shame in which they viewed themselves as inherently flawed because of their Indigenous identity. However, many Survivors were able to transform the solitude that followed from feelings of shame into a shared awareness of collective injustice. The mobilisation of groups of Survivors across the country became central to raising awareness and creating the momentum that led to civil litigation. In Nova Scotia in 1987, Nora Bernard began welcoming former students of the Shubenacadie Indian Residential School into her home, leading to the establishment of a group called Shubenacadie Indian Residential School Survivors. In 1998, this organization, now comprised of 900 members, brought a class action lawsuit against the Canadian government (Niezen, 2013).

In 1992, Chief Edmund Metatawabin of the Fort Albany Cree Band hosted a three-day 'healing conference' in which over 300 Cree people shared private testimonies about the abuse that they had experienced at St Anne's Residential School in Fort Albany, Ontario. The healing conference was advertised as an attempt to 'exorcise the demons' after learning that the federal Department of Indian Affairs would not be demolishing the building and replacing it with a new school building as promised. After the healing conference, 30 former students who had experienced abuse at St Anne's Residential School agreed to share their stories with a community-organized panel. The purpose of the panel was to investigate the lasting impact of the residential schools on the Cree community and to produce a report of its findings.

The watershed moment of public awareness about the dark history of residential schools was ushered in by a public disclosure by Phil Fontaine, leader of the Association of Manitoba Chiefs. This organization, together with the Roman Catholic Church, set up a committee to decide how to deal with alleged incidents of sexual, physical and emotional abuse at the 13 church-run residential schools in Manitoba. Fontaine demanded that the church acknowledge the abuse that students suffered at residential schools and he proceeded to speak about the physical and sexual abuse that he had experienced while attending a residential school (Stewart, 2001). The news coverage of this event reached a national audience, including many former students.

Thus, the movement towards civil litigation and the Indian Residential School Survivor Association (IRSSA) began, with former students recognising their position as Survivors and sharing their experiences with others. The networks that Survivors developed created the momentum to transform the perception of residential schools from a misguided enterprise of the past to a formative and horrific part of Canadian history of which the effects are widespread and ongoing.

Justice lobbying

In 1991, four aboriginal and three non-aboriginal commissioners were appointed to investigate the issues surrounding Canada's Indian policy and advise the government on their findings. The Royal Commission on Aboriginal Peoples' (RCAP) report, released in 1996, devoted an entire chapter to the residential school system. The ultimate recommendation of RCAP was a public inquiry into the history of the residential school program (Royal Commission on Aboriginal Peoples, 1996, Vol. 1, Ch. 10).

Rather than initiate a public inquiry, the government delivered an official acknowledgement of the harm that occurred in residential schools, published and posted online under the title *Statement of Reconciliation* (Canada, 1998). In spite of its shortcomings, the Statement of Reconciliation encouraged a wider public discussion about abuse in residential schools.

Collective healing

Part of the federal government's strategy to address the RCAP report's recommendation for a public inquiry was the establishment of the Aboriginal Healing Foundation (AHF) (Blackburn, 2012). From 1998–2012, the AHF engaged in research on the widespread impacts of residential schools, including post-traumatic stress disorder (PTSD), intergenerational trauma, substance abuse, depression and suicide and the abuse of students enacted on fellow students.

Civil litigation

Long before the Settlement Agreement was signed in 2006, the courts became the most important venue in which an alternative narrative about Indian residential schools began to take shape. Starting in 1989–90, prosecution of former residential school staff took place in British Columbia, Ontario and the Yukon Territories, initiating a widespread launch of investigations, indictments and prosecutions across Canada.

It is clear from these court decisions that the government's scepticism concerning the harm resulting from residential schools had become untenable. The practice of deflecting guilt onto specific individuals or extraordinary circumstances, instead of intentional government policy, was undermined as court judgments continued to accumulate. In 1998, with the failure of the government to adequately address the RCAP's recommendations, Survivors lost hope for a political resolution to the issue. This frustration with the lack of a political response prompted residential school Survivors to again turn to legal remedies for the harms they had suffered, a strategy that ultimately led to a negotiated solution. By October 2002, over 11,000 legal cases had been filed against the federal government and churches involved in the administration of residential schools (Llewellyn, 2002).

Indian Residential School Settlement Agreement

The RCAP report, together with mounting accumulation of testimony and evidence gathered through civil ligation, led to a reformulation of the Canadian government's strategy in addressing Survivors. In 1998, the government engaged in exploratory dialogues to discuss alternative models of litigation (Flisfeder, 2013). The resulting Alternative Dispute Resolution (ADR) process was an attempt to remedy the challenges of civil litigation through expediting casework and avoiding the re-traumatisation of victims through examination. Unfortunately, the ADR ultimately failed to provide a streamlined and effective process to address Survivors' needs.

In May 2005, the Canadian government, the churches and the Assembly of First Nations (AFN) signed an agreement in principle to negotiate a settlement to resolve the legal cases. After these negotiations deteriorated in August of 2005, the AFN launched a class action lawsuit against the federal government, which sought 12 billion dollars in general damages; 12 billion dollars for negligent harm, breach of fiduciary duties and treaty obligations; and 12 billion dollars in punitive damages. Although the settlement negotiations are ongoing, the submission of this suit was a strategic measure to ensure that the AFN would, as plaintiffs, be a legally vested participant in the process (Nagy, 2013). Through this position of strength, the AFN was able to mandate the inclusion of the Truth and Reconciliation Commission and its repository, the National Research Centre (now the National Centre for Truth and Reconciliation).

One of the outcomes of the Settlement Agreement's background of litigation and negotiation is that the federal government and the churches sought finality for judicial process and reparations, a circumstance that favoured limiting the judicial powers of the TRC. Under the terms of the Agreement, the TRC is prevented from holding formal hearings, acting as a public inquiry or conducting any type of legal process. It did not have subpoena powers and it had no legal mechanism to compel attendance or participation in any of its activities. It is prevented from identifying any person involved in its activities or reports without the consent of that individual – whether that individual is a participant or is named by an individual in the course of their participation.

The TRC is not concerned with identifying perpetrators since it is prevented from using its reports or testimony to recommend that either civil or criminal charges be sought. It has been from the outset deprived of any legal authority to pursue information about allegations of abuse or mistreatment beyond what is gathered through Survivor narratives. A goal of the IRSSA was to create an alternative to future litigation through the Common Experience Payment, which is applied to anyone who attended a federally operated Indian Residential School, and through the Independent Assessment Process (IAP), which adjudicates specific claims of abuse.

Although separate from the Commission's mandate of information gathering, the IAP has served as a focal point in the process of remembrance. Former students seeking compensation for particular abuses that took place at a recognised Indian Residential School are eligible to submit a deposition along with supporting evidence. These IAP records constitute narratives of personal experiences and conditions within the schools, shaped by the legal structures of abuse allegations. In April 2016, the Ontario Court of Appeal upheld a decision by the Supreme Court of Ontario that ordered the IAP records to be destroyed after a 15-year retention period, unless Survivors provide their consent for the documents to be transferred to the National Centre for Truth and Reconciliation (Fontaine v. Canada, 2017). More recently, the federal government has asked the Supreme Court of Canada to overturn the decision by the Ontario Court of Appeal, arguing that the IAP documents and testimonies are 'government records' and should remain in control of the government. The Supreme Court of Canada agreed to review the federal government's appeal (The Canadian Press, 2016). In October 2017, the Supreme Court of Canada unanimously ruled that the Independent Assessment process was meant to be a 'confidential and private process' and that 'claimants and alleged perpetrators relied on confidentiality assurance' meaning the 38,000 accounts will be retained for a 15-year period in which IRS Survivors can indicate they would like their records preserved. Those not identified for preservation will be destroyed (Harris, 2017).

The NCTR

The mandate of the National Centre for Truth and Reconciliation as defined in Schedule N is to create a 'research centre ... accessible to former students, their families and communities, the general public, researchers and educators who wish to include this historic material in curricula' (Canada, 2009). While truth and reconciliation commissions have become an essential tool for recognising human rights violations and avoiding their reoccurrence, there is no clear pathway for managing the impact of these events on Survivors and the rest of the nation. At the same time, there is no single answer to the organization, preservation and dissemination of information gathered through the TRC's activities.

The National Centre for Truth and Reconciliation must now operate as a realisation of the over two decades long journey to reform the state's dominant narrative of the Indian Residential School program. As such, it is important to conceive of the policy decisions of the NCTR as direct embodiments of this historic struggle. Under these circumstances, the NCTR faces some major challenges: it must convince non-Indigenous Canadians that the history of residential schools affects more than just Survivors and it must convince the public to bring the history of residential schools to life through education and national remembrance.

The research

From analysis of online policy developments and announcements as well as interviews with NCTR professionals, it was evident that incorporating plurality into the design, creation and use of the collection presented multiple challenges, namely:

- Who should own and maintain records housed within the NCTR database
- The trade-offs between privacy and access to these sensitive records
- The balance that needs to be established to satisfy competing information needs of researchers, Survivors, affected communities and the general public
- The affective dimensions of interacting with these records and the affective impacts on archivists and archival work

- The possibility of creating archives that not only preserves cultural memory but also helps affected communities and broader society understand, heal and move forward towards a society in which plural cultural understandings can co-exist.

Findings illuminate the complexity of trust and force consideration of its converse, distrust (Nathan, Shaffer and Castor, 2015). Of particular interest is the gap that was identified between stated intention and reality. For example, a goal of archival professionals contributing to the mission of the NCTR was to use archival description processes to facilitate Indigenous participation and ultimately to achieve reconciliation (Lougheed, Moran and Callison, 2015). The Centre had collected records from a range of different archives, including government- and church-run entities. The collection methodology was influenced primarily by budgetary considerations and resulted in a dataset that is characterised by different approaches to description, often with multiple metadata configurations (Lougheed, Moran and Callison, 2015). The Centre therefore faced significant challenges with respect to the need to try to normalise existing description as well as augment by facilitating the inclusion of Indigenous perspectives. The policy decisions made prioritised normalisation activities, which did not allow for the integration of alternative approaches to information management. For example, the metadata schema as it exists does not support a recon-ceptualisation of provenance that positions IRS Survivors as co-creators of records rather than subjects of the records. Furthermore, the metadata normalisation phase does not support participatory practices such as user annotations.

Other tensions related to collection development at the NCTR exist, particularly concern about whether the records housed in the NCTR database will adequately convey the descriptions of the originals housed in repositories across the country, from small church archives to Library and Archives Canada. The data also revealed a tension around the impossibility of establishing trust in a federated structure such as the NCTR when there are hundreds of First Nations, Métis and Inuit across Canada with distinct cultures, histories, and viewpoints. Moreover, the data revealed significant tension surrounding privacy concerns and the management of affect in a federated structure such as the NCTR.

New Zealand: impacts of Indigenous language collections

Researchers in New Zealand were similarly concerned with Indigenous perspectives, but in this case the motivator for their research was to contribute those perspectives to the overall findings of InterPARES relating to trust. Consequently, an attempt was made to explore the attitudes of Māori, the indigenous people of New Zealand, to the digitisation of te reo (Māori language) resources by cultural heritage institutions in New Zealand.

Background

New Zealand was one of the last habitable land masses to be settled, but it is thought that the first inhabitants were migrants from Polynesia more than 700 years ago, ancestors of today's Māori (Irwin and Walrond, 2016). European settlement, primarily from Britain, did not commence until the 19th century. In 1840, the Treaty of Waitangi, a written agreement between the British Crown and over 500 Māori chiefs, was signed. In 1975, legislation was passed to establish the Waitangi Tribunal, a permanent commission of inquiry to investigate breaches of the principles of the Treaty. Two claims made to the Tribunal are particularly relevant and important to the cultural heritage sector. The first of these was in relation to te reo māori, the Māori language. This claim resulted in the acknowledgement of te reo as a taonga, a treasure (New Zealand and Waitangi Tribunal, 1989). The second relevant claim was very significant and far reaching, concerning the role of Māori culture in legislation as well as government policies and practices (New Zealand and Waitangi Tribunal, 2011). The Tribunal decided that '[...] the Treaty envisages the Crown-Māori relationship as a partnership, in which the Crown is entitled to govern but Māori retain tino rangatiratanga (full authority) over their taonga (treasures)' (New Zealand and Waitangi Tribunal, 2011). This is of particular concern to the cultural heritage sector and issues are perhaps most evident when considering the te reo resources held by libraries and archives. Therefore, Māori attitudes to te reo digitised resources presented an obvious choice to use to explore issues relating to trust in the networked environment.

The research

The research project was conducted as a partnership between Māori and Pākehā researchers, reflecting the principles of the Treaty of Waitangi. The objective was to hear from as diverse a group of Māori as possible, so did not want to limit the research population to a particular tribe or region or occupation. Because of that, and because of the need to collect data within a limited time period, the decision was made to develop an online survey. The process of survey development involved much review, conversation and discussion with community partners, and the success of that process was reflected in the rich and detailed responses received. Distribution of the survey began with e-mailing links to researchers' networks and known contacts, with requests to distribute further if possible. A total of 80 responses were received, but because of the non-mandatory nature of the questions the total number of responses per question varied.

Findings from the project can be considered under three main headings: Whakawhanaungatanga, Wairua and Government Strategies.

Whakawhanaungatanga

Whanaungatanga is defined as 'relationship, kinship, sense of family connection – a relationship through shared experiences and working together which provides people with a sense of belonging. It develops as a result of kinship rights and obligations, which also serve to strengthen each member of the kin group. It also extends to others to whom one develops a close familial, friendship or reciprocal relationship' (Maori Dictionary, n.d., s.v. whanaungatanga).

This research found evidence that digitisation of te reo collections provides a significant societal impact by supporting a sharing and relationship system among communities and whānau (family). These relationships exist well beyond the bounds of the access interactions between the memory institutions and their customers and therefore beyond the traditional mechanisms of measuring and reporting on digitisation.

- 95% of respondents shared the digitised archives they found
- 60% of those shared archives were shared again by the recipient
- 67% liked being able to share the collection with friends and whānau
- 22% of respondents sourced their digitised collections from a friend
- 76% have used digitised collections received offline
- 25% of respondents stated they had added digitised archives to an iwi repository
- Throughout the survey, respondents cited a sense of obligation to whānau and community members to share information found in the archives, to those to whom it related.
- *'I have shared material with people who have a right to look at such material as being from an appropriate iwi'.*

This is the first time these relationships have been uncovered in archival research. However, more research is required to understand the extent of this sharing system, whether it differs from digital collections or from the use of digital collections in other cultures.

Wairua

This research sought to explore the extent to which the digitisation process and digital access and use activities affect the wairua (spirit or life force) and mana (power and prestige) of information and te reo in the collections. Generally, accessibility and ease of sharing outweighed concerns over adverse effects on wairua, with many respondents supporting open, sharable, usable digitised collections, while still providing caveats on that position.

- 93% of respondents felt that the digitised medium is appropriate for transferring te reo and mātauranga Māori
- 93% of respondents thought digitisation could help improve engagement with mātauranga Māori in New Zealand
- Over 80% of respondents felt more collections should be digitised, or that those collections partially digitised should be digitised in their entirety
- 44% of respondents thought digitisation did not affect wairua, with 37% stating it did affect the wairua (though many respondents felt greater access outweighed this), while 11% thought effects on wairua depended on the information being conveyed
- *'In most cases, [digitised information] loses the wairua that the original works possessed, such as the whakapapa korero that is specific to certain whanau/hapu/iwi and would lose its significance if the information were just passed out.'*
- *'Yes, [digitisation affects the wairua of collections], but if we don't have it somewhere we will lose that knowledge.'*
- *'I find [digitisation of te reo collections] appropriate with the caveat that institutions need to put effort into making sure users/researchers are aware of the rules for usage of the collections, and the difference between access and usage.'*

There is a complicated set of obligations and drivers to both share, use and protect collections at the same time. Non-Western views of the use of cultural heritage are increasingly discussed within the memory sector, but it is not a well-researched topic. This research only contributes a small amount to the understanding. More work is required to understand the role the wairua plays with the management and use of digitised te reo collections.

Government strategies

This research found evidence that use of digitised te reo collections supports the intended outcomes of several key government strategies, including the

Te Rautaki Reo Māori/Māori Language Strategy. The emphasis on understanding the impact of digitised collections on people and communities enables public institutions to draw on evidence and narrative to better tell their value proposition to their customers, stakeholders, senior leaders and funders.

- 65% of respondents used digitised te reo collections for language revitalisation initiatives
- 67% of respondents liked being able to share the collection with friends and whānau, which supports the Māori Language Strategy's result area of increasing the use of Māori language among whānau Māori and other New Zealanders, especially in the home
- There was a recurring narrative that the '...*digital collections of Māori language texts [have been] extremely valuable for developing the Te Aka online dictionary.*'
- '*koinei pea taku rauemi rangahau matua mō te reo Māori o mua.*' [Translation: 'this is perhaps my main research resource for the Māori language of the past.']

In addition, 24% of respondents experienced an outcome of being able to contribute to a Treaty of Waitangi settlement process.

The New Zealand Treasury's *Living Standards Framework* (2017) outlines social cohesion as a key pillar to supporting higher living standards. Social cohesion relates to the trust between citizen and state, social inclusion in decision-making and evidence of identity and inclusion in government activities.

- 49% of respondents experienced an outcome of personal enlightenment from use of digitised te reo collections
- 54% of respondents experienced an outcome of gaining family knowledge
- '[T]he convenience of this information has been pivotal to including some whanau in whanau decisions.'

In summary, findings from this research project highlighted complex preferences, attitudes and behaviours relating to digital and digitised information that need to be taken into account when considering issues relating to trust in the networked environment. These preferences, attitudes and behaviours may not be apparent if the focus is solely on Western knowledge paradigms and emphasise the critical need for the cultural heritage sector to take into account a plurality of perspectives.

Conclusion

Although the projects differed in terms of aims and objectives, there are two clear areas of commonality. The first is represented by the key roles played by policy. The Canadian study demonstrated a long-standing history of problematic policies. The disconnect between the aims articulated by professional archivists for the NCTR and the policies decided on to describe the collections has historical precedent in the stated aims of residential schools versus their practices. In contrast, findings from the New Zealand study were very encouraging for cultural heritage institutions as they demonstrated that digitisation activities were supporting government policies.

The second relates to plurality – the multiple and diverse perspectives that were present in the two projects. In the Canadian project, concerns were about how diverse voices were represented in the records. In the New Zealand study, the legislative environment had ensured that digitisation activities focusing on Indigenous content had been a core activity for cultural heritage institutions for some time, but the impact of all of that activity was still to be explored. Although the two research projects reported here are geographically specific, findings provide insights into the issues and challenges facing the cultural heritage sector worldwide in representing multiple and diverse perspectives.

References

Blackburn, C. (2012) Culture Loss and Crumbling Skills: The Problematic of Injury in Residential School Litigation, *Political and Legal Anthropology Review*, **35** (2), 288–306.

Canada (1998) *Statement of Reconciliation*. Government of Canada, https://www.edu.gov.mb.ca/k12/cur/socstud/foundation_gr9/blms/9-1-4e.pdf

Canada (2009) Schedule N —Mandate for the Truth and Reconciliation Commission. In *Indian Residential Schools Class Action Settlement. Residential Schools Settlement*, www.trc.ca/websites/trcinstitution/File/pdfs/SCHEDULE_N_EN.pdf

Flisfeder, M. (2013) A Bridge to Reconciliation: a critique of the Indian Residential School Truth Commission, *The International Indigenous Policy Journal*, **1** (1).

Fontaine v. Canada (Attorney General), 2017 SKQB 1 (CanLII) https://www.canlii.org/en/sk/skqb/doc/2017/2017skqb1/2017skqb1.html

Gilliland, A., McKemmish, S., White, K., Lu, Y. and Lau, A. (2008) Pluralizing the Archival Paradigm: can archival education in Pacific Rim communities address the challenge?, *The American Archivist*, **71** (1), 87–117.

Harris, K. (2017) *Supreme Court rules Indigenous residential schools' documents can be destroyed*. CBC News, https://www.cbc.ca/news/politics/indian-residential-schools-records-supreme-court-1.4343259 [accessed 13 July 2018].

Irwin, G. and Walrond, C. (2016) *When was New Zealand first settled? – The date debate*, https://teara.govt.nz/en/when-was-new-zealand-first-settled/page-1 [accessed 9 July 2018].

Llewellyn, J. J. (2002) Dealing with the Legacy of Native Residential School Abuse in Canada: litigation, ADR, and restorative justice, *The University of Toronto Law Journal*, **52** (3), 253–300. https://doi.org/10.2307/825996

Lougheed, B., Moran, R. and Callison, C. (2015) Reconciliation Through Description: using metadata to realize the vision of the National Research Centre for Truth and Reconciliation, *Cataloguing and Classification Quarterly*, **53** (5-6), 596–614.

Māori Dictionary, https://maoridictionary.co.nz/.

Miller, J. (1996) *Shingwauk's Vision: A History of Native Residential Schools*. Toronto: University of Toronto Press.

Miller, J. (2003) Troubled Legacy: a history of Indian Residential Schools, *Saskatchewan Law Review*, **66** (2), 357–383.

Milloy, J. (1999) *A National Crime: the Canadian Government and the Residential School System, 1879-1986*, Winnipeg, University of Manitoba Press.

Nagy, R. L. (2013) The Scope and Bounds of Transitional Justice and the Canadian Truth and Reconciliation Commission, *International Journal of Transitional Justice*, **7** (1), 52–73, https://doi.org/10.1093/ijtj/ijs034

Nathan, L., Shaffer, E. and Castor, M. (2015) Stewarding Collections of Trauma: plurality, responsibility, and questions of action, *Archivaria*, **80** (0), 89–118.

New Zealand Treasury (2017) *Living Standards Framework*, https://treasury.govt.nz/publications/presentation/living-standards-framework

New Zealand and Waitangi Tribunal (1989) *Report of the Waitangi Tribunal on the te reo Maori claim (WAI 11)*, Wellington, N.Z., Waitangi Tribunal, Department of Justice, https://forms.justice.govt.nz/search/Documents/WT/wt_DOC_68482156/Report%20on%20the%20Te%20Reo%20Maori%20Claim%20W.pdf

New Zealand and Waitangi Tribunal (2011) *Ko Aotearoa Tēnei: Report on the Wai 262 Claim Released*, https://www.waitangitribunal.govt.nz/news/ko-aotearoa-tenei-report-on-the-wai-262-claim-released/ [accessed 9 July 2018].

Niezen, R. (2013) *Truth and Indignation: Canada's Truth and Reconciliation Commission on Indian Residential Schools*, Toronto, University of Toronto Press.

Royal Commission on Aboriginal Peoples (1996) *Report of the Royal Commission on Aboriginal Peoples (RCAP)*, https://www.bac-lac.gc.ca/eng/discover/aboriginal-heritage/royal-commission-aboriginal-peoples/Pages/final-report.aspx

Stanton, K. (2010) *Truth Commissions and Public Inquiries: addressing historical injustices in established democracies*, PhD Thesis, University of Toronto Faculty of Law, Toronto, ON.

Stewart, P. (2001) Blind Spots: an examination of the federal government's response to the Report of the Royal Commission on Aboriginal Peoples. In Bianchi, E. (ed.), *Federal Government's Response to the Royal Commission on Aboriginal Peoples,* (49–62), Ottawa, Aboriginal Rights Coalition.

The Canadian Press (2016) Supreme Court to rule on fate of residential schools documents, *The Star,* https://www.thestar.com/news/canada/2016/10/27/supreme-court-to-rule-on-fate-of-residential-schools-documents.html [accessed 13 July 2018].

Troniak, S. (2011) *Background Paper: addressing the legacy of Residential Schools,* Library of Parliament, http://publications.gc.ca/collections/collection_2011/bdp-lop/bp/2011-76-eng.pdf

11

The role of the records professional

Editor: Tove Engvall
Contributors: Karen Anderson, Jenny Bunn,
Tove Engvall, Andrew Flinn, Georg Gänser,
Pekka Henttonen, Giovanni Michetti and Yingfang Cai

Introduction

Research conducted by the InterPARES Trust (hereinafter ITrust) has
addressed challenges relating to trust in a networked and digital context from
a variety of perspectives. This chapter will discuss the role of the records
professional in this context. ITrust defines records professional in the
following way:

> An individual who is trained in all aspects of managing records and information,
> including their creation, use, retention, disposition, and preservation, and is
> familiar with the legal, ethical, fiscal, administrative, and governance contexts of
> recordkeeping.
>
> (Pearce-Moses, 2018, s.v. records professional)

'Records professional' is often used as an umbrella term to include individuals working in various facets of records management and archives,
regardless of job titles. The main focus of and rationale for the existence of a
records professional rests on the idea of records as evidence of past activities
and it is this idea that has distinguished the records professional from ancient
times to modern days (Duranti and Franks, 2015, 105). Records are viewed
by the records professional as 'the currency of democracy' (Cunningham and
Phillips, 2005, 303) and as tools for creating trust through time and across
societies. In order for records to function in this way, in support of, for
example, accountability, the protection of rights and upholding of obligations
and informed decision-making, they need to be well-organized, managed and
accessible (International Organization for Standardization (ISO), 2016).
Ensuring accuracy and authenticity of data, documents and records, the

control of sensitive information, the maintenance of order and discoverability and the provision of access are some of the tasks that records professionals see as their role to undertake.

The identity of the records professional has to a large degree been constructed as one of a trusted custodian responsible for ensuring trustworthy records and the trustworthy management of records. The context in which records professionals act has always been complex, operating as they do within evolving legislative (e.g. Freedom of Information, Data Protection) and policy (e.g. Open Access) frameworks which sometimes contradict each other. For example, the good of open access to information and data can sometimes conflict with the good of protecting the privacy of individuals; and records professionals have to be proficient in balancing such conflicting interests and public goods. As the context in which they operate becomes increasingly networked and digital, the complexities faced by records professionals increase in parallel. Globalisation has become a force to be reckoned with in its impact on organizations, public administration, businesses and individuals towards multicultural, international and complex collaborative environments which cut across established structures and require new knowledge, competences, skills and mindsets (Vaillant, 2003).

Records professionals have recognised that there is a need for their identity to be reshaped in the digital context (MacNeil, 2011). They have traced a shift of emphasis towards access and use of records (Bastian, 2004; Menne-Haritz, 2001), pushed by the agenda of open access and the use of records as raw materials in innovation (McLeod, 2012). Nevertheless, they still stress the need for ensuring the evidential value of records and their long-term preservation to enable accountability and transparency (Tough, 2011). They point out that in order to meet demands for access to records, organizations needs to know what records they hold and where they are (Shepherd and Ennion, 2007; Crockett, 2009) and there has to be a robust and efficient records management system in place (Svärd, 2014). In order to provide access to records over long periods of time, preservation issues have to be considered at an early stage to ensure that records are generated and captured in ways that make them useful and accessible (McLeod, 2012). Records professionals have also noticed a tendency for development in the digital age to be dominated by technical perspectives, while issues related to processes, procedure and participation tend to be secondary (Craig, 2011).

Reshaping the records profession

InterPARES Trust defines a profession as:

A field of work that requires advanced education and training, adherence to a code of ethics, and the ability to apply specialized knowledge and judgement in a variety of situations.

(Pearce-Moses, 2018, s.v. profession)

Professions embody a field of knowledge in practice and are mediators for expertise about certain tasks and activities within a certain jurisdiction. This often leads to the development of standards, codes of ethics and professional values and rules (Abbott, 1988). The 'professional complex' includes research, teaching and practice, and is linked to legal and regulatory frameworks. Records professional roles can be different in different countries, but they are united by the same challenges around recordkeeping (Kallberg, 2013).

The context within which any profession works will affect its position, as will the efforts of the profession itself. Tasks are created, reshaped and changed (Abbott, 1988). Societal, technical and organizational changes may challenge the professional domain and require the development of new skills and education. Responsibilities have to be clarified and education has to meet current needs (Currall and Moss, 2008). Records professionals have highlighted that it is important for them to learn to communicate with stakeholders, to take a proactive and strategic role and to develop management and leadership skills (Kallberg, 2013). Increasingly, they need to work alongside and in collaboration with other professionals from outside their own profession.

This chapter presents an ontology of functions and activities carried out by records professionals, highlighting the development of areas of activity, such as Information Security Management, Governance and Monitoring and Auditing, which are taking on new or renewed importance within the digital environment. Traditional labels and roles such as records management and records manager are being subsumed into broader ones, such as information governance and information governance officer (Lomas, 2010). This chapter also presents case studies that show how this reshaping and relabelling of roles is being negotiated on the ground in an open government, as well as an enterprise context. In this way, we can see both top down and bottom up attempts by records professionals to identify their roles and responsibilities and what unique competences they can contribute.

Ontology of functions and activities for the profession

With a rapid transformation in established processes, the need to share responsibilities with new professions and a need for new methods and skills to perform tasks, the development of the online networked environment pushes for a re-formulation of the records professional's role and responsibilities. ITrust has developed an ontology to represent the functions and activities that are performed on records from creation to long-term preservation by records professionals. Presented in a graphical representation, the relationships among functions and activities are identified and understandable.

The ontology can help records professionals, stakeholders, users and clients to clarify the functions and activities that need to be implemented and performed in records and archives management. It will prove useful as a guideline for software and system development. In addition, it may be used to clarify the responsibilities of records professionals, to ensure transparency of records processes, to promote records professionals' active involvement in a wide range of different activities and to help understand the relationships among the diverse activities as well as the connections with other professions.

The diagrams are based on an analysis of the most relevant standards on records and management, such as the ISO 15489 series, the ISO 16175 series and the OAIS Reference Model, plus other relevant sources, leading to a total of 20 reference documents.[1] Standards play a fundamental role in the development of coherent criteria, vocabularies, methods, practices and processes in any scientific domain. They raise awareness and promote discussions about goals and values. Therefore, they are key to professionalisation (Davis, 2003). The ITrust ontology supports an understanding of the values standards convey, but it should always be remembered that standards are the result of a negotiation and harmonisation process, rather than neutral tools (Michetti, 2015).

The analysis of the reference documents has led to the production of short statements based on their content and modelled in the form of subject-predicate-object. The statements have then been represented in graphical form. Altogether they make up the ontology.

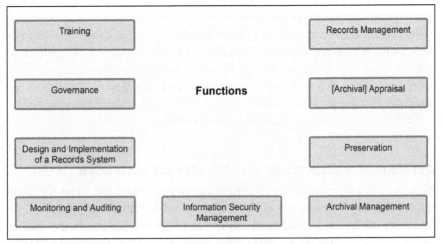

Figure 11.1 *Overview of high-level functions performed by records professionals*

The ontology consists of an overview map, featuring nine high-level functions, and 105 sub-maps, representing 105 functions and sub-functions in total. The overview map is the access point to the functions and sub-functions represented in the ontology. The nine high-level functions are: Records Management, [Archival] Appraisal, Preservation, Archival Management, Information Security Management, Monitoring and Auditing, Training, Governance, Design and Implementation of a Records System.

While Records Management, Appraisal, Preservation and Archival Management are identified as typical responsibilities of records professionals, this is not usually true for functions like Information Security Management, Governance, Monitoring and Auditing. The overview shows that the responsibilities of records professionals are growing and expanding, moving towards new fields. Attention to these changes is needed to provide successful integrated recordkeeping and preservation services.

From the overview map it is possible to explore the diagrams containing specific information about the functions and their relationships with other sub-functions. We will show here only a few high-level functions as illustration.

Records Management

Most of the standards analysed deal with the current phase of a record's lifecycle, so this is the most dense diagram – it contains the highest number of statements, hence relationships to other sub-functions. In particular, Records Management is articulated in a variety of different sub-functions and activities, including but not limited to traditional functions like Capture, Registration, Classification, Access Management and Disposition.

However, due to changing business environments – with particular reference to the requirements for digital records – functions like Metadata Management and Migration are included in the Records Management sub-functions as well. This development can be observed at all levels throughout the diagrams of the ontology. Many statements represented in the ontology deal with specific issues of the digital environment, so they reflect the technological shift in the records professions.

The Records Management function is related to some high-level functions either directly or through one or more sub-functions. For example, the sub-function Access is shared by the high-level functions Records Management, Archival Management and Preservation. This makes sense, because Access, along with its associated activities and tasks, assumes a relevant role throughout the whole of a record's lifecycle. Therefore, the diagrams in this ontology can be used to point out the shared responsibilities of all records professionals whether they operate in the records or in the archives management phase.

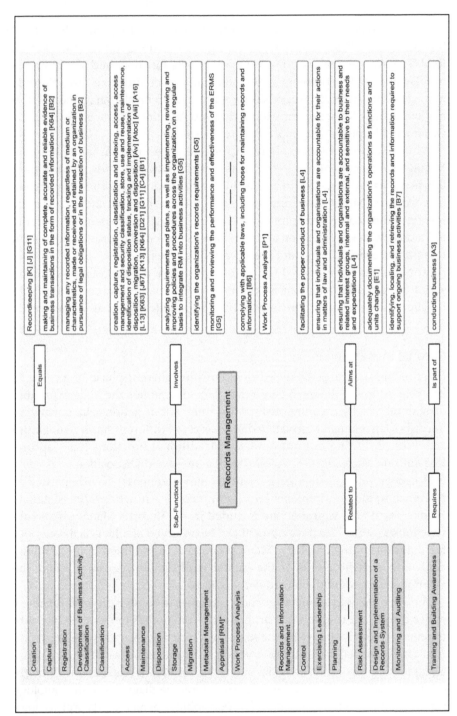

Figure 11.2 *Functions and activities related to Records Management*

Archival Management

Like Records Management, the sub-functions of Archival Management reflect the technological changes in the domain and the broader responsibilities of records professionals. Archival Management includes sub-functions that are carried out both in digital and non-digital domains, such as: Administration, Access, Controlling Archival Use and Promotion.

However, some sub-functions are associated mostly with the digital environment – see for example Data Management or Incorporation of metadata into archival systems. Archival Management is also related to Processing, which in turn contains the sub-functions Accession and Arrangement and Description and establishes a link between (digital) Preservation and Archival Management. Archival Management is linked to Preservation too (in addition to Governance and Digital Object Management) via the sub-function Preservation Planning.

Preservation

This function – along with the statements that are included in the diagram – deals mainly with long-term digital preservation. This reflects the relevance of this topic in archival practice and theory. Consequently, Preservation's sub-functions are mostly associated with long-term digital preservation: Conservation, Migration, Preservation Planning and Digitisation.

Sub-functions such as Migration, Capture, Access and Preservation Planning link the Preservation diagram to other diagrams in the ontology (e.g. Records Management, Governance, Archival Management) and thus, to the wider context of recordkeeping. Preservation is not isolated – the diagrams of the ontology show that it spans the entire life of a record.

Information and Security Management

This diagram illustrates the growing awareness of information security risks in the digital era. Traditionally, Information and Security Management has not been the focus of records professionals' action. However, the solid presence of this function in the ontology reflects development in the records profession. The ontology shows that this function has strong connections to Records Management, Archival Management and Preservation through its sub-functions. The Information and Security Management diagram contains the following sub-functions: Infrastructure and Security Risk Management, Risk Management, Risk Assessment and Risk Treatment.

The ontology shows that the functions performed on records during their life should not be interpreted as isolated entities. The graphical representation illustrates the connections and dependencies between records management

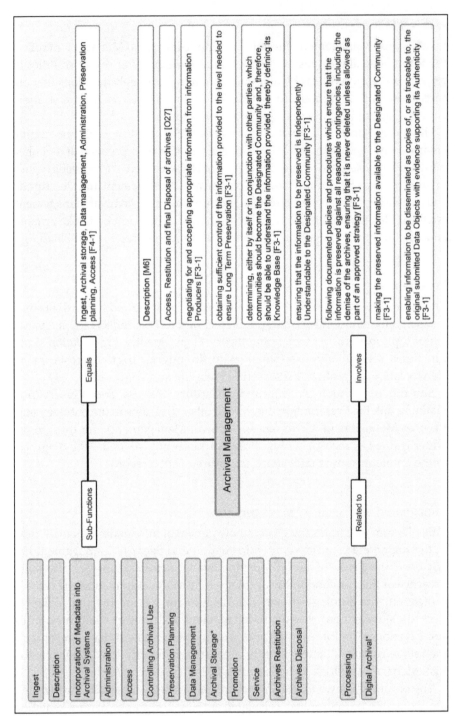

Figure 11.3 *Functions and activities related to Archival Management*

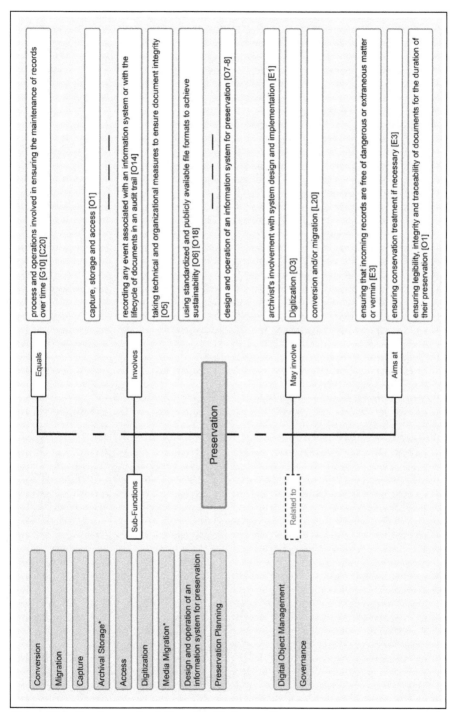

Figure 11.4 *Functions and activities related to Preservation*

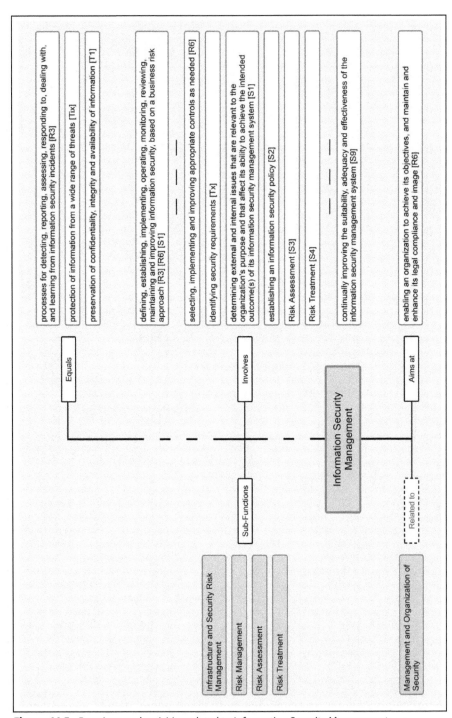

Figure 11.5 *Functions and activities related to Information Security Management*

and archival functions. The relationships in the ontology demonstrate that many of the functions are indeed continuous and integrated efforts. Several functions reappear throughout the ontology as either sub-functions or related functions. Thus, the ontology helps to understand that the management of records and archives is based on a network of functions that need to be performed continuously throughout a record's life. Neither archives nor records management are isolated endeavours – continuous and holistic approaches are needed and connections to other management areas have to be found and established. This is especially true in the digital environment – records professionals need to engage with new technologies in order to both deal with the recordkeeping issues arising from them and to find new solutions, practices and methods for old problems. At the same time, the digital environment (e.g. the cloud) challenges the traditional roles of records professionals, requiring an integrated and collaborative information management. The ontology shows the complex connections among records professionals' functions, activities and responsibilities. Therefore, it helps to promote a more comprehensive approach to the profession, suggesting that a broadened view of responsibilities is required. After this general overview, the next part will highlight some challenges related to some of these activities and the role of the records profession, as revealed in several case studies.

Contemporary patterns and challenges to the professional role

In the ITrust project, case studies have addressed challenges to the profession in the context of open government public administration in the United Kingdom and Sweden and in relation to an enterprise context in China. They address particularly some of the functions outlined in the previous section, such as information security, access, metadata management and archival functions.

As the examples will show, much of the emerging impetus towards open government and access to public-sector information has focused on the accessibility (and usability) of public-sector data and the control of any potential risk of sensitivity or privacy breaches. This can be compared to existing freedom of information (FOI) regimes but, in the case of FOI, the link between effective compliance and the exercise of citizen's rights and foundations of thorough and resilient records management policies and practice is more firmly established:

> Freedom of information legislation is only as good as the quality of the records and other information to which it provides access. Access rights are of limited value if information cannot be found when requested or, when found, cannot be

relied upon as authoritative. Good records and information management benefits those requesting information because it provides some assurance that the information provided will be complete and reliable. It benefits those holding the requested information because it enables them to locate and retrieve it easily within the statutory timescales or to explain why it is not held.

(Lord Chancellor, 2009)

If records professionals are to fully grasp the challenges and opportunities of the open government movement, then the profession will have to work with partners in groups such as the Open Government Partnership to demonstrate that the same link between recordkeeping and access to reliable and compliant information applies to open government as much as it does to freedom of information. The following section will raise perspectives, as well as certain issues, that were expressed in the case studies, but it is to be borne in mind that those discussed are only a part of the extensive tasks and challenges that the profession is facing.

The role of records professionals in digital development

With the development of open data agendas, there are new demands on public information, with new perspectives, as well as new roles and responsibilities, involved. How these are being worked out in relation to existing Freedom of Information regimes and the traditional records management function seems to vary in different contexts and to involve different strategic approaches. In case studies in the United Kingdom, both at national level in the National Health Service (NHS) (Harrison, Shepherd and Flinn, 2015) and at a local and more practical NHS Trust level (Chorley, Flinn and Shepherd, 2016), local government (Page, Flinn and Shepherd, 2014) and higher education (Brimble, Flinn and Shepherd, 2016), records management and open government data seemed to show separate rather than mutually supportive functions, with records management being deemed an 'everyday responsibility'.

In the study at the local NHS Trust (Chorley, Flinn and Shepherd, 2016), this 'everyday responsibility' did not include responsibility for the official statistics collected by the Trust, which were managed by a Business Intelligence Unit within the Informatics Directorate. Nor did it include a responsibility for patient records. The Trust was under some pressure to publish Open Government Data (OGD), but it was in an early stage of development and it was still unclear what this would come to mean for the Trust and for the interviewees' roles and responsibilities, how the task would be resourced and how it would work in practice. By contrast, in the study at the local authority level (Page, Flinn and Shepherd, 2014), work around OGD was more advanced and those involved in records management were involved in the development of policies responding to open government data obligations. They were hopeful that this involvement would extend the influence of records management within the authority, but also felt that records management was still generally seen as a traditional and 'everyday' paper-based function, rather than as a contribution to considerations of the management, preservation and quality assurance of the authenticity and reliability of datasets, essential to effective OGD initiatives.

In the study conducted at the Stockholm City Archives (Engvall, Liang and Anderson, 2015), records professionals had a much more strategic role in the work on open data. A digital archival strategy for the entire City dealt with matters including how open data should be managed and addressed aspects of accuracy, reliability and authenticity (Stockholm stadsarkiv, 2014). The City Archives took the lead in working with open data, with for example a Public Sector Information (PSI) lab. It was emphasised that records professionals had to take a proactive and strategic role and participate from the very beginning in the planning and creation of data, documents and records, or else others would take charge of the related questions. This strategic positioning demonstrated the City Archives' intention to make the e-archives a centre of information provision in the City.

Challenges raised in several of the case studies investigating open government and open data were the balance between security and openness, and democratic values and economic interests. At the Stockholm City Archives there was discussion about the institution's responsibility regarding re-use, particularly potentially negative re-use. Some argued that the City Archives' responsibility ended when the data was released, while others showed more concern for the potential harm in the re-use of data and interest in developing procedures to make sure that the City Archives brand would not be harmed by data potentially used for improper purposes (Engvall, Liang and Anderson, 2015).

In the case study in higher education in the UK (Brimble, Flinn and Shepherd, 2016), the priorities for records professionals were largely risk-based, focusing on protecting sensitive data, ensuring information security and complying with legal responsibilities. In the case of local government (Page, Flinn and Shepherd, 2014), the local authorities were keen to both meet their legal obligations for the publication of data and ensure that personal or sensitive data was not being published.

The case study in an enterprise context in China (Yingfang Cai, 2017) situated the archives in business processes, by discussing its role in e-commerce. In order to have an entirely digital business process, accounting records must be digital. This move towards digital accounting records has primarily been motivated by a desire to reap economic benefits and to reduce the administrative burden for enterprises in the e-commerce domain. In 2012, several state ministries and agencies issued a Notice on Further Promoting the Development of e-commerce and a pilot for the electronic management of accounting records was initiated (Writing Group of Explanation on Accounting Archives Management Measures, 2016). This work was further developed in 2015 when the State Council required the State Administration of Taxation, the Ministry of Finance, the State Archives Bureau, the National Standardization Administration and other departments to 'gradually implement electronic invoices and electronic accounting archives, and improve relevant technical standards and regulations' (State Council, 2015).

Following the new state requirements for filing and managing electronic archives, The State Archives Bureau has issued a number of policies to implement the relevant requirements (State Archives Administration of China, 2015). These policies have set requirements and rules around electronic records filing and archives management, as well as around metadata capture and management. As a result, the management of accounting records has been improved and more directed towards supporting the economic development of the country. Enterprises have sought to better meet accounting archives management requirements, increase electronic preservation and improve processes and procedures around electronic accounting archives. In 2016, the Thirteenth Five-Year Plan for national archives development strengthened digital records and archives management further, with the goals of enhancing the level of digital archives management, strengthening the management of digital records in business systems and developing standards and specifications for digital data capture and archival management (State Archives Administration of China, 2016; Yingfang Cai, 2017).

Democratic and economic motives

The digitisation of accounting archives in China has to a high degree been driven by economic motives, by the desire to contribute to the overall economic development of China and to make it easier for enterprises to operate in the e-commerce domain. The development has resulted in economic benefits, as well as more efficient work processes and archives management (Yingfang Cai, 2017). At the same time, improvements in the accounting of enterprises may also be seen to strengthen democratic transparency.

The open data agenda is also often discussed in terms of improving both democracy and the economy, as data is the raw material in innovation processes and the development of services and products and its openness is central to the overall strategy to develop a digital economy within the European Union. In the case study carried out in Stockholm, records professionals expressed the view that they tend to represent a democratic perspective, which can balance out the more economic and technocratic view of data. They felt it was important not to lose sight of both aspects and this was also reflected at the political level where there were different opinions of who should take responsibility for the work and what emphasis it should have. A leading politician in Stockholm expressed concerns about the risks of open data, including the potential for information overload and negative use, and advocated caution in maintaining awareness of these risks in order to develop an open government that is beneficial to everyone. In this case, the Stockholm City Archives had been given a central role in the work on open data, partly because they were seen as taking a democratically important role (Engvall, Liang and Anderson, 2015).

In the UK studies, such as the NHS Trust, there was uncertainty as to the benefit that would actually come out of open data once it was released and it was suggested that work should be initiated with researchers and other users. Participants stated that the argument for OGD being a public good should be strengthened; one records professional expressed the view that 'there are more pressing things than releasing data for third parties to make money out of' (Chorley, Flinn and Shepherd, 2016, 45). Lack of a defined policy with regards to OGD, as well as a lack of resources, were also mentioned as challenges (Brimble, Flinn and Shepherd, 2016).

Competencies, skills and guidance required

The case studies in the UK and Sweden clearly showed the need for collaboration with other domains and professions. Records professionals have to learn other professionals' language, especially IT, in order to be able to communicate (Engvall, Liang and Anderson, 2015; Harrison, Shepherd and Flinn, 2015). In the transition to wholly digital information management, records managers have much to offer in terms of knowing about digital continuity and preservation, as well as about ensuring that data are contextualised, reliable and authentic. If they are to realise this potential and to play a more prominent role in responding to OGD initiatives, however, they will have to adopt the language and broader collaborative functions as required by a 'holistic, and ethically-sensitive approach to information governance' (Harrison, Shepherd and Flinn, 2015, 46).

Contemporary inconsistencies in the management of metadata across NHS England, with the consequent difficulties this brings in tracing back processed data to the original raw data, can serve as one example of what greater involvement by records managers could improve (Harrison, Shepherd and Flinn, 2015, 52–3). What is to be emphasised is the importance of strategic and managerial skills to take a proactive role and to develop common and coherent frameworks and strategies from the very beginning for the management of records (Engvall, Liang and Anderson, 2015). As the work on open data requires collaboration, it is important that responsibilities are clarified and shared and records professionals be more confident about their role and contributions in relation to other professions.

In the emerging arena of open data, further guidance is needed, particularly around issues such as appraisal (decisions about what should be retained and made available, to whom, in what format and at what time); risk assessments and ethical considerations regarding access; balancing security and openness with considerations of privacy; legal and procedural issues; assurance of the quality and trustworthiness, as well as the contextualisation of data; awareness of user needs; and development of tools for users to assess the authenticity of information online. It was also emphasised that, even though there are benefits to automation, from an ethical perspective it is important that humans are involved to make certain decisions and that decisions are not left entirely to machines (Engvall, Liang and Anderson, 2015).

In the UK case study, a desire was expressed for national guidance and assistance (for example, by The National Archives) in developing local policies and guidelines because there were gaps between nationally formulated policies and implementation at local level (Harrison, Shepherd and Flinn, 2015; Chorley, Flinn and Shepherd, 2016). In China, as mentioned earlier, a guide has been issued on enterprise digital records and archives management that sets out the rules and normative documents and plans and formulates steps for enterprises to carry out digital records management, addressing aspects of authenticity, long-term management and requirements for metadata capture. The implementation of these rules and procedures has also identified some key processes for digital record and archives management in practice, including the determination of the scope of digital recordkeeping for business systems, selection of formats for storage, determination of metadata, authenticity and long-term protection, treatment of different carriers of the same record and business system infrastructure conforming to archives management (State Archives Administration of China, 2016).

Records professionals' contribution

In the Stockholm City Archives study, the participants expressed their contribution in the following way:

> ... the archivist's role is to control and support how information comes about and is handled to meet everyone's needs; the archivist also considers the future and the rest of the world in their work – their perspective is hence much broader geographically and time-wise. They also help with creating frameworks and processes for what must be documented and acquired – appraisal of information – as well as what gets published and disseminated to the public.
>
> (Engvall, Liang and Anderson, 2015, 9–10)

What the case studies in the UK and Sweden show is that the major concerns around open data centre on privacy and security versus openness; data and metadata management, to make the data meaningful and trustworthy and to enable traceability from processed to raw data; ethical issues; and the navigation of varying interests for democratic concerns and economic benefits. This, as well as compliance with regulations, digital continuity and holistic strategies and frameworks for information provision, are some of the functions records professionals contribute to. Using records professionals' expertise to ensure trustworthy open government data is crucial for enabling open government to reach its goals of openness and trustworthiness (Brimble, Flinn and Shepherd, 2016), but it requires records professionals to improve their digital skills and expertise and to develop further guidance regarding the new complex environment.

The case studies indicate that questions at different levels of the diagrams in the ontology, such as security, access, control and legal compliance, data and metadata management, appraisal, archival preservation and more, are addressed. Challenges raised in the studies can be mapped onto the ontological diagrams to define responsibilities and to identify required improvements in skills and expertise. This would bring different tasks and challenges into focus and identify which profession should have responsibility for what. Relationships between records management, information governance, data protection, FOI and open government data, as well as responsibilities, should be clarified.

The example in China shows that records professionals have an important role to play if the digital records workflow is to function in its entirety, in this case in the e-commerce domain. Well managed, authentic accounting records are vital to ensure audit and inspection, risk control, internal control and internal and external supervision. The need for the standardised management of electronic accounting records has been fulfilled and the digital accounting archives project has led to the development of policies, standards, methods and practical tools, as well as to a discussion of the archives' role in societal development. Improvements have been made in digital records management and The Accounting Archives Management Measures lay a firm foundation for further steps, introducing relevant standards and norms, which can be extended to other types of digital records and archives management (Yingfang Cai, 2017). In relation to the ontology, this study has considered questions at different levels, for example on records and archival management; requirements on submission and ingest; disposal, control and audit; and preservation. It has also gone beyond the diagrams, showing the archives' role in a societal and business process context.

Examples put forward in the studies of the challenges, competencies needed and the contributions of records professionals are summarised below.

Table 11.1 *Examples of the challenges, competencies needed and contribution of records professionals in an open government context*

Challenges	• Balancing interests of openness versus security • Balancing a technocratic approach • Clarification and sharing of responsibilities • Coherence of different agendas • Resources • Data and Metadata management • Ensuring Reliability, Authenticity and Traceability of data • Prejudices against recordkeeping and records professionals.
Competencies needed	• Understanding of IT language • Digital skills • Collaboration with other professions • Proactivity • Management and strategic skills • Appraisal and risk assessment • Knowledge about users and development of tools for users • Ethical and value guidelines.
Contribution	• Compliance with regulation • Digital continuity and preservation • Data and metadata management • Security and Control of sensitive information • Holistic strategies and frameworks for records provision • Contextualised, authentic and reliable records • Trusted and impartial third party • Standardisation and systematisation of electronic records management • Facilitation of risk control, audit and transparency • Enabling digital workflows.

Conclusion

This chapter highlighted the perspective of records professionals as they try to define their role and responsibilities in the face of a rapidly changing technological and social environment. Their primary concern remains the maintenance of a persistent digital memory and evidence base that are trusted as both an accurate record of past events and transactions and a solid grounding for future decisions and action. Their primary challenge is to work out how this can be achieved in increasingly networked, yet distributed, technologies, in connected but distrustful and polarised social landscapes. Neither this concern nor this challenge are or should be of records professionals alone. They will be able to address them on their own, but, if they are to maintain their collective sense of identity, they will need to negotiate and define what their own role and contribution can and should be towards meeting this challenge.

At a high level, the ITrust work summarised in this whole book can be seen as one such contribution, but, more specifically within this chapter, the ontology of functions and activities that has been developed is another one, building as it does from the experience of the profession to model the extent and complexity of the task of maintaining trustworthy records.

In this chapter, we also show that records professionals in a number of national contexts are wrestling with complexities on a daily basis. Anxiety over increasing workload were clearly expressed, as was the necessity of building working relationships with other professionals and participating in new conversations about, for example, information governance and open government data. For some, this seems an uphill battle as others see them as entrenched in a more traditional paper-based past rather than an exciting digital future. For others, it is natural to take an active leading role and use new developments as opportunities to extend their role. Nevertheless, those interviewed were all involved in practically negotiating the meaning and implications of the new conversations opening up. This meaning could be seen broadly as a renegotiation of the boundary between public and private, and more specifically as a resolution of the tensions felt among managing individual organizations' risk in a public accountability context, protecting personal information while still making data public, and in balancing democratic goals with those for business innovation. These themes were also considered in Chapter 3, putting to the fore questions regarding values and ethics.

This chapter also serves to remind records professionals of the importance of context in the way conversations are developing. For example, the studies reported show that, even within the same national context, the conversation around open government takes slightly different forms in different sectors, namely health, local government and higher education. Then again, comparing the national contexts of Sweden, the UK and China reported here, it is clear that the Chinese conversation is more focused on economic development than on open government and open government data in the way Sweden and the UK are. Records professionals are not the only ones having to negotiate this complex situation. How they choose to do so – and how others define their role – is open to question, but they undoubtedly do have a contribution to make.

References

Abbott, A. D. (1988) *The System of Professions: an essay on the division of expert labor.* http://public.eblib.com/choice/publicfullrecord.aspx?p=3563014

Bastian, J. (2004) Taking Custody, Giving Access: a postcustodial role for a new century, *Archivaria*, **53**, 76–93.

Brimble, S., Flinn, A. and Shepherd, E. (2016) *The Role of the Records Manager/Records Management in an Open Government Environment in the UK: higher education.* EU32, Phase 1 Final Report. InterPARES Trust. https://interparestrust.org/assets/public/dissemination/EU32InterPARESReport.pdf

Chorley, K., Flinn, A. and Shepherd, E. (2016) *The Role of the Records Manager/Records Management in an Open Government Environment in the UK: the National Health Service (local records).* EU27, Final Report. InterPARES Trust. https://interparestrust.org/assets/public/dissemination/InterPARESTrustResearchReportEU27.pdf

Craig, B. L. (2011) The Past May Be the Prologue: history's place in the future of the information professions, *Libraries and the Cultural Records*, **46** (2).

Crockett, M. (2009) A Practitioner's Guide to the Freedom of Information Act 2000, *Journal of the Society of Archivists*, **30** (2), 191–225. https://doi.org/10.1080/00379810903444995

Cunningham, A. and Phillips, M. (2005) Accountability and Accessibility: ensuring the evidence of e-governance in Australia, *Aslib Proceedings*, **57** (4), 301–17. https://doi.org/10.1108/00012530510612059

Currall, J. and Moss, M. (2008) We Are Archivists, But Are We OK?, *Records Management Journal*, **18** (1), 69–91. https://doi.org/10.1108/09565690810858532

Davis, S. E. (2003) Descriptive Standards and the Archival Profession, *Cataloging and Classification Quarterly*, **35** (3–4), 291–308. https://doi.org/10.1300/J104v35n03_02

Duranti, L. and Franks, P. (eds) (2015) *Encyclopedia of Archival Science*. Lanham: Rowman & Littlefield Publishers.

Engvall, T., Liang, V. and Anderson, K. (2015) *The Role of the Archivist and Records Manager in an Open Government Environment in Sweden*, EU11, Final Report, InterPARES Trust, https://interparestrust.org/assets/public/dissemination/EU11_20150707_RoleRMOpenGovSweden_EUWorkshop5_FinalReport_Final.pdf

Gänser, G. and Michetti, G. (2018) *Ontology of Functional Activities for Archival Systems.* TR05, Final Report. InterPARES Trust. https://interparestrust.org/assets/public/dissemination/TR05-FinalReport-20180526.pdf

Harrison, E., Shepherd, E. and Flinn, A. (2015) *A Research Report into Open Government Data in NHS England.* EU19, Final Report. InterPARES Trust. https://interparestrust.org/assets/public/dissemination/EU19_20150421_UKNationalHealthService_FinalReport.pdf

International Organization for Standardization (ISO) (2016) *ISO 15489-1 Information and Documentation – Records Management, Part 1 Concepts and Principles.* Geneva:

ISO, https://www.iso.org/standard/62542.html

Kallberg, M. (2013) *The Emperor's New Clothes: recordkeeping in a new context*, PhD Thesis, Mid-Sweden University.

Lomas, E. (2010) Information Governance: information security and access within a UK context, *Records Management Journal*, **20** (2), 182–98, https://doi.org/10.1108/09565691011064322

Lord Chancellor (2009) *Lord Chancellor's Code of Practice on the Management of Records Issued under Section 46 of the Freedom of Information Act 2000*, Ministry of Justice and The National Archives, www.nationalarchives.gov.uk/documents/foi-section-46-code-of-practice.pdf

MacNeil, H. (2011) Trust and Professional Identity: narratives, counter-narratives and lingering ambiguities, *Archival Science*, **11** (3–4), 175–92, https://doi.org/10.1007/s10502-011-9150-5

McLeod, J. (2012) Thoughts on the Opportunities for Records Professionals of the Open Access, Open Data Agenda, *Records Management Journal*, **22** (2), 92–7, https://doi.org/10.1108/09565691211268711

Menne-Haritz, A. (2001) Access – The Reformulation of an Archival Paradigm, *Archival Science*, **1** (1), 57–82, https://doi.org/10.1007/BF02435639

Michetti, G. (2015) *Unneutrality Of Archival Standards And Processes (Short Version)*, https://doi.org/10.5281/zenodo.17937

Page, J., Flinn, A. and Shepherd, E. (2014) *The Role of the Records Manager in an Open Government Environment in the UK*, EU03, Final Report. InterPARES Trust, https://interparestrust.org/assets/public/dissemination/EU03_20141105_RoleRMOpenGovUK_FinalReport.pdf

Pearce-Moses, R. (2018) *InterPARES Trust Terminology*, InterPARES Trust, www.interparestrust.org/terminology.

Shepherd, E. and Ennion, E. (2007) How Has the Implementation of the UK Freedom of Information Act 2000 Affected Archives and Records Management Services?, *Records Management Journal*, **17** (1), 32–51. https://doi.org/10.1108/09565690710730688

State Archives Administration of China (2015) *Guide for Corporate Electronic Document Filing and Electronic Records Management*. http://daj.hanzhong.gov.cn/nry2014.jsp?urltype=news.NewsContentUrl&wbnewsid=12689&wbtreeid=1023

State Archives Administration of China (2016) *The 13th Five-Year Plan for National Archives Development*, www.saac.gov.cn/news/2016-04/07/content_136280.htm

State Council (2015) *State Council's Opinions on Developing E-Commerce to Accelerate the Cultivation of New Economic Dynamics*, www.gov.cn/zhengce/content/2015-05/07/content_9707.htm

Stockholm stadsarkiv (2014) *Dig In – Digital Arkivstrategi För Stockholms Stad [Dig In – Digital Archival Strategy for the City of Stockholm]*, http://insynsverige.se/stockholm-kultur/dagordning?date=2014-08-26#agenda-8

Svärd, P. (2014) The Impact of Information Culture on Information/Records Management: a case study of a municipality in Belgium, *Records Management Journal*, **24** (1), 5–21, https://doi.org/10.1108/RMJ-04-2013-0007

Tough, A. (2011) Accountability, Open Government and Record Keeping: time to think again?, *Records Management Journal*, **21** (3), 225–36, https://doi.org/10.1108/09565691111186894

Vaillant, S. (2003) The Complexities of Working in the International Records Management Business – RM Isn't Rocket Science, or Is It?, *Records Management Journal*, **13** (3), 111–16, https://doi.org/10.1108/09565690310507310

Writing Group of Explanation on Accounting Archives Management Measures (2016) *Explanation on Accounting Archives Management Measures – Revised*, Beijing, China Financial and Economic Publishing House.

Yingfang Cai (2017) Research on System of Policies, Legislation, Regulations and Standards about Electronic Records Management on E-Commerce, *Archives Science Study*, s1, 108–15.

Note

1   The complete set of reference documents includes: the series ISO 15489, ISO 16175, ISO 23081, ISO 27000 and ISO 30300; the standards ISO 14641-1, ISO 14721 and ISO 16363; the Technical Reports ISO 26122 and ISO 15801; and ARMA International's Generally Accepted Recordkeeping Principles as well as the Society of American Archivists' list of Core Archival Functions (Gänser and Michetti, 2018).

12

Education

Victoria Lemieux and Darra Hofman

Introduction

In this chapter, we return to reflect upon the goal of the InterPARES Trust (hereinafter ITrust) project, which was:

> . . .to generate the theoretical and methodological **frameworks** that will support the development of integrated and consistent local, national and international **networks of policies, procedures, regulations, standards and legislation concerning digital records entrusted to the Internet**, to ensure public trust grounded on evidence of good governance, a strong digital economy, and a persistent digital memory [in relation to models of education for records professionals.] [emphasis in original text]
>
> (Duranti, 2013)

Based on evidence generated from ITrust studies conducted during the period 2013–2018, this chapter advances the argument that, owing to changes in the characteristics of records and the context of record making and recordkeeping (e.g. the introduction of cloud technology) and in the range of tasks and functions that records professionals now perform over the course of their careers, the education of records professionals requires an updated educational framework that draws upon diverse sources of knowledge and recognises that the application of archival knowledge and thinking will take place in an increasingly broad range of professional contexts.

The studies conducted under the auspices of the ITrust project demonstrate that records professionals now work in diverse settings: cultural heritage institutions, government agencies, international organizations, private for or not-for-profit entities and as independent consultants. The nature of the work is also increasingly diverse, ranging from that of the traditional archivist to that of the digital archivist, digital preservation specialist, records manager, information manager, privacy officer, access to information officer and archival science researcher and educator, to identify but a few of the possible career pathways open to those who possess graduate level archival education. Further, records and archival professional careers increasingly span all levels of organizations, from entry-level junior positions to the most senior executive levels (see Figure 12.1).

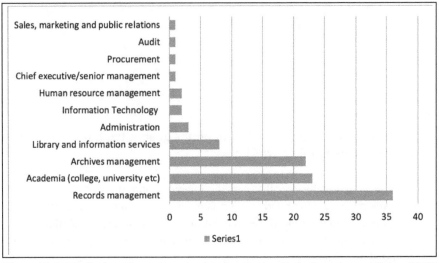

Figure 12.1 *Distribution of records and archival professional roles* (Ngoebe and Katuu, 2017)

The technical and policy challenges that records and archives professionals face are also growing in complexity: changing technical forms of records, digital preservation, protection of privacy, indigenous rights, trust in information and institutions, open government and access to public information all mean that the daily practices and decisions of these professionals have an increasing impact upon society now and in the future. Thus, education, whether pre-appointment, pre-university or university-based undergraduate or graduate, on-the-job or continuing post-appointment (Katuu, 2009), must prepare them for diverse careers, contexts of professional practice and responsibilities.

Analytic framework
The analysis presented in this chapter takes a competencies-based approach

to understanding the educational requirements needed as a foundation for records and archival work. For the purposes of this study, knowledge, skills and attitudes (or, in some variations, abilities) are all considered to be aspects of 'competence' or 'competency'.

There is a large, diverse literature on each of these terms, their meaning and their usefulness; generally speaking, however, a competency framework is 'a descriptive tool that identifies the skills, knowledge, personal characteristics, and behaviors needed to effectively perform a role in [an] organization and help the business meet its strategic objectives' (Lucia and Lepsinger, 1999, 5). In their widely cited article on the subject, Le Deist and Winterton (2005) developed a model that aligns the American Knowledge, Skills and Abilities (KSA) model, the French model of *savoir*, *savoir-faire* and *savoir-être* and the German model of Beruf, Qualifikation and Kompetenz:

	Occupational	*Personal*
Conceptual	Cognitive competence	Meta competence
Operational	Functional competence	Social competence

Figure 12.2 *Model of Competency Framework*

Cognitive competence, which aligns with knowledge, consists of the cognitive frameworks, knowledge and understanding necessary in an occupation. Functional competence encompasses the functional, psychomotor and applied skill competences of a profession. Social competence captures attitudes or savoir-être, the appropriate social behaviours to be successful in an occupation. Meta-competence, which is often beyond the scope of a graduate educational program, is the ability to learn and to acquire and integrate the other competencies.

Cheetham and Chivers (1996, 1998) have a model of five inter-connected competences:

- **Cognitive competence**, including underpinning theory and concepts, as well as informal tacit knowledge gained experientially. Knowledge (know-what), underpinned by understanding (know-why), is distinguished from competence.
- **Functional competence** (skills or know-how), those things that a person who works in a given occupational area should be able to do and be able to demonstrate.
- **Personal competence** (behavioural competence, or know how to behave), defined as a relatively enduring characteristic of a person causally related to effective or superior performance in a job.
- **Ethical competence**, defined as the possession of appropriate personal and professional values and the ability to make sound judgements based upon these in work-related situations.
- **Meta-competence**, concerned with the ability to cope with uncertainty, as well as with learning and reflection.

For the purposes of this project, the Cheetham and Chivers meaning of cognitive competence, functional competence and ethical competence provide the broad structure to which the research team adhered in looking for professional competencies used by records and archives professionals. While 'personal values' as such, were beyond the scope of this project, the research team did look at capturing information about records managers' and archivists' professional values and the competences necessary to be able to make sound ethical judgements.

It is important to note that competencies exist at different levels. The DigCurV Curriculum Framework, which was designed for 'supporting the professional development across [market] sectors' (DigCurV, 2013), categorises skill levels simply and hierarchically into 'basic, denoted by "is aware of"', 'intermediate, "understands"', and 'advanced, "is able to"'. While such organization is fairly intuitive and common, it is by no means definitive. A commonly used tool for organizing pedagogical goals is *Bloom's Taxonomy of Educational Objectives*, first published in 1956, which categorised learning goals, from the simplest and concrete to the most complex and abstract, as knowledge, comprehension, application, analysis, synthesis and evaluation (Bloom et al., 1984). Figure 12.3 opposite shows the original taxonomy, a pyramid with knowledge at the base.

Bloom's Taxonomy was revised by Anderson and Krathwohl (2001) in *A Taxonomy for Teaching, Learning, and Assessment* to emphasise the dynamism of learning and educational objectives, as well as the iterative nature of learning (note the spiral in the middle of the revised taxonomy):

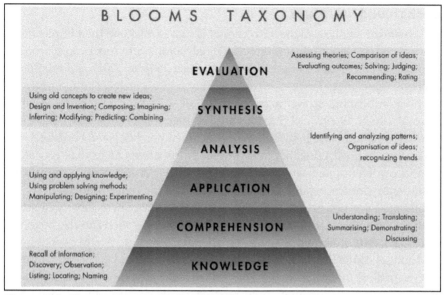

Figure 12.3 *Blooms Taxonomy* (Alford, Herbert and Frangenheim, 2006)

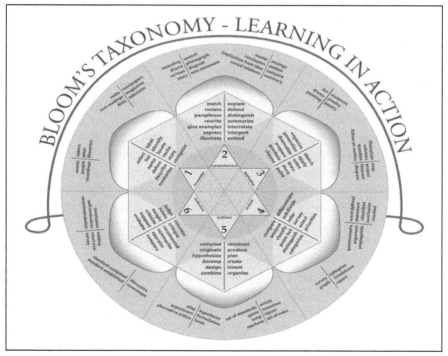

Figure 12.4 *'Bloom's Rose'* (Aainsqatsi, n.d.)

Background literature

To situate our analysis of the outcomes of ITrust studies and their implications for archival education, we undertook an analysis of North American, European and African archival literature written between 2001 and 2017 and relating to archival education. There is no journal devoted exclusively to literature on archival education, so writings on this topic are found in general archival journals, such as *Archival Science* and *The American Archivist*, as well as in journals on library and information science, documentation and heritage. Since 2008, the Archival Education and Research Initiative (AERI) has run as an annual conference dedicated to archival research and education; although the conference does not publish proceedings, and therefore papers from the conference are not always widely available, such papers have generated material on archival education. Papers on archival education can also be found amongst those presented at the International Council on Archives' Congress and annual conferences. Over the past six years, there has been steady, though not overriding, interest in archival education in the literature, as reflected in the number of articles on that topic relative to articles on other topics. Not surprisingly, authors of articles on archival education usually are associated with a graduate archival education programme.

An article by Langmead (2015) discusses who these archival educators are. Her thesis is that there have been two distinct generations of leaders in the field of archival education. The first consisted of the archival pioneers who, while educated as historians, taught archival matters while still working as archivists. The second generation of educators, currently at the helm, consists in large part of professionals who left their work in order to become full-time academics. Only a few of these educators hold degrees in archival science, mostly from Europe, while most have tended to have backgrounds in history or in library and information science. There is now a third cohort of archival educators assuming the leadership of the field who moved directly from their academic studies to teaching positions. This group includes the first archival educators in North America who earned doctorates in the independent academic discipline of 'archival studies'. To Langmead's typology we may also add a smattering of educators who have earned doctorates in computer science and then gone into archival education, while still working either as archival practitioners or as full-time educators.

One of the dominant themes in the writings on archival education is the growth and use of digital records and archives, expressing anxiety about the degree to which archival education is adequately preparing professionals to deal with these changes. Katuu (2009, 2015) discusses this concern in the African context, calling for recognition that North American and European education and training models may not be suited to the African context, where organizations are still struggling to address dilapidated records systems for paper records.

Marciano et al. (2018) call for the formation of, and education in, a new transdiscipline of 'Computational Archival Science'. This call comes amidst and in response to the rise of 'big' digital data in the archives and 'records as data', as well as of new approaches to engaging with archival materials that draw upon data science tools and techniques (e.g. information visualisation and visual analytics, natural language processing, machine learning, etc.). It opens up a novel current of archival discourse by introducing ideas from computer and data science as a perspective on the mission and identity of archives and archivists. The observation from a review of the literature on archival education that development of technological competencies is of increasing importance in the education of archivists supports findings from other sources reviewed for this study. For example, a study by Lyon et al. (2015) draws attention to the rise of data-related job descriptions and advertisements for data librarians, data stewards/curators and data archivists. In relation to the knowledge and skills required of data archivists, the researchers observed that employers were calling for, among other things, disciplinary knowledge (e.g. science, health) and knowledge of data collection procedures, metadata standards and data integration techniques, as well as skills in statistical software packages and web authoring tools and research experience. They further note that the job of data archivist did not arise as often as that for data librarian or data steward/curator, possibly suggesting that the traditional job of archivists is being renamed and reclassified in different job sectors today.

In terms of recruitment, they suggest that programmes need to consider recruiting STEM graduates who have strong technical and quantitative skills and are able to manipulate tabular data or perform statistical analyses of datasets using a software package such as R or SPSS. This raises the question of how best to support development of such competencies amongst records and archives professionals. Anderson et al. (2011) discuss the value of lab-based education in the development of digital expertise. This supports evidence from a review of archival education programmes which indicates that the creation of labs – virtual or physical – is a central part of the archival education offering in an increasing number of archival programmes.

Pat Franks' 2013 paper on infusing digital curation competencies into the SLIS program discusses the unprecedented growth and demand for digital skills, but acknowledges that education and training programs are inadequate to meet the demand (Franks, 2013). She goes on to describes how digital curation competencies have been integrated into San Jose State University's SLIS program and how one course, a course designed to provide professional experiences through internship, has been used as a way for students to apply their knowledge and hone their digital skills.

Franks' observations are supported by other articles that discuss the value of practice as part of archival education in order to apply theoretical knowledge learned in taught courses. Access to practical experience is necessary as students typically struggle with the application of abstract knowledge, especially as it relates to technical skills needed to deal with digital records and archives. This is a theme reflected in other sources of evidence considered for this study and suggests that experience-based learning opportunities must remain a prominent part of archival education.

Another dominant theme arising from an analysis of the literature is the growing influence of critical perspectives in currents of archival thinking. This strand of thinking has encouraged archivists to challenge traditional conceptions of their professional mission and identity. It is a perspective reflected in archival discourse in relation to memory, power (e.g. colonialism/post-colonialism), culture, identity (e.g. queering the archives, indigenous sovereignty) and inclusivity. Terry Cooks' 2013 essay is indicative: he argues that archival paradigms over the past 150 years have gone through four phases, from juridical legacy to cultural memory to societal engagement to community archiving (Cook, 2013). The archivist, he says, has been transformed, from passive curator to active appraiser to societal mediator to community facilitator. The literature on this theme reflects, furthermore, a focus on 'the archive' as opposed to archives and on the 'archival multiverse' as opposed to a single archival paradigm (The Archival Education and Research Institute (AERI) and Pluralizing the Archival Curriculum Group (PACG), 2011). Authors of these papers call for a move away from a preoccupation with evidence in archival education to one that reflects on issues of memory, identity and community, as the broader intellectual currents of a shift from pre-modern to modern to postmodern to contemporary thought. Also reflective of this theme, and its implications for archival education, is a focus on possibilities for healing conflicting discourses within the archival profession, as exemplified by literature and discussions on processes of truth and reconciliation between First Nations peoples and white settlers (White & Gilliland, 2010). These strands of archival thought have also led to calls for greater emphasis on ethical reflection and frameworks in archival education. Caswell observes, however, that even as critical theoretical perspectives discuss 'the archive', they reflect no acknowledgement of the discipline of archival science and its contribution to managing 'the archives' (Caswell, 2016).

A few articles also discuss approaches to archival education integrated with other fields, a perspective motivated by the fact that these fields have a shared mandate to collect, acquire and preserve cultural heritage materials. A 2007 article by Anna Maria Tammaro explores ways that iSchools can participate in research and education relevant to the employment of information professionals in libraries, archives and museums to provide access to and preservation of the collections held by these institutions (Tammaro, 2007). Tammaro argues that the education of information professionals for each of these institutions has primarily been separate, with diverse tracks and traditions, and notes that while some schools educating librarians do offer courses that include discussion of the application of library and information science skills to archival and museum collections, few offer full specialisations in this area. Tammaro correctly notes that, in the North American context, archival education has traditionally been based on degrees in history but, as archives have increased digitisation to provide preservation and expand access to the content, the need for staff with more technical knowledge and skills related to the preservation and expansion of access to archives has grown. She notes similar trends in museum studies and library and information science and uses this as a basis for a case for more integrated approaches to education. A paper by Australian Bob Pymm (2012) also echoes this theme, calling for more collaborative educational offerings that draw in 'kindred sectors'.

Other papers discuss archival education in relation to the users of archives, with Vilar and Šauperl (2014) arguing that archival literature has, by and large, paid relatively little attention to user studies. Duff, Yakel and Tibbo (2013) propose an Archival Reference Knowledge (ARK) Model based on their research. Archival reference competencies suggested in these two articles include:

- Research knowledge (domain knowledge, especially)
- Collection knowledge (i.e. knowledge of holdings and the context of records creation)
- Interaction knowledge (i.e. user behaviour and institutional practices).

Duff, Yakel and Tibbo note that some of the knowledge required of reference archivists cannot be easily taught through formal education (e.g. knowledge of holdings); however, archival education can include instruction on how to read finding aids and link the information in these representations of archival holdings back to the context of archival creation.

It is noteworthy that articles on archival education such as those discussing the value of integrated approaches take a vocational view of archival education, focusing on its role as providing training for the archivist destined to work in a traditional archives or memory/cultural institution. The focus of the literature stands in contrast to the fact that, increasingly, graduates of archival education programmes are working in contexts outside of these traditional institutions. There thus appears to be a gap in scholarly writing on education for other types of roles, which perhaps reflects a failure on the part of archival educators to reflect sufficiently upon the need to develop education that transcends a specific occupational locus. By its nature, this type of 'transcendent' education would have to rely on a strong archival theoretical foundation, even as students may choose to also learn about theories from other relevant disciplines or particular schools of thought – such as law, information science, management or critical theory and post modernism – each of which may be more relevant in one locus of archival work than in another.

Methodology

This study is based upon the findings (at time of the analysis) of the other studies undertaken under the auspices of ITrust. The ITrust studies reports provided the source for examining archival competencies for several reasons. Firstly, the studies, although not directly focused on archival competencies, nonetheless capture the work and concerns of records professionals in a diversity of organizations, roles and contexts, including diverse juridical contexts. Two coders, both enrolled in archival education programs at the University of British Columbia (Coder 1 is a Master of Archival Studies student; Coder 2 is a PhD student in Library, Archival and Information Studies, specialised in archival studies), divided the final reports evenly and coded each report, using NVivo qualitative analysis software, for the occurrence of professional competencies needed by archivists. Although both coders used the broad categories of the Le Deist and Winterton model as their conceptual framework (and as *de facto a priori* codes), the codes beyond that were entirely grounded or emergent. Those codes were then analysed and queried to reveal the education model that emerged from each coder's work. From those models, common categories and themes were identified. While the methodology took significant inspiration from grounded theory (Strauss and Corbin, 1990), the ultimate goal of this research deviated from that of pure grounded theory (the generation of theory from data) and the methodology thus deviated as well.

Findings

Despite the two coders working independently, there was significant convergence in the themes that emerged. The coders' functional coding exhibited the most diversity, in part due to the nature of the studies each researcher happened to code (Coder 2 coded several reports addressing open government initiatives, leading to a substantial amount of codes related to the legal functions of records and archives professionals). Research skills, however, featured prominently in both coders' results. Finally, the coders commenced the study sceptical as to the likelihood of finding social competences in the results of the other ITrust studies findings; instead, both coders' results identified ethics, including the particularly challenging 'making hard decisions' (termed 'leadership' by Coder 2), as an important emergent theme.

Building on the coding done by each coder, as well as close analysis of the codes nested under the high-level categories, a (relatively broad) hierarchy of cognitive competencies arose fairly clearly (see Figure 12.5).

Cognitive competencies relate to theories and concepts that support records

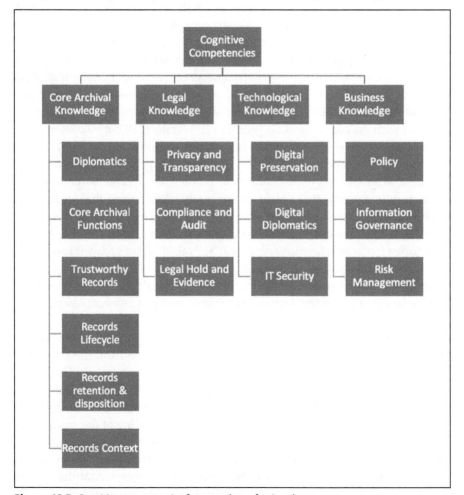

Figure 12.5 *Cognitive competencies for records professionals*

and archives professional work, as well as informal tacit knowledge gained experientially. It is hardly surprising that the model that emerged from analysis of ITrust studies identified core archival knowledge, including diplomatic theory (see, e.g. Duranti, 1998), a theoretical framework that underpins the ITrust research project, as a significant component of required professional cognitive competency. Aside from diplomatic theory, competency in core archival functions (e.g. appraisal, arrangement and description and reference and outreach) is necessary, as is knowledge of what constitutes trustworthy records and recordkeeping (i.e. for evidentiary purposes), knowledge of the theory and processes associated with administering the records' life cycle, including retention and disposition of records, and, finally, competency in analysis of the context of records creation and keeping.

Functional competencies (i.e. necessary skills and know-how), by contrast, were more challenging to identify, in part because of the varied functions that records and archives professionals in the studies fulfil for their organizations. However, in-depth analysis of the coding revealed that, while not every professional would fulfil every function, there were nonetheless clear categories of functions that records and archives professionals could be asked to, and need the skill to, perform. Perhaps unsurprisingly, these functions aligned with the cognitive skills required (this reflects *Bloom's Taxonomy*; one cannot practice a skill without the knowledge underlying that skill). Again, the hierarchy below is broad-stroke, reflecting the general themes raised in the data; after all, 'risk management' or 'privacy' are literatures, courses and even professions unto themselves. However, the data reveals that records and archives professionals need a fundamental level of competence in those areas. The hierarchy shows the most commonly occurring examples in the sub-categories (such as reference/access and appraisal under archival functions), but these are illustrative, as opposed to exhaustive or exclusive; thus, the data demonstrated that records and archives professionals must have functional competency in all of the archival functions (not just reference/access and appraisal).

The research team was surprised that contract management and negotiation as well as business case development did not emerge from the coding as required functional competencies for records and archives professionals, especially since the context of the ITrust project was the long-term preservation of authentic records in online environments. The absence of this competency may be attributable to the fact that the coding of the studies was carried out before all final study reports, in particular 'Preservation as a Service for Trust' (PaaST) (Thibodeau, 2018), were completed and available. Anecdotally, feedback on the results of this study suggests that these skills also are gaining importance as archival professional competencies.

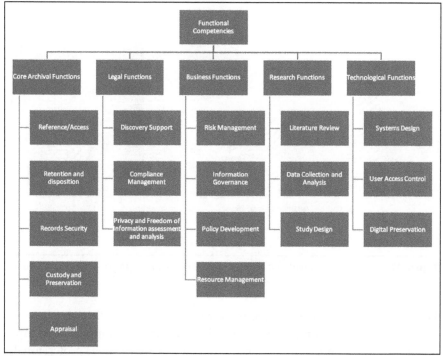

Figure 12.6 *Functional competencies for records and archives professionals*

A survey of records and archives professionals in 15 countries, primarily located in Kenya, Zimbabwe, South Africa and Botswana, 'Curriculum Alignments at Institutions of Higher Learning in Africa: Preparing Professionals to Manage Records Created in Networked Environments', indicates that educational programmes do not yet cover the full range of topics and skills needed by professionals to respond to the complex and diverse range of issues raised in the other ITrust studies (see Figure 12.7 on the next page) (Katuu, 2018). Figure 12.7 represents the results of a survey conducted by the ITrust African Team that asked respondents to indicate the extent to which their educational programmes covered four cognate areas: introduction to information technology, legal aspects of the records profession, current records management and introduction to digital preservation. Survey respondents indicated that in all but current records management, course coverage was moderate to non-existent. It remains to be seen whether these survey results also reflect the experience of European, North American, Latin American and Asian records professionals, but our intuition based on anecdotal evidence is that the results from these regions would be broadly aligned with the results of the survey conducted for this study.

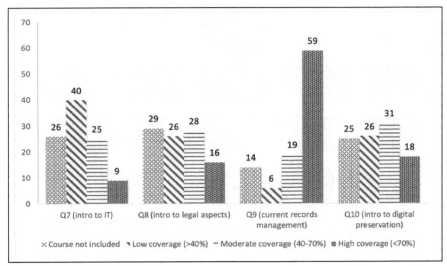

Figure 12.7 *Courses and extent that were covered in respondents' programmes* (Katuu, 2018)

Finally, the data and codes were reviewed to develop a (fairly constrained) hierarchy of social competencies. While significantly more social competencies are likely necessary for successful records and archives professionals, those below were captured by the ITrust research results at hand at the time that the coding was carried out.

Ethical competencies identified in the ITrust study, which encompass the possession of appropriate personal and professional values and the ability to

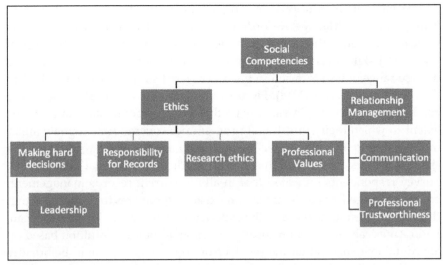

Figure 12.8 *Social competencies for records and archives professionals*

make sound judgements based upon these in work-related situations, included competency in making decisions around ethical choices and conflicting values. This competency, in turn, was viewed as being associated with having leadership competency. Responsibility for records, and even a Jenkinsonian 'duty' to the records (Jenkinson, 1937), still emerged as an important social competency for records and archives professionals. Given the importance of functional competency in research, it is not surprising that social competence related to research ethics emerged from the analysis of the ITrust studies. Naturally, professional values also emerged as being important, although a limitation of this study is that the coding did not focus on analysing an emergent set of concepts to define the broad parameters of a shared set of professional values. Similar to other professions, communication and professional trustworthiness were also identified as key social competencies for records professionals.

After the above hierarchies of core categories were developed, the researchers compared them to an existing standard of archival education, as well as an allied discipline's curriculum, the DigCurV. They began with the Society of American Archivists' (SAA) recommended curriculum for Graduate Programs in Archival Studies (GPAS) because it was the most recently revised (Society of American Archivists, 2016). Although SAA does not organize their GPAS into a formal hierarchy, these researchers have done so for ease of comparison (see Figure 12.9 on the next page).

It is gratifying – though not necessarily surprising – that the SAA guidelines align closely with the results of the research. Although hierarchies that emerged out of this study treated the legal category as a separate cognitive and functional area of competence from the archival areas, it is so fundamental that the SAA has subsumed it under 'core archival knowledge'. The ITrust research did not identify a central role of financial systems, unlike the SAA model, which focuses on the fairly narrow category of 'organizational theory'. The ITrust research revealed that practising records and archives professionals require a fairly broad base of business knowledge, including risk management, information governance, policy development and implementation and relationship management, in addition to organizational theory. The study also did not reveal the direct connections to allied fields, such as library and information science, but a number of codes and categories (such as those related to metadata) draw on work from both library and information science and other allied professions, such as computer science. However, the allied professional competences required are likely to depend upon the career path of an individual records professional.

The framework also aligns well with the DigCurV curriculum for digital curation. DigCurV organizes digital curation skills into four categories:

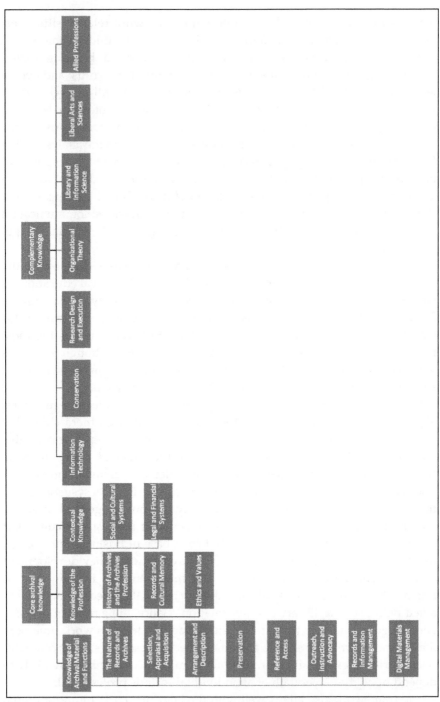

Figure 12.9 *Hierarchical representation of the Society of American Archivists' Graduate Program in Archival Studies Guidelines* (SAA, 2016)

Knowledge and Intellectual Abilities (KIA), Personal Qualities (PQ), Professional Conduct (PC) and Management and Quality Assurance (MQA), which consists of risk management, audit and certification, and resource management (2013). The competences identified are highly similar; the differences arise primarily in categorisation. Thus, the DigCurV curriculum's 'Professional Conduct' skill includes legal knowledge and skill (regulatory requirements knowledge and regulatory compliance skills), along with ethics, principles and sustainability (which our framework emphasises as being primarily social). Similarly, while the MQA skillset was quite important to archival practice in this study, it was not broken out separately, but was rather understood in both its cognitive and functional modes.

Implications

This chapter has presented an analysis of evidence generated from ITrust studies conducted between 2013 and 2018. The chapter advances the argument that, owing to changes in the characteristics of records and the context of recordkeeping (e.g. the rise of computerised information processing and communication) and in the range of tasks and functions that records and archives professionals now perform over the course of their careers, as discussed in the ITrust studies, the education of such professionals now requires an updated educational model that draws on more diverse sources of knowledge to support the features of today's records and archives and the diverse professional contexts in which records and archives professionals now work.

The analysis is not without its limitations: given the timeline for completion of the analysis, coding had to be carried out before all final study reports were available. In addition, the research team was unable to drill down into every concept that emerged from the coding exercise (e.g. professional values) to develop a comprehensive understanding of the composition of the concept grounded in the research studies. Nevertheless, the analysis points in some useful directions.

For educators, the models of the competencies now needed by records and archives professionals can be used to develop educational programme guidelines and guide curriculum design. We hope, for example, that the framework presented in this chapter will help to inform the creation and updating of graduate programme guidelines for archival studies in the various jurisdictions in which the ITrust project has undertaken research. We also suggest that educators use the models in the design or updating of educational offerings by translating the cognitive, functional and some of the social competencies into courses that build the theoretical knowledge and skills required of today's professionals. The scope of the topics in each course and the depth of coverage would, of course, vary according to the nature of the educational programme (i.e. whether it is a pre-appointment certificate programme, a university-based undergraduate or graduate programme or a continuing education short course). We refer readers to the AF01 study report for an example of how some of the cognitive and functional competencies may be represented in four distinct courses, 'Introduction to IT', 'Introduction to Law for Archives and Records Professionals', 'Management of Current Records' and 'Introduction to Digital Preservation', in the context of university-based graduate professional education. In-class interactions and assignments can be designed to further strengthen students' functional and social competencies.

We also hope that this analysis will be useful in the diverse organizational contexts where records and archives professionals now seek and find employment. The human resources departments of these organizations can use the competency models presented in this chapter to develop job descriptions and evaluate candidates for new roles based on their cognitive, functional and social competencies. Typically, it is still difficult to find one individual who possesses all the competencies we identified; however, the framework can help organizational leaders ensure that they have staff with the knowledge and skills to cover all the competencies.

For records and archives professionals, the framework of competencies that has emerged from the ITrust studies will serve to help them assess the competencies they currently possess against the broad range of competencies required of today's professionals. Where there are areas of weakness, professionals can then seek out professional educational offerings to address gaps in knowledge or skills.

Finally, we suggest that the educational model presented in this chapter will help those from other professions, such as accountants, computer programmers and software developers, lawyers, etc., appreciate the knowledge and skills possessed by records and archives professionals and identify when the expertise of a records and archives professional is needed on a project or within ongoing operations.

Conclusion

The ITrust studies analysed for this chapter point to the growing complexity of records and archives records work and the rising expectations and demands on the records and archives professionals. As society moves further into the digital era, with greater reliance on cloud and other emerging forms of technology (e.g. blockchain and distributed ledgers) for recordkeeping, it is clear that the competencies that these professionals must possess to perform effectively in their jobs is neither trivial nor easy obtained. Collectively, the records and archives professional community around the world faces an enormous and urgent challenge to ensure that their profession receive the education they need to succeed.

References

Aainsqatsi, K. (n.d.) *Bloom's Rose*, CC BY-SA 3.0 (https://creativecommons.org/licenses/by-sa/3.0) or GFDL (www.gnu.org/copyleft/fdl.html)], from Wikimedia Commons, https://commons.wikimedia.org/wiki/File:Blooms_rose.svg

Alford, G., Herbert, P. and Frangenheim, E. (2006) *Innovative Teachers' Companion 2006*, Toowoomba, Qld, ITC Publications.

Anderson, K., Bastian, J., Harvey, R., Plum, T. and Samuelsson, G. (2011) Teaching to Trust: how a virtual archives and preservation curriculum laboratory creates a global education community?, *Archival Science*, **11** (3–4), 349–72, https://doi.org/10.1007/s10502-011-9157-y

Anderson, L. W. and Krathwohl, D. R. (eds) (2001) *A Taxonomy for Learning, Teaching, and Assessing: a revision of Bloom's taxonomy of educational objectives*, Complete edn., New York, Longman.

Bloom, B. S., Engelbart, M. D., Furst, E. J., Hill, W. H. and Krathwohl, D. R. (1984) *Taxonomy of Educational Objectives: the classification of educational goals, Handbook 1: the cognitive domain*, New York, Longman.

Caswell, M. L. (2016) 'The Archive' Is Not an Archives: on acknowledging the intellectual contributions of archival studies, *Reconstruction: Studies in Contemporary Culture*, **16** (1), https://escholarship.org/uc/item/7bn4v1fk

Cheetham, G. and Chivers, G. (1996) Towards a Holistic Model of Professional Competence, *Journal of European Industrial Training*, **20** (5), 20–30, https://doi.org/10.1108/03090599610119692

Cheetham, G. and Chivers, G. (1998) The Reflective (and Competent) Practitioner: a model of professional competence which seeks to harmonise the reflective practitioner and competence-based approaches, *Journal of European Industrial Training*, **22** (7), 267–76, https://doi.org/10.1108/03090599810230678

Cook, T. (2013) Evidence, Memory, Identity, and Community: four shifting archival paradigms, *Archival Science*, **13** (2–3), 95–120, https://doi.org/10.1007/s10502-012-9180-7

DigCurV (2013) *DigCurV – Skills in Digital Curation Curriculum Framework*, https://www.digcurv.gla.ac.uk/index.html [accessed 14 July 2018].

Duff, W., Yakel, E. and Tibbo, H. R. (2013) Archival Reference Knowledge, *The American Archivist*, **76** (1), 68–94.

Duranti, L. (1998) *Diplomatics: new uses for an old science*, Scarecrow Press.

Duranti, L. (2013) *Introduction to InterPARES Trust*, Slide presentation, InterPARES Trust, https://interparestrust.org/assets/public/dissemination/IPT_20131204_ IntroductionInterPARESTrust.pdf

Franks, P. (2013) Infusing Digital Curation Competencies into the SLIS Curriculum. In Casarosa, V., Cirinnà, C., Fernie, K. and Lunghi, M. (eds), *Proceedings of the Framing the Digital Curation Curriculum Conference*, Florence, Italy, CEUR Workshop Proceedings, digcur-education.org

Jenkinson, H. (1937) *A Manual of Archive Administration*, New and revised edn, London, Percy Lund, Humphries & Co., www.archive.org/details/manualofarchivea00iljenk

Katuu, S. (2009) Archives and Records Management Education and Training: what can Africa learn from Europe and North America?, *Information Development*, **25** (2), 133–45. https://doi.org/10.1177/0266666909104714

Katuu, S. (2015) *Managing Records in a South African Health Care Institution – A Critical Analysis*. PhD Thesis, University of South Africa.

Katuu, S. (2018) *Curriculum Alignments at Institutions of Higher Learning in Africa: preparing professionals to manage records created in networked environments*, AF01, Final Report, InterPARES Trust, https://interparestrust.org/assets/public/dissemination/AF01-FinalReport.pdf

Langmead, A. (2015) The History of Archival Education in America: what's next? In Cox, R. J., Mattern, E. and Langmead, A. (eds), *Archival Research and Education: selected papers from the 2014 AERI Conference*, Sacramento, CA, Litwin Books.

Le Deist, F. D. and Winterton, J. (2005) What Is Competence?, *Human Resource Development International*, **8** (1), 27–46, https://doi.org/10.1080/1367886042000338227

Lucia, A. D. and Lepsinger, R. (1999) *The Art and Science of Competency Models: pinpointing critical success factors in organizations*, San Francisco, Calif, Jossey-Bass/Pfeiffer.

Lyon, L., Mattern, E., Acker, A. and Langmead, A. (2015) Applying Translational Principles to Data Science Curriculum Development, iPRES. In *iPRES 2015 Proceedings*.

Marciano, R., Lemieux, V., Hedges, M., Esteva, M., Underwood, W., Kurtz, M. and Conrad, M. (2018) Archival Records and Training in the Age of Big Data. In Jaeger, P. T. and Sarin, L. C. (eds), *Re-Envisioning the MLS*, Bingley, Emerald Group Publishing, http://dcicblog.umd.edu/cas/wp-content/uploads/sites/ 13/2016/05/submission_final_draft.pdf

Pymm, B. (2012) *Education for the Profession: convergence or divergence in the digital world*. Presented at the International Council on Archives Congress 2012, Brisbane, Australia.

Society of American Archivists (2016) *Guidelines for a Graduate Program in Archival*

Studies, https://www2.archivists.org/prof-education/graduate/gpas [accessed 14 July 2018].

Strauss, A. L. and Corbin, J. M. (1990) *Basics of Qualitative Research: grounded theory procedures and techniques*, Sage Publications.

Tammaro, A. M. (2007) A Curriculum for Digital Librarians: a reflection on the European debate, *New Library World*, **108** (5/6), 229–46. https://doi.org/10.1108/03074800710748795

The Archival Education and Research Institute (AERI) and Pluralizing the Archival Curriculum Group (PACG) (2011) Educating for the Archival Multiverse, *The American Archivist*, **74** (1), 69–101.

Thibodeau, K. (2018) *Preservation as a Service for Trust (PaaST)*, NA12, Final Report, InterPARES Trust, https://interparestrust.org/assets/public/dissemination/PreservationasaServiceforTrust1_0-FINAL.pdf

Vilar, P. and Šauperl, A. (2014) Archival Literacy: different users, different information needs, behaviour and skills. In Kurbanoğlu, S., Špiranec, S., Grassian, E., Mizrachi, D. and Catts, R. (eds), *Information Literacy, Lifelong Learning and Digital Citizenship in the 21st Century* (Vol. 492, 149–59). Cham, Springer International Publishing, https://doi.org/10.1007/978-3-319-14136-7_16

White, K. L. and Gilliland, A. J. (2010) Promoting Reflexivity and Inclusivity in Archival Education, Research, and Practice, *The Library Quarterly*, **80** (3), 231–48. https://doi.org/10.1086/652874

APPENDIX 1

InterPARES Trust Terminology

Richard Pearce-Moses

The InterPARES Trust Terminology is drawn from the evolving intersection of recordkeeping and information technology, exploring aspects of trust in networked environments. Established social conventions of trusting archives has been based, in large part, on the notion of tangible records in the custody of an archival repository. If an archives delegates custody of its records to a third party, such as a cloud service provider, assumptions underlying those social conventions have changed and should be re-examined.

This terminology is a starting point to clarify the meaning of the words and phrases that represent not only the emerging technical concepts, but also those underlying assumptions. The meaning of a term representing a relatively new concept is often ambiguous because it is not yet well established or may be used with a variety of senses. Over time, especially as the implications and implementations of these new concepts mature, they take on a consensual meaning. For example, when first introduced, 'cloud' was particularly nebulous. Some argued that it was merely a new word for existing technologies such as distributed storage. Others argued that it was substantially different, incorporating notions of storage as a service independent of implementation. Marketers often used 'cloud' to promote existing products and services as new and innovative. In the past several years, the notion of cloud computing has been clarified and expanded.

At the same time, terms with established meanings are often learned through use in context, rather than formal study. As such, terms may be used imprecisely or without a full understanding of their meaning. For example, many individuals have a working sense of 'trust', but they might not be able to provide a concise or considered definition. While many of these terms can be found in standard reference works, the terminology includes definitions and notes written specifically in context of archives and technology.

The terminology's definitions are descriptive, reflecting how a term is used in the literature. The online version typically includes examples used to justify the definition. At the same time, those citations often provide explanation beyond what is appropriate for a concise definition. In addition to these citations, terms often have a note that provides a gloss on meaning and usage.

The print edition is abridged from the online version available at https://interparestrust.org/terminology. In general, it does not include terms included in the InterPARES 2 Glossary (2018). Neither does it include terms used in the Preservation as a Service of Trust (PaaST) model (Thibodeau et al., 2018).

The terminology was developed as part of the InterPARES Trust research project, Luciana Duranti, principal investigator. Richard Pearce-Moses was the editor. Alicia Barnard provided translations to Spanish and Rosely Rondinelli provided translations to Portuguese. This work reflects many individuals' collaborative research on cloud issues.

Notes

InterPARES 2 (2018) Glossary.
  http://interpares.org/ip2/ip2_term_pdf.cfm?pdf=glossary [accessed 21 March 2018].
Thibodeau, K., Prescott, D., Pearce-Moses, R., Jansen, A., Timms, K., Michetti, G., Duranti, L., Rogers, C., Johnson, L., Butler, J. R., Mumma, C., Lemieux, V., Romkey, S., Hamidzadeh, B., Evans, L., Tennis, J., Seller, S., McGuirk, K., Powell, C., Crocker, C. and Rovegno, K. (2018) *Preservation as a Service of Trust (PaaST) Functional and Data Requirements for Digital Preservation*, InterPARES Trust.

access n. ~ 1. The opportunity or ability to find, retrieve, or use documents or information. ~ 2. IP2: The right or permission to find, retrieve, or use documents or information. ~ 3. PaaST (Access): A capability that enables an actor to request or receive preservation targets, heuristic information or preservation management information, or to exercise interactive functionality that implements one or more PaaST requirements.
  Note: PaaST does not address the full range of access services associated with dissemination of information, but focuses on those that are a direct consequence of preservation.
access control n. ~ COMPUTING: High-level policies and mechanisms designed to secure a system by authorizing users to find, retrieve, use, or store information or other resources to which they need access.
  Note: In the context of computing, resources may include things like applications and devices.

anonymous adj. ~ 1. Of unknown authorship. ~ 2. Lacking a known name or identity.

— (anonymity, n.) ~ 3. The state of being anonymous.

Note: In some instances, individuals may seek anonymity by consciously concealing their identity to protect themselves from retribution for their acts or expressions. In other instances, someone may protect others' anonymity for similar reasons. For example, computer users may use a proxy server and virtual private network to mask identifying information, such as an IP address, provided by the server. Such uses are not necessarily malicious; many libraries use a proxy server to represent many authenticated users to a service using a single identity. Anonymity is generally distinguished from pseudonymity, as the identity of an individual using a pseudonym may be commonly known; for example, Charles Lutwidge Dodgson writing as Lewis Carroll.

archival cloud n. ~ A trustworthy, cloud-based service that replicates the traditional functions of in-house archives, including secure storage, search and retrieval, and preservation.

Note: An archival cloud is more than data storage. The system requirements must be driven by the needs of the records creators and archival principles, rather than by any specific technology.

archives n. ~ 1. ARCHIVES, IP2: The whole of the documents made and received by a juridical or physical person or organization in the conduct of affairs, and preserved. ~ 2. ARCHIVES: A place where records selected for permanent preservation are kept. ~ 3. ARCHIVES: An agency or institution responsible for the preservation and communication of records selected for permanent preservation.

— (archive, v.) ~ 4. COMPUTING: To save digital data, documents, and records, typically those that are not current, offline.

Note: Archive[4], as used in information technology, connotes migrating seldom-used data to offline or nearline storage. Where traditional archival science emphasizes protecting the authenticity, reliability, and integrity of the records for an indefinite period, information technologies often focus on a more limited period – often 10 to 20 years – and may not include processes to protect the records' trustworthiness.

Archiving as a Service (AaaS) n. ~ A service offered by a provider that supports the full range of functions necessary to store, access, and preserve records of long-term value while protecting the records' authenticity, reliability, and integrity.

Note: Many providers offering archiving as a service do little more than provide offline storage.

audit n. ~ A systematic assessment of compliance with established policies, procedures, laws, and standards.

Note: Audits may be conducted for individuals or organizations. An internal audit is conducted by an organization's staff; an independent audit (also called an external audit) is conducted by a party not connected with the entity audited.

authentication n. ~ IP2, ARCHIVES: A declaration of a record's authenticity at a specific point in time by a juridical person entrusted with the authority to make such a declaration (e.g. public officer, notary, certification authority).

— (authenticate, v.) ~ To declare, either orally, in writing, or by affixion of a seal, that an entity is what it purports to be, after having verified its identity.

Note: Archivists use the term to describe the process of demonstrating, generally through internal and external evidence, that a document is genuine and free from tampering. Computing/IT uses the term to describe the process of granting an authorized user access to a system.

availability n. ~ 1. Capability of being accessed or used. ~ 2. COMPUTING: Ensuring timely and reliable access to and use of information (NIST, 2013, citing 44 USC 3542).

Note: In computing, availability refers to the ability to access and use a system, and is often dependent on many components within a complex system, including software, hardware, and networking. Systems designed for high availability may require expensive redundancies.

big data n. ~ A dataset – often an aggregation of datasets from different sources, made for different purposes, and with different structures – that is so large that performance requirements become a significant factor when designing and implementing a data management and analysis system.

Note: Usage is ambiguous as 'big data' is often used more for marketing than as a defining concept. The volume of 'big data' varies with context, and is not determined by a specific, quantitative measure. 'The key feature of the paradigmatic change is that analytic treatment of data is systematically placed at the forefront of intelligent decision-making. The process can be seen as the natural next step in the evolution from the "Information Age" and "Information Societies"' (Hilbert, 2013, 4).

blockchain n. ~ An open-source technology that supports trusted, immutable records of transactions stored in publicly accessible, decentralized, distributed, automated ledgers.

Note: Because blockchain technology relies on disintermediated access to multiple copies of distributed ledgers, the need for a centralized authority (such as a bank) to approve transactions is not necessary. Trust in the security of a blockchain is based on the notion that each block inherits the root hash of all previous transactions, and altering a given transaction would require simultaneous alteration of all subsequent blocks in all copies of the distributed ledgers created since the transaction took place. Blockchain technology is designed to confirm records' integrity, existence at a certain point in time, and sequence to support their non-repudiation. Bitcoin is an example of a technology that uses blockchain technology to store information about cryptocurrency.

certification (records) n. ~ 1. A process to assess some quality or expectation of a record, frequently its authenticity. ~ 2. An attestation that a record has some quality or meets some expectation.

Note: A record may be certified as to a number of qualities, including trustworthiness, reliability, authenticity, accuracy, integrity, identity, precision, correctness, truthfulness, or pertinence. Typically an archives certifies that a record is, in fact, the record received and that it has not been altered. Certification of other qualities are often done by individuals with particular, relevant expertise, such as forensics or questioned documents. In a legal context, certification may relate to the admission of copies in lieu of originals or admissibility of evidence.

certification (systems) n. ~ 1. A process to assess whether a system meets expectations typically established in a standard. ~ 2. An attestation that a system meets expectations.

Note: Examples of standards that may be used to certify systems include Electronic Records Management Software Applications Design Criteria Standards (DoD 5015.2-STD) and Audit and Certification of Trustworthy Digital Repositories (ISO 16363). However, not all standards must be as rigorously vetted.

chain of custody n. ~ A chronology of entities that held records over time that can be used to demonstrate the authenticity of records.

Note: In a legal context, each entity in the chain of custody may be expected to attest to their receipt, proper safekeeping and handling, and disposition of the records.

citizen engagement n. ~ Efforts to actively empower citizens in government decision-making processes through transparent dialogue and communication among individual citizens and with the government in order to increase trust in the government and to ensure decisions reflect citizens' interests.

classification n. ~ 1. The process of assessing whether a document or other information asset contains sensitive information and assigning a level indicating the risk associated with that information. ~ 2. The process of assigning some thing to a specific class within a hierarchy, based on the thing's characteristics.

Note: The fact that a document is classified indicates that it – at one time – contained sensitive information. However, classification alone does not indicate the degree of sensitivity. Classified documents are assigned a classification level, which may range from confidential to top secret.

cloud n. ~ A broad range of infrastructures and services distributed across a network (typically the internet) that are scalable on demand and that are designed to support management of high volumes of digital materials.

Note: Because 'cloud' – as a general term – is used in so many contexts and implemented in a variety of ways, its meaning is so broad that it is exceptionally nebulous. To the extent the term has been appropriated by marketing, a specific technical definition may be lost in hype. Often it connotes outsourcing some or all aspects of an organization's information technology services.

cloud broker n. ~ An entity that manages the use, performance and delivery of cloud services, and negotiates relationships between cloud providers and cloud consumers (Liu et al., 2011, 20).

cloud computing n. ~ A model for enabling ubiquitous, convenient, on-demand network access to a shared pool of configurable computing resources (e.g. networks, servers, storage, applications, and services) that can be rapidly provisioned and released with minimal management effort or service provider interaction (Mell and Grance, 2011, 2).

Note: This cloud model is composed of five *essential characteristics*, including on-demand self-service, broad network access, resource pooling, rapid elasticity, and measured service; three *service models*, including Software as a Service (SaaS), Platform as a Service (PaaS), and Infrastructure as a Service (IaaS); and four *deployment models*, including private cloud, community cloud, public cloud, and hybrid cloud (Mell and Grance, 2011, 2).

cloud provider n. ~ An entity offering management and support to cloud consumers for access to a range of ubiquitous, convenient services, including infrastructure, platform, and applications, that can be rapidly provisioned with minimal effort by the consumer.

Note: Services offered fall into the categories Infrastructure as a Service (IaaS), Platform as a Service (PaaS), and Software as a Service (SaaS). Providers may be part of different deployment models, including public, private, community, and hybrid models.

cloud service n. ~ Functionality offered by a cloud provider that supports infrastructure, platform, software, or other services.

Note: A cloud service may be implemented using a public, private, hybrid, or community model.

cloud storage n. ~ A cloud service to house and retain digital information that typically can be rapidly and easily provisioned for use by the consumer.

Note: May sometimes be referred to as Data Storage as a Service (DSaaS).

community cloud n. ~ A cloud infrastructure deployment model in which a specified group of organizations with common privacy, security, or legal concerns, collaborate to share resources that may be managed by the organizations or a third party, on or off premises.

confidence n. ~ Belief in the reliability or trustworthiness (of some thing or person).

Note: Confidence is an expectation of a positive outcome, as distinguished from competence, which is a measure of dependability and capability.

confidentiality n. ~ The expectation that private facts entrusted to another will be kept secret and will not be shared without consent.

consortium n. (consortia, consortiums, pl.) ~ A group of entities working in a formal partnership towards a common objective.

Note: Consortia typically have some type of written agreement that outlines their purpose, membership, and procedures. The agreements may be more or less formal, depending on the complexity of the work and associated risks.

context n. ~ IP2: The framework in which a record is created, used, and maintained.

data anonymization n. ~ A process to protect personal information by removing or obfuscating personally identifiable information (US) or personal data (EU) that relates to an individual or that could allow the individual to be identified.

Note: Data anonymization is often used to make restricted datasets more widely accessible, while simultaneously protecting sensitive or personally identifiable information (US) or personal data (EU). It may use a combination of techniques, such as deleting, encrypting, or obfuscating specific data elements that are unique to and that could directly identify an individual, such as name, Social Security Number, or e-mail address. Effective data anonymization is particularly challenging, as a group of seemingly unrelated elements can identify individuals indirectly. For example, birth date, sex, and ZIP code can identify many individuals, even in large data sets (Sweeney, 2000). Unlike data obfuscation, data anonymization does not require that the resulting dataset has the same functionality as the original dataset. Some sources suggest that anonymization is distinguished from pseudonymization. Anonymization is limited to a specific dataset, making it impossible to link information about the individual to other datasets. Pseudonymization creates an artificial identifier for individuals that can be used to link information about the individuals in multiple datasets.

data management n. ~ An operational-level structure that focuses on the day-to-day, routine implementation of data governance strategies, including acquisition, control, protection, and delivery of data.

data mining n. ~ An approach to discover implicit patterns, often non-obvious, in very large data sets (big data) through a variety of techniques of analysis, categorization, clustering and correlation.

data protection n. ~ EUROPEAN UNION: Regulations and practices that control the collection, processing, access, and use of personal information.

declassification n. ~ The process of removing the security classification from a record or other information asset.

denial of service n. (DoS, abbr.) ~ An attack on an online service that seeks to make the service unavailable to legitimate users by overwhelming the service with spurious requests or network packets.
Note: Traffic in a denial of service (DoS) attack generally comes from a single source. Traffic in a distributed denial of service attack (DDoS) will originate from many sources that are part of a botnet, a collection of compromised devices running attack software.

digital forensics n. ~ 1. COMPUTING: The use of techniques and technologies to identify, preserve or recover, and analyze computer data as part of an investigation in a manner that ensures that it is admissible as evidence at trial. ~ 2. ARCHIVES: The use of such techniques and methods to assist in the acquisition, processing, preservation, and dissemination of computer files in archives.
Note: Cloud forensics is a specialized application of digital forensics[1] in a cloud environment.

disclosure n. (disclosive, adj.) ~ Actions taken to make known secret or previously unknown information.

discovery n. ~ 1. The means of locating something through a search. ~ 2. The initial identification or observation of something. ~ 3. LAW: The compulsory process of producing relevant documents to opposing parties in litigation.

disintermediation n. ~ The elimination of third-party agents in transactions between two parties, often through the use of automated services to facilitate a direct interaction between the two parties.

duty to remember n. ~ An ethical obligation to actively preserve and keep current events of the past, especially social evils such as genocide and slavery, so that they may serve as a moral compass and prevent repetition of similar acts.

e-governance n. ~ The use of technology to support and automate a governing body's internal processes and delivery of services, but also to promote transparency and participation in the process by those governed.

e-government n. ~ IP2: The use of information technologies, especially the internet, to improve government services for and interactions with citizens (G2C), businesses and industry (G2B), and different division of government (G2G) by simplifying processes, and by integrating and eliminating redundant systems.
Note: Often used synonymously with electronic government, e-gov, Internet government, digital government, online government, or connected government.

forensics n. ~ The use of scientific techniques to examine, gather (or recover), and analyze information in a way that maintains its integrity.
Note: Developed in large part to gather evidence during investigations of potential criminal activity, forensics can be used in other contexts to more fully understand the nature of materials being studied for a wide range of purposes.

governance n. ~ A senior-level administrative structure that sets strategy for an organization by identifying roles, responsibilities, decision-making processes, policies, and procedures and that monitors outcomes and compliance.
Note: In a corporate environment, boards of directors are responsible for governance. Stockholders appoint the directors and auditors to satisfy themselves that an appropriate governance structure is in place.

hybrid cloud n. ~ A deployment model in which two or more clouds (private, community, or public) remain unique entities, but are connected by standardized or proprietary technology that enables data and application portability.

identity n. ~ 1. Characteristics that distinguish one entity from another and that make them recognizable. ~ 2. IP2: The whole of the characteristics of a document or a record that uniquely identify it and distinguish it from any other document or record; with integrity, a component of authenticity.

identity management n. ~ 1. COMPUTING: Policies, procedures, and techniques designed to enhance security by ensuring only authorized individuals can access systems and information resources they have permission to use. ~ 2. BUSINESS: Policies and procedures to monitor and protect a corporate brand in the public sphere.

information governance n. ~ A senior-level administrative structure that establishes roles and responsibilities, decision-making processes, policies and procedures that promote effective decisions regarding the effective and efficient creation, storage, use, and disposition of information resources that align with business outcomes.

Note: Information governance relies on data governance to ensure that decisions are based on data that is sufficient and high quality. In some organizations, information governance seeks to integrate and co-ordinate a range of relative activities, such as data management, knowledge management, and records management.

information management n. ~ 1. An operational-level structure that focuses on the day-to-day, routine use of information to achieve the organization's goals and objectives, including IT service delivery, information security, and relevant business standards. ~ 2. PAAST (Information Management): Capabilities that support creating and maintaining preservation management information, about controls, objects, processes, and actors.

Note: Information management capabilities include categorizing information, extracting data from information sources, generating data from the execution of a preservation action, associating data with preservation targets or data objects, and collecting data generated in inspection and verification of objects.

information security n. (infosec, abbr.) ~ Policies, procedures, and other controls to protect data assets from unauthorized access, modification, disclosure, or other use to ensure data integrity, confidentiality, and availability.

Infrastructure as a Service (IaaS) n. ~ A low-level cloud service, with fundamental resources, such as processing, storage, and networks, managed by the provider, giving the consumer the ability to rapidly and conveniently deploy the platform and software.

InterPARES Authenticity Metadata n. ~ A metadata profile with functional requirements to ensure that metadata is necessary and sufficient to support the presumption of the authenticity of records, is interoperable between systems and across time, is adequate for archival description, and is useful for both the retrieval and meaningful display of records (Tennis and Rogers, 2012, 42).

legal hold n. ~ A directive issued to individuals who may have custody of records relevant to potential litigation, investigation, or audit that suspends routine destruction of records otherwise allowed under an approved records retention schedule.

Note: Also called a hold order or preservation order.

liability n. (liable, adj.) ~ 1. An obligation or responsibility by law, contract, or equity. ~ 2. A debt or financial obligation.

maturity model n. ~ A process to rank the reliability and sustainability of an entity's behaviors, practices, and processes, relative to some function or outcome.
Note: Capability is described in terms of maturity levels, such as none, initial, repeatable, defined, managed, and optimizing. Other descriptors may be used, such as nominal, minimal, intermediate, advanced, and optimal.

media sanitization n. ~ COMPUTING: A process to destroy data stored on media in a way that makes it irretrievable.

on-demand self-service n. ~ Computer capabilities a consumer can unilaterally and automatically provision, such as server time and network storage, as needed without requiring human interaction with each service provider (Mell and Grance, 2011, 2).
Note: An essential characteristic of cloud computing.

open adj. ~ 1. Available and accessible for use due to an absence of restrictions. ~ 2. Available and accessible for use as the result of license.
Note: While the term 'license' often suggests restrictions, some, such as Creative Commons licenses, are designed to be permissive. Open Knowledge International's definition of 'open' stresses 'a robust commons in which anyone may participate, and interoperability is maximized' noting 'knowledge is open if anyone is free to access, use, modify, and share it – subject, at most, to measures that preserve provenance and openness' (Open Knowledge International, 2014).

open data n. ~ Data available to anyone that may be used for any purpose and that is in a structure that facilitates its use at little or no charge.
Note: The Open Data Institute asserts that works must be licensed to be open and considers a work to be open in terms of how the license addresses key principles, including: access, redistribution, re-use, absence of technological restriction, attribution, integrity, no discrimination against persons or groups, no discrimination against fields of endeavor, distribution of license, license must not be specific to a package, and license must not restrict the distribution of other works. Any charge should be limited to a reasonable, one-time reproduction cost.

open government n. ~ An approach designed to provide greater access to unrestricted information held by public bodies in order to promote transparency, accountability, and citizen engagement and participation, to accomplish a larger outcome of building and enhancing citizens' trust in their governments.

open government data n. ~ Data that is created or accumulated in the public sector and is available to anyone, and that may be used for any purpose and is in a structure that facilitates its use at little or no charge. *Note:* Open government data is distinguished from open data on the basis that it must meet different expectations, based on principles that the data must be complete, primary, timely, accessible, machine processable, non-discriminatory, non-proprietary, and license free.

open source n. ~ IP2: A computer program in which the source code is available to the general public for use and/or modification from its original design free of charge (open).

— adj. ~ COMPUTING: A method and philosophy for software licensing and distribution designed to encourage use and improvement of software written by volunteers by ensuring that anyone can copy the source code and modify it freely.

operational risk n. ~ A level of risk that results from inadequate or failed internal processes, people, and systems, or from external events.

permission n. ~ 1. Authorization, either tacit or explicit, allowing some thing or action. – 2. COMPUTING: Access controls that grant users the ability to perform specific, often limited, actions in a system.
Note: Creative Commons exemplifies permission[1], in that it is a license that authorizes the reproduction and use, within limits, of intellectual properties. File systems that control whether an individual can create, read, update, or delete a file are an example of permission[2].

person n. ~ An individual or legally defined entity who is the subject of rights and duties, and who is recognized by the juridical system as capable of or having the potential for acting legally.

personal data n. ~ Any information relating to an identified or identifiable natural person ('data subject') . . . who can be identified, directly or indirectly, in particular by reference to an identification number or to one or more factors specific to his physical, physiological, mental, economic, cultural or social identity (EU Council Directive 1995/46/EC, 1995).

personally identifiable information n. (also personally identifiable information, personal identifying information, personal identifiable information; PII, abbr.) ~ 1. Data that allows a specific individual to be recognized. – 2. Restricted, private data that can be linked to a specific individual.
Note: Examples of distinguishing data include information that (taken individually or as a small set) can be tied to a unique person, such as a Social Security Number, e-mail address, mother's maiden name, and date of birth. Examples of data that are restricted because they are

private include medical, educational, or financial information.

Platform as a Service (PaaS) n. ~ A mid-level cloud service with fundamental infrastructure resources, along with an operating system and commonly with basic utilities such as support for web services, databases, and programming languages that are managed by the provider, leaving the consumer to rapidly and conveniently deploy applications.

preservation n. (preserve, v.) ~ 1. The whole of the principles, policies, rules, strategies, and activities aimed at prolonging the existence of an object by maintaining it in a condition suitable for use, either in its original format or in a more persistent format, while leaving intact the object's intellectual form. ~ 2. Retention for a limited period of time. *Note:* Preservation has two distinct senses tied to the length of time the records are to be kept. Preservation[1] (sometimes called continuing preservation or archival preservation) connotes long-term actions to protect records from damage or deterioration, or to ensure that they remain accessible far into the future. Preservation[2] refers to short-term restrictions on records destruction. However, actions often associated with long-term preservation may be required for records with long, but not permanent, retention periods. For example, tangible records made using fragile materials or virtual records that use obsolete software formats may need treatment to ensure they remain accessible before they are scheduled for destruction.

Preservation as a Service for Trust (PaaST) n. ~ 1. A project of InterPARES Trust that investigated requirements for preservation of digital information in a manner independent of both the technology used and the assignment or division of responsibilities. – 2. A set of functional and data requirements that specify the actions and information needed for preservation of digital information, while supporting customization for different types of information and different policies, objectives and constraints on preservation. *Note:* The Open Archival Information System (OAIS) reference model is abstract and lacks sufficient detail for implementation. By contrast, PaaST describes a model and specifications that can be implemented in software.

privacy n. ~ 1. A quality or state of seclusion, of keeping to one's self, and being free from intrusion or public scrutiny. ~ 2. Control over access and use of one's personal information. *Note:* In US law, invasion of privacy includes an unauthorized appropriation of an individual's name or likeness for personal benefit; the interference in a person's seclusion or personal affairs that is offensive and intentional; the public disclosure of private information, especially for offensive purposes; and presenting to the public information that places another person in a false light. A person's right to privacy is the basis for protection against invasion of privacy. A person's right to privacy is not absolute secrecy, but based in the autonomy of an individual to determine a circle of intimacy. Similarly, invasion of privacy is not absolute, and is generally tied to unwarranted interference, an attempt to outrage or cause mental suffering or humiliation by a person of ordinary sensibilities.

private cloud n. ~ A deployment model in which a provider manages and supports infrastructure, platform, or software as a service for the exclusive use of a consumer.

Note: The boundary between provider and consumer may be blurred in some contexts. The provider may be a part of the consumer's organization. Also, the consumer may be an organization that grants different business units or individuals access to its cloud.

profession n. ~ A field of work that requires advanced education and training, adherence to a code of ethics, and the ability to apply specialized knowledge and judgement in a variety of situations.

Note: Some professions require certification by a board or a government issued license.

public cloud n. ~ A deployment model in which services (infrastructure, platform, or software) are managed by a third-party provider and made available to the general public.

reclassification n. ~ The process of decreasing or downgrading, or increasing the security classification level of a record or other information asset.

records professional n. ~ An individual who is trained in all aspects of managing records and information, including their creation, use, retention, disposition, and preservation, and is familiar with the legal, ethical, fiscal, administrative, and governance contexts of recordkeeping.

Note: 'Records professional' is often used as an umbrella term to include individuals working in various facets of records management and archives, regardless of job titles.

redaction n. ~ Masking confidential or offensive information in a document.

Note: Redaction may make it impossible to discover masked information, completely obscuring a word or block of text. In other instances, especially to flag offensive content, information may leave a few letters that allow the reader to infer the hidden word.

retention n. ~ 1. The act of keeping something by preventing its disposal or alteration. – 2. Maintaining records for a period of time until their authorized disposition by destruction or transfer.

Note: Retention is often defined as the preservation of records for a

period of time, based on the records' ability to provide useful information or to document legal compliance. When that period expires, records
are often transferred to an archives or sometimes to another entity. In
this context, preservation refers primarily to efforts to protect records
from premature destruction because of their value or relevance to litigation or investigation.

retention period n. ~ The period of time records should be kept before
disposition, either by destruction or transfer to an archive.
Note: A retention schedule lists record series and their retention period.
To prevent charges of spoliation, a hold order may suspend destruction
of records that have passed their designated retention period if they are
relevant to litigation or investigation.

retrieval n. ~ 1. Activities and processes to get or bring (something) back. –
2. INFORMATION RETRIEVAL: A process of searching, browsing, selecting,
and accessing information.
Note: Retrieval^2 techniques may use specialized techniques for different
types of information, such as text, images, audio, or datasets. Retrieval
may be based on metadata assigned to digital objects that hold the
information, on automated analysis of the content of those objects, or a
combination.

right to be forgotten n. ~ An individual's claim of privilege to control his or
her personal information by demanding that access to such information
must be restricted unless there are particular reasons justified by a pre-
ponderant interest of the public, including freedom of expression and
freedom of information.
Note: The European Court of Justice limits this right to information 'that
is inaccurate, inadequate, irrelevant, or excessive in relation to data processing' (EU Commission, 2014, 2).

risk n. ~ Uncertainty associated with results arising from intentional or
unanticipated events, threats, or vulnerabilities, and their impact or
probability.
Note: The ISO 31000 (2009) standard on risk management changes the
previous definition of risk (in ISO Guide 73) from the 'chance or
probability of loss' to 'the effect of uncertainty on objectives', suggesting
that risk could have either positive or negative consequences. Risk may
have a variety of financial and operational consequences, including
mission, functions, image, and reputation.

risk assessment n. ~ A process of determining the relative likelihood and
impact of risks.
Note: The National Institute of Standards and Technology (NIST) considers risk analysis and risk assessment as synonymous. However, some

distinguish risk assessment from risk analysis, the latter focusing on identification of risks. A part of risk management, risks assessment considers the impact of threats, vulnerabilities, and mitigations, as well as any existing risk mitigation controls to determine the level of risk and whether additional or improved controls are needed.

risk management n. ~ A program and its supporting, integrated activities to identify the likelihood of some event (typically a threat or vulnerability) occurring, assess its impact and priority, and plan a variety of responses.

Note: Risk management aims to prevent loss and capitalize on opportunities to improve the operations of an organization.

risk mitigation n. ~ A process to implement controls and countermeasures to reduce the consequences of risk.

security n. ~ The state of being protected from attack, risk, threat, or vulnerability.

Note: In the context of computing, security includes protection against unauthorized access to systems, the destruction or alteration of information, or denial of service, whether caused by malice or unintended act.

semi-structured data n. ~ Information resources that rely on tags or markers, rather than a data model, to indicate different semantics elements.

sensitive data n. ~ A special class of personal information that relates to racial or ethnic origin, political opinions, religious or philosophical beliefs, or trade union membership; health or sex life; or offenses, criminal convictions, or security measures.

Note: Defined in 'On the Protection of Individuals with Regard to the Processing of Personal Data and on the Free Movement of Such Data', Sec. III, Art. 8 (1) (EU Council Directive 1995/46/EC, 1995).

sentiment analysis n. ~ Techniques to determine whether attitudes or emotions underlying an expression are positive, negative, or neutral, often through an analysis of tone and affect.

service level agreement n. (SLA, abbr.) ~ An agreement between a service provider and a customer that documents minimum expected performance, often in terms of operations, such as availability (up time) and response time, and in terms of policy, such as security and privacy.

social capital n. ~ Intangible assets such as trust, goodwill, and collective benefits realized by individuals' participation in and respect for the norms of social networks.

social media n. ~ Online services intended to promote open-ended discussion and sharing among voluntary members of a community based on common interests, rather than seeking task-oriented goals by select individuals.

Note: Examples include Facebook, Twitter, and Instagram, as well as public comments on websites, blogs, and wikis. Discussion and sharing may include any format, including text and graphics.

Software as a Service (SaaS) n. ~ A high-level cloud service, managed and hosted by the provider, that offers consumers on-demand access to applications.

Note: 'The consumer does not manage or control the underlying cloud infrastructure including network, servers, operating systems, storage, or even individual application capabilities, with the possible exception of limited user-specific application configuration settings' (Mell and Grance, 2011, 2).

threat n. ~ 1. A possible danger that may cause damage ~ 2. COMPUTING: A possible danger to a system or information stored on the system, typically connoting a malicious act that breaches security or exploits a vulnerability.

Note: Threat is a specific type of risk that connotes malicious intent, as distinguished from unintentional acts that may cause damage or other risks, such as accident or natural disaster.

transparency n. ~ (The condition of) timely disclosure of information about an individual's or organization's activities and decisions, especially to support accountability to all stakeholders.

Note: Beyond its basic sense of 'allowing light to pass' and 'the ability to see through', Louis Brandeis anticipated the modern sense of transparency when he said, 'Publicity is justly commended as a remedy for social and industrial diseases. Sunlight is said to be the best of disinfectants; electric light the most efficient policeman' (Brandeis, 2014, 92). In government, transparency assures that citizens have the information they need to hold officials accountable. Similarly, in computing, transparency allows users the ability to ensure that services perform as promised.

trust n. ~ 1. Confidence of one party in another, based on alignment of value systems with respect to specific actions or benefits, and involving a relationship of voluntary vulnerability, dependence and reliance, based on risk assessment.

— v. ~ 2. To have confidence in another party with respect to specific actions or benefits.

Note: Trust is subjective, as indicated by the fact that one describes individuals on a scale that ranges from trusting (to the point of gullibility) to skeptical (to the point of paranoia or conspiracy theory).

trusted digital repository n. ~ A trusted digital repository is one whose mission is to provide reliable, long-term access to managed digital resources to its designated community, now and in the future (Trusted Digital Repositories, 2002, i).

Note: In the context of big data, the veracity of publicly available datasets should not be assumed. Ballard (2014, 8) gives examples of a compilation of information about individuals that gives incorrect information because its data was not verified using other authoritative datasets, as well as datasets on customer reviews that contain false, malicious reports.

vulnerability n. ~ A weakness or flaw that, if exploited, would expose an entity to risk.

Bibliography

Note: All URLs accessed 10 May 2018. Broken URLs accessible through the Internet Archive Wayback Machine (https://web.archive.org/) are marked with an asterisk.

Ballard, C., Compert, C., Jesionowski, T., Milman, I., Plants, B., Rosen, B. and Smith, R. (2014) *Information Governance: principles and practices for a big data landscape*, IBM, www.redbooks.ibm.com/redbooks/pdfs/sg248165.pdf

Brandeis, L. (1914) *Other People's Money and How the Bankers Use It*, Frederick A. Stokes, https://archive.org/details/otherpeoplesmone00bran

Cohen, F. (1987–2008) *Enterprise Information Protection*, Fred Cohen and Associates, http://all.net/books/EntInfoPro.pdf

EU Commission (2014) Factsheet on the 'Right to be Forgotten' ruling (C-131/12), http://ec.europa.eu/justice/data-protection/files/factsheets/factsheet_data_protection_en.pdf*

EU Council Directive 1995/46/EC (1995) On the Protection of Individuals with Regard to the Processing of Personal Data and on the Free Movement of such Data. 24 October 1995, OJ L281/3, http://eur-lex.europa.eu/legal-content/EN/TXT/PDF/?uri=CELEX:31995L0046&from=en

Fiedler, K. and McNamee, J. (2014) *The Charter of Digital Rights*, 10th edn, European Digital Rights, https://edri.org/wp-content/uploads/2014/06/EDRi_DigitalRightsCharter_web.pdf

Federal Rules of Evidence (2013) United States House of Representatives, Committee on the Judiciary, www.uscourts.gov/uscourts/rules/rules-evidence.pdf

Hilbert, M. (2013) Big Data for Development: from information to knowledge-societies, https://papers.ssrn.com/sol3/papers.cfm?abstract_id=2205145.

InterPARES 2 (2018) *Glossary*, InterPARES, http://interpares.org/ip2/ip2_term_pdf.cfm?pdf=glossary

Liu, F., Tong, J., Mao, J., Bohn, R., Messina, J., Badger, L. and Leaf, D. (2011) *NIST*

Definition of Cloud Computing: recommendations of the National Institute, National
Institute of Standards and Technology,
http://csrc.nist.gov/publications/nistpubs/800-145/SP800-145.pdf

Mell, P. and Grance, T. (2011) *The NIST Definition of Cloud Computing: Special Publication 800-145*, National Institute of Standards and Technology,
https://nvlpubs.nist.gov/nistpubs/Legacy/SP/nistspecialpublication800-145.pdf

NIST Public Affairs Office (2017) NIST General Information.
https://www.nist.gov/director/pao/nist-general-information

NIST Cloud Computing Security Working Group (2013) *Cloud Computing Security Reference Architecture: special publication 500-299*, NIST,
http://collaborate.nist.gov/twiki-cloud-computing/pub/CloudComputing/
CloudSecurity/NIST_Security_Reference_Architecture_2013.05.15_v1.0.pdf

NIST Joint Task Force Transformation Initiative (2012) *Guide for Conducting Risk Assessments: SP 800-30, rev. 1*, National Institute of Standards and Technology,
https://nvlpubs.nist.gov/nistpubs/Legacy/SP/nistspecialpublication800-30r1.pdf.

NIST Joint Task Force Transformation Initiative (2013) *Security and Privacy Controls for Federal Information Systems and Organizations: SP 800-53, rev. 4*, National
Institute of Standards and Technology, http://nvlpubs.nist.gov/nistpubs/
SpecialPublications/NIST.SP.800-53r4.pdf

Open Knowledge International (2014) Open Definition 2.1,
https://opendefinition.org/od/2.1/en/

Oracle (2011) Enterprise Information Management: best practices in data
governance, www.oracle.com/technetwork/articles/entarch/oea-best-practices-
data-gov-400760.pdf

Oxford English Dictionary (2018) Oxford University Press, www.oed.com/

Pearce-Moses, R. (2005) *A Glossary of Archival and Records Terminology*, Society of
American Archivists. http://www2.archivists.org/glossary/

Sweeney, L. (2000) Simple Demographics Often Identify People Uniquely. Data
Privacy Working Paper 3, Carnegie Mellon University,
http://dataprivacylab.org/projects/identifiability/paper1.pdf

Tennis, J. (2013) Data, Documents, and Memory: a taxonomy of sources in relation
to digital preservation and authenticity metadata. In Duranti, L. and Shaffer, E.
(eds), *The Memory of the World in the Digital Age: digitization and preservation*,
UNESCO, http://ciscra.org/docs/UNESCO_MOW2012_
Proceedings_FINAL_ENG_Compressed.pdf

Tennis, J. and Rogers, C. (2012) Authenticity Metadata and the IPAM: progress
toward the InterPARES Application Profile. In *Proceedings of the International
Conference on Dublin Core and Metadata Applications*, 38-45,
http://dcevents.dublincore.org/IntConf/dc-2012/paper/view/109

Thibodeau, K., Prescott, D., Pearce-Moses, R., Jansen, A., Timms, K., Michetti, G.,
Duranti, L., Rogers, C., Johnson, L., Butler, J. R., Mumma, C., Lemieux, V.,

Romkey, S., Hamidzadeh, B., Evans, L., Tennis, J., Seller, S., McGuirk, K., Powell, C., Crocker, C. and Rovegno, K. (2018) *Preservation as a Service of Trust (PaaST) Functional and Data Requirements for Digital Preservation*, InterPARES Trust.

Trusted Digital Repositories (2002) RLG, https://www.oclc.org/content/dam/research/activities/trustedrep/repositories.pdf.

APPENDIX 2

Products of InterPARES Trust research
Corinne Rogers

All results of the research studies undertaken as part of InterPARES Trust (hereinafter ITrust) are made freely available for use through a Creative Commons Attribution – NonCommercial – ShareAlike 4.0 International Public License (http://creativecommons.org/licenses/by-nc-sa/4.0/). These results, as well as many presentations, published articles, books and book chapters may be found at https://interparestrust.org/trust/research_dissemination.

ITrust research products include annotated bibliographies, literature reviews, final and status reports, checklists and guidance documents, survey instruments, reports and analysis. The checklists and guidance documents will be briefly described here. These and all other research products can be found on the ITrust website.

Each document is identified by a code consisting of two letters followed by two numbers. The letters indicate the regional team that led the study; the numbers indicate the order in which the studies were proposed and approved. For example, AF01 indicates the first study undertaken by Team Africa.

- AA – Team Australasia
- AF – Team Africa
- AS – Team Asia
- EU – Team Europe (including Israel and Turkey)
- LA – Team Latin America (including Mexico)
- NA – Team North America
- TR – Transnational Team (comprised of international organizations).

Checklists and guidance documents

EU08 (2016) Checklist for Ensuring Trust in Storage in Infrastructure-as-a-Service – Hrvoje Stančić, Edvin Bursic and Adam Al-Harari (English, Spanish)

This checklist offers guidance for individuals, businesses, government agencies or other organizations to assess the security and ongoing trustworthiness (i.e. authenticity, reliability and accuracy) of their data when stored in an Infrastructure-as-a-Service (IaaS) platform. The goal of the study was to establish the minimum amount of information necessary to support users' trust in an IaaS provider and also position the provider as a trusted service provider. This checklist can be used by records managers and archivists when assessing a Cloud Service Provider (CSP) offering IaaS, as well as by CSPs as a guideline for providing online information about their service. This document can also be found as part of the final report for EU08.

EU09 (2016) Comparative Analysis of Implemented Governmental e-Services: a Checklist for Assessment – Hrvoje Stančić, Hrvoje Brzica, Ivan Adzaga, Ana Garic, Martina Poljicak Susec, Kristina Presecki and Ana Stankovic

This checklist offers guidance to records professionals in businesses, government agencies or other organizations, as well as service providers, to assess the implemented governmental e-services in the context of trusting those services and the data they hold and preserve. The questions in the checklist are sufficient to provide enough information on an e-service in order for the users to consider the service to be responsible, reliable, accurate, secure, transparent and trustworthy.

EU15 (2016) Checklist for Single Sign-On Systems – Hrvoje Stančić, Tomislav Ivanjko, Nikola Bonic, Ana Garic, Ksenija Loncaric, Ana Lovasic, Kristina Presecki and Ana Stankovic

This checklist offers guidance to records managers and archivists in businesses, government agencies or other organizations to assess single sign-on (SSO) systems, as well as by SSO developers to ensure that they have provided sufficient information on the system they are developing in order to detect the possibilities of exchanging identification and authentication credentials. Single sign-on systems and their key components were analyzed in 28 European countries: Austria, Belgium, Bulgaria, Croatia, Cyprus, Czech Republic, Denmark, Estonia, Finland, France, Germany, Greece, Hungary,

Ireland, Italy, Latvia, Lithuania, Luxembourg, Malta, Netherlands, Poland, Portugal, Romania, Slovakia, Slovenia, Spain, Sweden and the United Kingdom. This analysis built on findings by the research team that there was an absence of publicly available information important for establishing trust in e-Services, particularly information about 'Storage and long-term content availability' and 'System operation transparency'. This document can also be found as part of the final report for EU15.

NA06 Retention & Disposition in a Cloud Environment – Functional Requirements (March 2015)

This study was designed to contribute to a better understanding of the difficulties encountered when managing records in a cloud environment by answering two questions: (1) How does the use of cloud services affect an organization's ability to retain and dispose of records in accordance with the law and other guidelines? and (2) What can be done to mitigate the risks that arise from the gaps between the ability to apply retention and disposition actions to records residing within the enterprise and those residing in the cloud? The checklist offers guidance for individuals and organizations in evaluating specific cloud products and/or services to assess ability to meet retention and disposition requirements.

NA08 (2016) Managing Records of Citizen Engagement Initiatives: A Primer – Grant Hurley, Valerie Léveillé and John McDonald

The primer is a tool designed to help guide the drafting, execution and/or evaluation of government-citizen engagement initiatives as they relate, specifically, to the open government initiatives within an organization and, more generally, to recordkeeping needs and requirements and internal information management culture. Open government and citizen engagement are defined, the role of records and recordkeeping in the context of citizen engagement is discussed, and issues and strategies are proposed at levels of policy, governance and management, people, standards and practices, technology and awareness.

NA12 (2018) Preservation as a Service for Trust (PaaST): Functional and Data Requirements for Digital Preservation – Kenneth Thibodeau, Daryll Prescott, Richard Pearce-Moses, Adam Jansen, Katherine Timms, Giovanni Michetti, Luciana Duranti, Corinne Rogers, Larry Johnson, John R. Butler, Courtney Mumma, Vicki Lemieux, Sarah Romkey, Babak Hamidzadeh, Lois Evans, Joseph Tennis, Shyla Seller, Kristina McGuirk, Chloe Powell, Cathryn Crocker and Kelly Rovegno

Just as the Cloud is not a specific technology or even a family or configuration of technology, the primary challenges it poses for digital preservation are not technological. Rather, the challenges stem from the loss of control over, and even knowledge of, what hardware and software are used and how they are used. PaaST defines a comprehensive set of functional and data requirements that support preservation of digital information regardless of the technologies used or who uses them. The requirements are intended to enable authentic digital preservation in the Cloud; nevertheless, the requirements are valid in other scenarios as well, including in-house preservation and situations where digital preservation includes both in-house and contracted services. PaaST requirements supplement the Open Archival Information System (OAIS) Reference Model (now an ISO standard). They are applicable to cases that include heterogeneity in the types of information objects being preserved; variety in applicable directives, such as laws, regulations, standards, policies, business rules and contractual agreements; varying conditions of ownership, access, use and exploitation; variation in institutional arrangements and relationships between or among the parties involved; and as wide a spectrum of circumstances as possible, from best practices to worst cases.

NA14 Cloud Service Provider Contracts Checklist – Jessica Bushey, Marie Demoulin, Elissa How and Robert McLellan (February 2016) (English, French, Dutch, Spanish)

This checklist supports records managers, archivists, chief information officers and others who are assessing cloud services for their organization. It is a tool for users to gain an understanding of the terms in boilerplate cloud service contracts, verify if potential cloud service contracts meet their needs, with particular emphasis on requirements for records and archives, clarify recordkeeping and archival needs to legal and IT departments, and communicate recordkeeping and archival needs to cloud service providers. This checklist is a tool for consideration only and does not constitute legal advice, nor does it recommend for or against any particular cloud service provider (or the use of cloud services in general).

TR03 (2017) Security Classification Checklist – Ineke Deserno, Eng Sengsavang, Marie Shockley, Shadrack Katuu and Julia Kastenhofer

This checklist supports organizations in the development or revision of policies and procedures for managing security classified information assets, especially digital information, to ensure the reliability, authenticity, confidentiality, integrity and availability of security classified records and their long-term preservation. It supports best management of these assets throughout their lifecycle, from creation through active and controlled business use, to secondary use, eventual declassification and archival control.

Index